THE HUNGER GAMES COMPANION

ALSO BY LOIS H. GRESH FROM MACMILLAN

The Twilight Companion: The Unauthorized Guide to the Series

THE UNOFFICIAL GUIDE
TO THE BESTSELLING
HUNGER GAMES SERIES

THE
HUNGER
GAMES
COMPANION

LOIS H. GRESH

MACMILLAN

First published in the US 2011 by St. Martin's Press

This edition published in the UK 2011 by Macmillan Children's Books
a division of Macmillan Publishers Limited
20 New Wharf Road, London N1 9RR
Basingstoke and Oxford
Associated companies throughout the world
www.panmacmillan.com

ISBN 978-1-4472-0997-3

5 7 9 8 6 4

A CIP catalogue record for this book is available from
the British Library.

Book design by Richard Oriolo
Printed and bound by CPI Group (UK) Ltd, Croydon CR0 4YY

CONTENTS

DOOMSDAY PREDICTIONS

A TIMELINE TO THE APOCALYPSE

THE HUNGER GAMES TRILOGY

SURVIVING THE END OF THE WORLD

In dystopian post-apocalyptic novels, a remnant of humanity survives against the odds in situations ranging from nuclear wars to environmental meltdowns; invasions by aliens, zombies, and other monsters; plagues; chemicals; genetics gone wild; supermassive black holes that devour us; earthquakes; volcanoes; and even human-eating plants. Many of these scenarios are man-induced horrors: the nukes, biological and chemical wars, genetic engineering, global warming, pollution, corporate and government greed. In the real world, if a few people survive such an apocalypse, then there's only one way to completely obliterate the human race: The survivors must kill each other off.

Enter author Suzanne Collins's *The Hunger Games* and its two sequels, *Catching Fire* and *Mockingjay*. While the first two books in the series focus on annual gladiatorial Hunger Games and then the Quarter Quell, the third book is essentially about war. Originally aimed at teens aged twelve and up, the series quickly grabbed hold of everyone: twelve, thirteen, fourteen, twenty-five, thirty-five, fifty. It doesn't matter how young or old you are, the messages are the same. If humans aren't careful, we may blow ourselves into oblivion by wars, cruelty, the lust for power, and greed. Children are the future of the human race. If we kill our children, who will be left?

What better way to make these points than to postulate an apocalypse followed by war and rebellion, and then to pit the losers' children against each other in the Hunger Games—annual battles to the death? As if the Hunger Games don't kill enough children, the Capitol then pits the survivors against each other in the Quarter Quells.

In general, dystopian post-apocalyptic fiction is wildly popular these days. The novels are bleak, dismal, poignant, sad. These aren't comedies. The genre tends to send the warning that, if we don't wake up and stop killing each other, if things don't change—and soon—we might face the nightmares of the characters in the books.

Suzanne Collins's warnings are dished out to us up front and close as if through a magnifying lens. She gives us a heroine, Katniss Everdeen, who is remarkably like many young girls hope to be: She's brave, considerate, kind, intelligent, quick-witted, courageous, and very resourceful. Yet she lives in a world where all hope has been lost, where people eat pine-needle soup and entrail stew just to survive; where Peacekeepers beat and whip her neighbors and friends for nothing more than hunting and sharing much-needed food; where children are selected each year by lottery to slaughter each other in the Hunger Games, a gladiatorial arena that merges the ancient Roman games with reality television. Truly, this is a world in which the term, "survival of the fittest," has immediate and lethal meaning.

The books are international bestsellers, and Suzanne Collins has been applauded by everyone from Stephen King to *The New York Times Book Review* to *Time* magazine. As of this writing, more than 8 million copies of all three books in the trilogy are in print. The first novel, *The Hunger Games*, has been on *The New York Times* Bestseller List for 130 weeks. Suzanne Collins is one of *Entertainment Weekly*'s 2010 Entertainers of the Year. The books are #1 *USA Today* bestsellers, #1 *Publishers Weekly* bestsellers, and top many other prestigious literary award lists, as well.

By the time you start reading this book (the one in your hands now), you'll be anxiously anticipating the first Hunger Games movie. You may read *The Hunger Games Companion* multiple times, especially after March 2012 when *The Hunger Games* film is in theaters, with Lionsgate at the helm, Jennifer Lawrence starring as Katniss Everdeen, Josh Hutcherson as Peeta Mellark, and Liam Hemsworth as Gale Hawthorne.

This book, *The Hunger Games Companion*, is an unauthorized guide to Suzanne Collins's excellent trilogy. It examines all the subjects that I find fascinating about the books, topics not covered anywhere to date on the Internet or in any other book.

I assume that readers of this book have already devoured The Hunger Games series—many of you multiple times. I assume you know the plots, you know about Katniss and Peeta and Gale, about Buttercup and Prim and Rue, and so forth.

My goal is to generate discussion about The Hunger Games trilogy: the characters, the settings, the storylines, and also about subjects ranging from war to repressive regimes to hunger to the nature of evil itself. Every topic is set against the backdrop of and intertwined with The Hunger Games books and characters.

For example, chapter 2 parallels the Capitol of Panem with repressive regimes in our real world. Along with detailed examples, I pose the question: Could the world depicted in The Hunger Games really happen? Are we facing Big Brother, the end of privacy, dehumanization, and too much government control over our lives? Have the rich become too rich, and are most of us much too poor? You'll be surprised at the answers.

Another example: Chapter 4 draws direct and in-depth parallels between the real gladiators in ancient Rome and the tributes of

Panem. While the Capitol is indeed evil to send twenty-four children into the arena every year, the ancient Romans were much worse: They killed many thousands of men, women, children, and animals at a time using torture techniques that go well beyond the horrors of The Hunger Games trilogy. Their vanity and banquets were on par with the Capitol's: They feasted and laughed, drank wine and fussed with their clothing.

And how about hunger? Is the starvation in all the districts of Panem any different from starvation in our own, all-too-real world? Is it possible to live on meager amounts of grain and oil? In chapter 3, you'll learn how long a typical person can exist on such small allotments of food and the effects on children of this level of malnutrition and starvation. If the Capitol needs the districts to provide it with textiles, food, coal, and other goods, shouldn't it feed its slave workers sufficiently to enable them to work?

As for reality television, public relations experts, paparazzi, fashionistas and stylists, and obfuscation of the truth, chapter 9, "Hype Over Substance," shows you how The Hunger Games is a mirror of modern times.

In this book, you'll learn about the muttations and how they might be engineered, the mockingjays and how they might mimic elaborate melodies and sounds, the trackerjacker poison and how it might work, and many other topics.

To open discussion among fans of The Hunger Games, this companion guide offers opinions about matters relating to the characters, their relationships, the storylines. For example, I thought long and hard about Katniss's vote of "yes" for a Capitol children's Hunger Games at the end of *Mockingjay*. Later in this book, I'll provide my conclusions and the reasons for them.

As another example, we'll discuss why Katniss becomes suicidal and hooked on morphling in *Mockingjay*: Does it make sense in the context of her personality in both *The Hunger Games* and *Catching Fire,* and if so, why?

Before you dive into the rest of this book, pause and indulge me for a moment or two. Let's start our entire Hunger Games discussion with a look at the apocalypse that presumably occurs before the opening chapter. How could The Hunger Games apocalypse have happened? Where are the people from all the other countries? Also, how far into the future might The Hunger Games be?

These are the clues from Suzanne Collins: The seas rose dramatically and "swallowed up so much of the land" that people went to war over "what little sustenance remained" (*The Hunger Games,* 18). District 13 was leveled by "toxic bombs" (*The Hunger Games,* 83). Fearing war or complete destruction of the Earth's atmosphere, the government leaders planned to race to their underground city (now District 13) (*Mockingjay,* 17).

My guess is that the author might be suggesting that an environmental disaster caused the apocalypse. One possibility is the melting of the ice caps. Various scientists believe that the destruction of Earth's atmosphere and the rise in carbon dioxide and other pollutants may very well cause the ice caps to melt and the world to flood.

If the world floods to this extent, then people in high areas such as mountains might survive. Pockets of survivors may be in the Himalayas, the Alps, the Andes, and elsewhere. They may be in lower-lying areas such as the portions of North America that survived the floods.

The Hunger Games shows us no Internet capability, no satellites circling the globe. Due to the global war, I assume that the satellites cannot be maintained. I assume that survivors in other countries cannot communicate with Panem, that the floods have destroyed the required infrastructures, that shortwave radios possibly exist but little else. If we remember that the Soviets jammed shortwave radio transmissions from the United States during the Cold War (so its citizens couldn't communicate with the outside world), then it's an easy jump to think that Panem has done the same thing. It's possible that the survivors in other countries don't step in and help the citizens of Panem because they have their own problems due to the environmental apocalypse.

How long might it take for the ice caps to melt and flood the Earth sufficiently to cause an apocalypse of this magnitude? Maybe five hundred years from now? One hundred years from now?

Scientists don't really have a definitive answer about global warming and the melting of the ice caps. According to *Time*/CNN, "By some estimates, the entire Greenland ice sheet would be enough to raise global sea levels 23 ft., swallowing up large parts of coastal Florida and most of Bangladesh. The Antarctic holds enough ice to raise sea levels more than 215 ft."[1] Explains Spencer Weart, former director of the Center for History of Physics of the American Institute of Physics:

> Specialists in glacier flow worked up increasingly elaborate ice-sheet models. . . . The models failed to answer the question of how fast a major ice sheet could surge into the ocean. The improved models did show, reassuringly, that there was no plausible way for a large mass of Antarctic ice to collapse altogether during the 21st century. According to these models, if the West Antarctic Ice Sheet diminished at all, it would discharge its burden only slowly over several centuries, not placing too heavy a burden on human society.[2]

So let's suppose it takes a few hundred years for the seas to rise 238 feet (23 feet from Greenland plus 215 feet from Antarctica). If these speculations are accurate, the world of The Hunger Games might take place several hundred years from now.

Keep in mind, of course, that other scientists provide varying speculations about whether global warming will cause this catastrophe at all, how high the seas might rise, how long this could take, and what the consequences could be. Debates rage all over the world about these subjects.

So hypothetically, in a few hundred years, we could have a society with advanced technologies such as muttations, force fields, and high-speed trains; but with the world basically flooded.

The war after the apocalypse may have decimated the cities and suburbs, as we see no evidence in The Hunger Games books of sky-scrapers, mall strips, gas stations, and other buildings beyond the village square, the mayor's house, and the Victor's Village. We also see no rubble from crushed buildings. It's possible that the trains have been routed around the rubble, so tributes don't see cities where people back home could possibly hide and later rebel. This, again, is all speculation on my part.

Having addressed the question of what might have caused the apocalypse preceding *The Hunger Games* (and only Suzanne Collins, her agent, and her editors know for sure what she had in mind), I'd like to close this introductory chapter with a few speculations about the end of the entire series: What happens long after the *Mockingjay* war? Specifically, why does Katniss marry Peeta and have children? This ending surprised a lot of readers, myself included, and so I've given it a lot of thought.

We first meet Katniss as a kindhearted and strong-willed girl who must provide for her family: her mother, little sister, Prim, and even (after an initial near-demise of the cat) Buttercup. I like Katniss from the first page, and when her best friend Gale is introduced, I also like him. Similar to Katniss, Gale provides for his family, and the two of them join forces to bring food home.

After being thrust into her first Hunger Games, Katniss must pre-tend to share a romance with another boy, Peeta, and this charade continues throughout *Catching Fire*. Peeta is basically a selfless ro-mantic saint with a backbone. Other than when his brain is hijacked, he's completely devoted to Katniss and her well-being.

Katniss and Gale remain good friends, but everything changes after Katniss experiences the gruesome reality of the Games. She's caught between the two boys—Peeta the super-sweet, uber-devotional baker and Gale the super-macho, childhood friend.

But in *Mockingjay,* Prim is killed by bombs, and we also learn that Gale has become a bomb maker. Hence, it seems that the author has set up a scenario in which Katniss can never choose Gale as her lover-husband. The choice is made for her: Peeta, or nobody.

I believed in Katniss as a three-dimensional (i.e., *real*) character throughout the trilogy. She develops over time from a fairly innocent and sweet young girl into a warrior who tries to save herself and Peeta, to one who tries to save everyone in all the districts. She is forced to become a killer of other children, which permanently alters her personality, as it would anyone in the real world subjected to the Games. She hardens herself sufficiently to take on the role of the Mockingjay to save the people of Panem. She does what she has to do. But it all takes a serious toll on her, just as war takes its toll on many soldiers. A teenager enduring what Katniss endures might very well suffer from depression, suicidal thoughts, and drug addictions. In the end, when Katniss realizes that President Coin is no better than President Snow, there's no way she can do anything other than kill Coin. Her life has not been pretty.

When Katniss marries Peeta and has children, the one thing she swore she'd never do, is this Suzanne Collins's way of telling readers that there's always hope at the end of even the darkest tunnel? This is possibly the one bright spot in an otherwise extremely bleak world the author paints for us.

The bottom line is that The Hunger Games series is powerful and brilliant. From the beginning, the prose is luscious: "Prim's face is as fresh as a raindrop, as lovely as the primrose for which she was named" (*The Hunger Games*, 3). The action is fast, the pace even swifter. Reading the first book is like catapulting down waterfalls at top speed. Katniss is drawn with precision clarity; possibly, more distant in *Mockingjay* than in the first two books, but ultimately, as mentioned above, very believable and intensely sympathetic. The zaniness of the stylists and fashionistas gives the reader a little relief from the horrors, but overall, the books maintain a grim look at the ugly face of humanity. There's no way that sprays, spritzes, dyes, and plastic surgeries can erase that ugliness. The juxtaposition of Capitol excesses against the impoverished, starving masses is brilliantly drawn time and time again through Katniss's eyes.

In short, these are some of the best books I've read in a long time. They make me think about the human condition, and that's the mark of fine literature.

If you're reading this book, *The Hunger Games Companion,* then I suspect you feel the same way.

DOOMSDAY PREDICTIONS

2800 BC, Assyria

This may be one of the earliest examples of prophets foretelling the end of the world due to moral decay. An Assyrian clay tablet from approximately 2800 BC bore the doomsday prophecy that "Our earth is degenerate in these latter days. There are signs that the world is speedily coming to an end. Bribery and corruption are common."

REPRESSIVE REGIMES AND REBELLIONS

COULD THE HUNGER GAMES REALLY HAPPEN?

When thinking of The Hunger Games trilogy, core issues immediately pop to mind. The reader can't help but wonder if our society is heading toward the same problems depicted in the world of The Hunger Games. Perhaps this is a central reason why the series affects readers so much: We identify with the central characters and can actually envision—with great horror—a future reality that is not too different from Katniss's reality. We're already heading down the path leading to these aspects of society we see in the novels:

- Big Brother
- Government control over citizens, harassment of citizens

- Lack of privacy and erosion of civil liberties
- Legal penalties for invoking freedom of speech
- Using people to spy on each other
- Dehumanization
- Ultimately, rebellion.

In subsequent chapters, we establish that there's a huge disparity between the people in the Capitol who have too much to eat, who focus on what they look like, and spend money on plastic surgeries and style, versus everyone else—the starving, the hounded, the impoverished, those lacking even basic human comforts. The "haves" versus the "have nots"—we see them clearly in the world of The Hunger Games, but we also see them clearly in our society.

In our real world, in the United States, the top 1 percent of all households controls 43 percent of the wealth, and the next 19 percent controls 50 percent of the wealth; hence, it's estimated that *20 percent of all households in the United States control 93 percent of the wealth*.

What does this leave for everyone else, the 80 percent of citizens of the United States? Unfortunately, *80 percent of households have only 7 percent of the nation's financial wealth*. And even worse, as Professor G. William Domhoff of the University of California at Santa Cruz tells us, "[T]he bottom forty percent of the population . . . holds just 0.3% of the wealth in the United States."[1] These are enormous disparities in resource distribution between the rich and everyone else.

Business Insider puts it bluntly: "The rich are getting richer and the poor are getting poorer. Cliché, sure, but it's also more true than at any time since the Gilded Age. If you're in that top 1%, life is grand."[2] Statistics show that the disparities are starting to look like what we saw right before the Great Depression. For example, in 1928 the "top one-hundredth of 1 percent of U.S. families averaged 892 times more income than families in the bottom 90 percent," and in 2006, "the top 0.01 percent averaged 976 times more income than America's bottom 90 percent."[3]

People have lost their homes at a shocking pace, and some reports suggest that the "housing crisis could peak in 2011, as the number of homeowners receiving foreclosure notices climbs to about 20%."[4] Indeed, as of February 2011, CNN tells us that foreclosures are responsible for a whopping 26 percent of current house sales. Further, "nearly thirty percent of mortgage borrowers are underwater on their loans, owing more than their homes are worth"[5] and estimates place the losses to banks on mortgages at possibly more than $700 billion.[6] People are unemployed with no hope of ever finding jobs again. The understated statistics from the government suggest that the nation's unemployment rate is 9 to 9.5 percent as of January 2011. However, as many analysts are quick to point out, the unemployment numbers do not include those who have given up all hope of finding work. Estimates place the hopelessly unemployed at 6 million of the supposed 15 million jobless Americans. In addition, 1.5 million people have been out of work for more than ninety-nine weeks. Explains Harvey Katz of Value Line, which does investment research:

> Worse, the aforementioned unemployment rate of 9.4% is just a fraction—perhaps half—of the overall jobless rate. That is because this so-called official rate includes only those considered to be technically unemployed . . . the cumulative total is probably closer to 18%—or just under one in five Americans who want fulltime, permanent employment, who are unable to secure such work.[7]

To avoid a major Depression akin to the one the United States suffered in the 1930s, the U.S. government gave $700 billion to the banks. The government also bailed out the auto industry to the tune of some $25 billion.

Branko Milanović, lead economist at the World Bank's research division in Washington D.C., recently told *U.S. News & World Report* that the wealth of the world has never been as unequally distributed between the rich and everyone else as it is now. He says that the countries with the widest disparities are in Latin America and Africa.[8] Professor Domhoff cites a 2006 study by the World Institute for Development Economics Research, whose data is pretty old at this point, from the year 2000, to point out that the financial disparities exist worldwide.[9] The study concluded that the top 10 percent of all households in Switzerland owned more than 70 percent of the country's wealth; in Denmark, they owned 65 percent; France, 61 percent; Sweden, 58 percent, England, 56 percent; and so forth. Again, these are older statistics, and also, as Domhoff points out, the data is "spotty" for many countries. Still, no matter how lenient we are in looking at the numbers, hoping to reduce the inequalities, we can't get around the fact that the disparities are absurdly wide.

As we all know, wealth leads to power. Before the 2008 presidential election, CNN noted that "The herd of candidates vying for the White House in 2008 may have different positions on abortion, gun control, climate change and taxes, but there is one thing most of them have in common—they're millionaires."[10] *Money* magazine wrote that the "seven front-runners, those with the highest standings in the polls and the biggest campaign troves, all have assets that would place them in the nation's top 10% of households, and most of them in the top 0.5%."[11] In 2002, *Forbes* magazine listed the ten richest politicians in America, and among them were Michael R. Bloomberg, mayor of New York City, with close to $5 billion; Winthrop Rockefeller, lieutenant governor of Arkansas, $1.2 billion; B. Thomas Golisano, then gubernatorial candidate of New York, $1.1 billion; and John Kerry, then senator of Massachusetts, $550 million.[12]

Says Branko Milanović, ". . . you have an entrenched elite that basically maintains its own high position to the detriment of others."[13]

How different is our real world, then, to what we see in The Hunger Games? The rich have all the resources. The rich have all the powerful jobs. The rich control everyone else. These are factors, as we'll soon see, that lead to repression and in many cases, revolutions and rebellions. Perhaps the future as reflected in The Hunger Games series posits a collapse of our civilization as inequalities take hold and the government clamps down on civil liberties and human rights. It's not all that farfetched.

GEORGE ORWELL'S *1984* AND BIG BROTHER

The term, "Big Brother," is well known in this country. It symbolizes government power and the collapse of civil liberties and rights. It personifies government surveillance.

In George Orwell's 1949 novel, *1984,* Big Brother is the figurehead of the Party; he may be a real person, he may be just a symbol. He appears as the dictator of Oceania on gigantic telescreens and posters in order to issue propaganda. In The Hunger Games, President Snow, Caesar Flickerman, and the Games are force-fed to citizens via televisions set up in all the Districts. The propaganda is constant.

The Oceania government controls and harasses citizens, spies on everyone, dehumanizes people, and penalizes those who invoke freedom of speech. The same is certainly true in the world of The Hunger Games. A classic dystopian novel, *1984* shows us a future that follows a global war. After the war, three super-states divide the land masses up and then control everyone in their provinces. The individual must do as the government wants, and the government controls everyone and everything. The Proles, or Proletariats, constitute 85 percent of the population, and as in our real world and in the world of The Hunger Games, this vast majority has no power and no wealth, and they serve the whims of the rich. The Inner Party, representing only 2 percent of the population, are like the super-wealthy in our population who have the most power. They are also like the Gamemakers, Peacekeepers, and Mayors in The Hunger Games. Citizens are so dehumanized that they're known as "unpersons." And children are used as spies, even against their own parents. As in The Hunger Games, children are pawns of the evil empire, which forces them to do the government's will and destroy any semblance of free thought and speech by their parents. Remember, the children are tools of the government in The Hunger Games; if the Capitol controls the children and tortures/executes them at whim, then the evil empire has an iron grip on the adults. Basically, the Party in *1984* keeps people impoverished and desperate for basics such as food and shelter, just as the Capitol does in The Hunger Games. Poverty, hunger, and misery: tools that the governments in both books use to control the people.

Winston Smith in *1984* is "lucky" to belong to the somewhat middle-class Outer Party, which affords him with "luxuries" such as black bread and gin. He lives in a small apartment, where he's forced to watch Big Brother on the telescreen; if caught "thinking" rebellious ideas, he could be executed.

He eventually rebels against the Party, which arrests, imprisons, and subjects him to beatings, electric shocks, and psychological torture. The Party also arrests and tortures his illegal lover, Julia. The Capitol in The Hunger Games uses similar techniques, and then some (see chapter 6, "Torture and Execution").

In *1984,* the government controls love affairs, as well. Winston and Julia aren't supposed to be involved in a romance; hence their imprisonment and torture. The two end up discarding each other, both caving into Big Brother.

In The Hunger Games, the government straight up to President Snow, tries to control the romance between Katniss and Peeta to the point of picking out her wedding dress. Both Katniss and Peeta are keenly aware throughout all three books that their romance may be their key to survival. Finally, after shifting out of the severity of tracker jacker hijacking, Peeta clings to his love of Katniss.

Perhaps the most fascinating difference between *1984* and The Hunger Games lies in the conversations between Winston Smith and Julia. Remember, Katniss and Peeta are paranoid about each other's loyalty during their battles to the death; Katniss tries to save Peeta's life numerous times; and Peeta is willing to sacrifice himself to save

Katniss. But in *1984,* Winston and Julia betray each other. She explains that "they" (the government) threaten the people with things that nobody can "stand up to" or "even think about." She says that, in the end, "all you care about is yourself." Sadly, Winston agrees, and they both comment that, after a betrayal in which you're willing to sacrifice someone else to save your own neck, "you don't feel the same" about the other person any longer.

Yet perhaps the *major* difference is that in *1984,* the police make sure people do not even *think* subversive things. The government controls *thoughts.* Unfortunately, as shown in chapter 9, "Hype Over Substance," in the real world, much of what people think is controlled by mass media, gossip rags, and news conglomerates. In many cases, we know more about Michelle Obama's fashions than her husband's politics. We rarely read or view hard facts about the war in Iraq the same way we accessed the same types of facts during the Vietnam War. Back then, we couldn't go a day without seeing soldiers wounded, fighting, and dying; without reading the appalling statistics about the number dead, the hopeless war situation, and so forth. We were inundated with facts by news organizations. Today, we have to dig to find out the truth about casualties of war; the number wounded, fighting, and dying. Instead of hard journalism, we're subjected to hundreds of television channels and thousands of Internet news sites that feed us trivia about gossip, fashion, and style. In *1984,* the government controls the people's view of reality in order to control the people. Nobody in *1984* really knows what's going on around the world. The use of the Big Lie is rampant in *1984,* whereby Newspeak words can possess meanings that contradict each other.

If the government hides the truth long enough and if news sources hide the truth long enough, then what are we left with? Will anyone remember why civilization collapsed? They don't remember the reasons in The Hunger Games, nor do they remember history in *1984;* indeed, Winston Smith's job is to revise the past as reported by news organizations. And in our real world, as the media becomes looser and less able to provide us with real facts, what will happen to our civilization? I leave you with *this*:

> [Hitler's] primary rules were: never allow the public to cool off; never admit a fault or wrong; never concede that there may be some good in your enemy; never leave room for alternatives; never accept blame; concentrate on one enemy at a time and blame him for everything that goes wrong; people will believe a big lie sooner than a little one; and *if you repeat [a lie] frequently enough people will sooner or later believe it.*
>
> —The United States Office of Strategic Services,
> *Hitler As His Associates Know Him.*[14]

In general, dystopian fiction portrays a bleak world in which everything is pretty much hopeless. A dystopia is not a fun place to live: people are oppressed, dehumanized, and frightened. Typically, the government is highly centralized and totalitarian. The Hunger Games trilogy is an example of dystopian fiction: The world is bleak, everything is pretty much hopeless, people are oppressed, dehumanized, and frightened; and the government is centralized and totalitarian.

Historically, dystopian novels are indictments against frightening social trends. The authors are warning us that our futures will be terrible if these trends persist.

Perhaps one of the earliest dystopian novels was 1921's *We* by Yevgeny Zamyatin, which focused on an oppressive social order complete with terrorist force and the elimination of any individuality. Along with George Orwell's *1984*, the novel *We* is considered a classic example of dystopian fiction.

Aldous Huxley's *Brave New World* differs somewhat from both *We* and *1984*, in that Huxley's novel shows the oppressive results of brainwashing, blind faith in the government and technology, and a conscious reduction by the government in the intellectual and individual liberties of citizens.

Fahrenheit 451 by Ray Bradbury is another classic dystopian novel, very similar to *Brave New World* in that it also shows the oppressive results of brainwashing, blind faith in the government and technology, and a conscious reduction by the government in the intellectual and individual liberties of citizens. Suzanne Collins references *Fahrenheit 451* in *Mockingjay* when she assigns Katniss to Squad 451.

The key difference among the three works might be that *Brave New World* gives us a World State without any war yet with extremely stultifying social stability. In *1984* and *Fahrenheit 451*, things are quite different: everyone's afraid of enemy attacks and war, and torture and deprivation are commonplace. While people don't worry about enemy attacks and war in the world of The Hunger Games, they do worry constantly about torture, starvation, and being selected to participate in the Games.

A central idea in *Fahrenheit 451* is that people no longer remember history because the government has obliterated it using technology. People watch television rather than talk to and have fun with friends. They believe whatever propaganda the government is spewing on the television screen, and they no longer have a clue as to what's real and what isn't real.

In the The Hunger Games world, people no longer remember what caused the apocalypse, though they do remember—thanks to all the government propaganda on the television screens—why they are being oppressed. The know very little about the actual Dark Days, however, and when subjected to government torture tactics, they fail to differentiate between what's real and what isn't real. Peeta, of course, is the prime example of this problem.

Both in *Fahrenheit 451* and The Hunger Games trilogy, the free flow of information is totally censored, and hence, people don't know what's happening in the world. In Katniss's world, nobody really knows what happens in the other districts, and indeed, they don't even know that District 13 still exists. When Rue tells Katniss about the harsh living conditions and punishments in District 11,

Katniss thinks about how little she knows about people outside of District 12, and "because even though the information seems harmless, they don't want people in different districts to know about one another" (*The Hunger Games,* 203).

It's interesting to note that in the The Hunger Games trilogy as well as in *Brave New World,* religion no longer exists. When their children are selected for the Games, parents don't fall to their knees and wail to God. When Katniss is in her darkest moments, depressed and suicidal, being forced to kill other children, wondering if Peeta will survive his leg injury and subsequent infection, wondering if her sister will survive, and so on, she does not pray to God. It's as if all religion has disappeared from Panem. In *Brave New World,* religion is actually taboo, and people are supposed to do little other than make goods and buy them. And yet the goal of government in *Brave New World*—in addition to maintaining an iron grip on everything and everyone—is to keep everyone dulled down and controlled, "happy" as if on tranquilizers. The leaders of Panem definitely aren't interested in the happiness of its citizens, even if that happiness is fake.

As an aside, rather than using the term, "dystopia," to describe *Brave New World,* it's often considered a form of utopian fiction. People are so brainwashed and controlled that they don't know that they're being oppressed. Sure, they have no religion, no art, and no science, but do they know what they're missing? No.

Along with no religion, the oppressed people in The Hunger Games districts do not enjoy art, music, poetry, dance, organized sports, or intellectual endeavors that involve science, history, etc. They are completely stifled. Peeta's artistic abilities emerge from his experiences as a baker. Because he's decorated so many cakes, the story tells us, he has a knack for painting and camouflage. Only after winning the Games is Katniss encouraged to design clothes. While Rue loves music, particularly bird songs, she does not play a musical instrument, nor is she exposed to symphonies, choruses, operas, and so forth. About the most we see, in terms of music, are some simple tunes and folk melodies. Culture is totally stifled, yet the beauty of these simple tunes endure and offer small glimpses at hope and a different way of life.

Beetee, the inventor, creates a tiny musical chip that holds hours of songs; clearly, the people of District 12 will never stroll around while listening to hours of music, so perhaps the chip is intended for citizens in the Capitol. These lucky few have music, design, fashion, and art; they live for entertainment. But the oppressed masses have nothing.

Aleksandr Solzhenitsyn's *One Day in the Life of Ivan Denisovich* is yet another classic tale of dystopian fiction, except in this case, it drew upon the real experiences of the author and exposed the repressive Stalin regime for what it was: this was no far-in-the-future post-apocalyptic scenario; rather, it was drawn from real life. If we compare basic elements of *The Hunger Games* and *One Day in the Life of Ivan Denisovich,* the world of the former becomes even more terrifying because we start realizing that it could happen someday if we're not careful to encourage and maintain civil liberties, human freedom, and culture. *One Day in the Life of Ivan Denisovich* is a fictionalized portrait of an era in which the government controlled and harassed citizens, civil liberties and privacy were ignored, torture and extreme punishments were doled out to those who dared to voice opinions, and people were dehumanized. We'll walk through a few parallels between *One Day in the Life of Ivan Denisovich* and The Hunger Games, keeping in mind that *Ivan* reflects an all-too-real time period in Soviet history, and then we'll take a hard look at that time period to bring the The Hunger Games world into sharp focus.

Aleksandr Solzhenitsyn was born in 1918 and fought in the Red Army against the Nazis, who had invaded Russia. In the Battle of Leningrad, he served as a captain, but when in 1945 (at the age of twenty-seven), he criticized Stalin in letters to a friend, the Soviets arrested and sentenced him to eight years of hard labor and exile in a correctional labor camp. Refusing to cooperate with the secret police, he ended up in a labor camp in Siberia, where he decided to write a novel about his experiences.

By 1929, more than 1 million citizens were imprisoned in these harsh labor camps, called GULAGs. By 1940, more than 13 million people were in the GULAGs. The crimes leading to punishment in the GULAGs were vaguely defined in Article 58 of the Soviet laws and included unproven espionage, suspected espionage, and simply talking to another person suspected of espionage; letting weeds grow, failing to produce sufficient crops, and allowing machines to break down; perceived expression of intent to perform a terrorist act; and the most common crime: creating, distributing, writing in a letter or personal diary about, discussing, or otherwise hinting at anything related to propaganda or agitation against the Soviet government.

In The Hunger Games series, we might think of the districts as prison camps. Certainly, District 11 operates as a prison camp, with its thirty-five-feet-tall barbed wire fences, watch towers, and armed guards. As civil unrest grows and new Peacekeepers come into District 12, if these new police even think someone is acting subversive, they torture him with public beatings and whippings. The attitude of the government is clear, as stated by President Snow in *Catching Fire*: "And if a girl from District 12 of all places can defy the Capitol and walk away unharmed, what is to stop [all of the people] from doing the same?" (*Catching Fire*, 21.) Further, just as the evil leaders in Stalin's era and in Ivan's labor camp think, Snow believes that letting Katniss go unpunished could lead to an uprising and possibly a full revolution.

Solzhenitsyn's novel begins when Ivan wakes up in the Siberian GULAG, feeling sick and facing another grueling day. *The Hunger Games* begins when Katniss wakes up to face Reaping Day.

In Solzhenitsyn's novel, we learn that the only way Ivan can survive is to fend for himself and not worry about his fellow prisoners. Violence is necessary for self-preservation. And what do the tributes have to do in order to survive the Hunger Games? The same thing.

Like Ivan, Katniss is basically a kind, gentle, and decent human being, but when pitted against other people for her own survival in the Games, she must maim and kill.

Ivan and everyone else is starving in the prison camp. The guards take portions of his meager bread allotment every day, because without the food thefts, even the guards can't survive. Fighting for food is essential if Ivan is to live. In the world of The Hunger Games, food is carefully rationed by the government, with people getting basically less than is needed to survive. Despite the fact it's illegal, Peacekeepers, the Mayor, and other local officials gladly take hunted game from Katniss. To get more grain, children throw their names into the Reaping lottery multiple times. Greasy Sae doles out ladles of stew made from bark, mice, and entrails.

Toward the end of Solzhenitsyn's novel, Ivan comments that the only reason Stalin's regime remains in power is because Stalin has divided all the people against each other. This is how the government controls everyone. The same happens in The Hunger Games trilogy, where the Capitol divides everyone into districts that are never allowed to communicate with one another.

Stalin, whose birth name was Iosif Vissarionovich Dzhugashvili, was born in 1879, and rose from the lowest classes of pre-Russian Revolution society. His father was a violent alcoholic cobbler, his mother a washerwoman; both were serfs in Georgia before their homeland was conquered by the czar. Stalin actually trained to be a priest, but leaving the church to become a revolutionary activist, he ended up in prison. The czarist government exiled Stalin to Siberia.

After the overthrow of the czar, Stalin became a high-ranking leader in the Communist Party. He collectivized agriculture throughout the Soviet Union in the 1920s and '30s. When unrest broke out because affluent *kulak* peasants weren't sharing their farm animals with the collective, the government shipped a million *kulak* families to Siberia. Other peasants, those who were grumbling about collectivization, were shipped off to become laborers. During the early 1930s, millions of people died from starvation under Stalin's rule. This is a clear case in reality where a brutal government dictator starves his own people to death, and this is not the only case by far.

Paranoid that citizens were thinking about staging upheavals or rebellions, Stalin tortured people, imprisoned them, exiled them, starved them; and he deported millions to the GULAGs, where many died. Overall, Stalin was responsible for the deaths of 4 to 10 million of his own people, plus another 6 to 8 million from forced starvation. These are actually conservative numbers, as some historians suggest that Stalin was responsible for as many as 20 million deaths.

President Snow tortures people, imprisons them, and starves them. He deports children to the Games, where they die. While not responsible for slaughters approaching 10 or 20 million people, he's as cold, impassive, and cruel as Stalin. His regime is as repressive as Stalin's government. And Snow's main reason for cruelty is to squash any uprisings or rebellions.

People have rebelled against repressive regimes since the dawn of civilization. Spartacus's revolt against Rome during the time of the gladiator games (see chapter 4, "Tributes") is similar to Katniss's revolt, except of course, that Spartacus ultimately was defeated whereas Katniss succeeds.

As I write this book in February 2011, rebellions against repressive regimes are raging across the Middle East. A major trigger was the revolt of Mohamed Bouazizi on December 17, 2010 when he set fire to himself in Tunisia. Living in an agricultural region, he was unemployed and trying to sell vegetables with a street cart, when government officials told him it was against the law. His act sparked demonstrations from other Tunisians against the mass unemployment under the repressive government, which retaliated by sending police to open fire on the citizens. As the rebellion spread and police violence continued, close to eighty citizens ended up dead. At first, President Zine El Abidine Ben Ali backed the police brutality and murders, but later, he started reversing his position. He promised to create jobs, lower food costs, and allow freedom of speech. Eventually, he had to flee the country, and as of this writing, is in Saudi Arabia. He had ruled Tunisia for twenty-three years.

In February 2011, hundreds of thousands of Egyptians gathered to protest the government policies of President Hosni Mubarak. After thirty years of power, he fled Cairo for Sharm el-Sheikh, and millions of people packed the streets of Cairo to celebrate. Like Ben Ali, Mubarak tried to hold onto his power by promising jobs, higher wages, and freedom of speech, but after being repressed for so many decades, the mobs weren't buying it.

Also in February 2011, police fought thousands of protestors in Bahrain, yet another recent example of anti-government unrest in the Middle East. The leader of Bahrain, Hamad bin Isa Al Khalifa, is a Sunni Muslim whose family has ruled the country since the eighteenth century. The majority of people in Bahrain, however, are not Sunni Muslims; rather, they are Shia. Sheikh Hamad promised to institute reforms, but as many as 10,000 protestors gathered in the streets, demanding jobs and housing, civil and political rights, and the removal of Prime Minister Sheikh Khalifa bin Salman Al Khalifa, who had held his position for forty years. As this book goes to print in early May 2011, government forces have arrested 800 people; tortured, imprisoned, and killed civilians; and fired 1,000 citizens from their jobs.

Also in February 2011, hundreds of thousands of people throughout the Middle East held demonstrations on behalf of the Libyans who are trying to overthrow the repressive regime of Colonel Muammar el-Qaddafi. In Libya, military forces shot gunfire into unarmed civilian crowds, including thousands of people leaving mosques after praying. Qaddafi warned his people that Libya would become a hell if the protests against his government didn't cease. As of February 2011, tens of thousands of citizens were participating in demonstrations, with soldiers defecting from Qaddafi to guard the masses from police attack. As of late March 2011, the United Nations voted to enforce "no-flying" zones in Libya and to help the country's oppressed people. As this book goes to print in early May 2011, NATO continues bombing Libya in hopes of diminishing Gaddafi's military power.

These various examples share some obvious commonalities: government control over citizens, harassment of citizens; erosion of civil liberties; penalties for invoking freedom of speech; and ultimately—at least in the cases cited—repressive regimes face rebellions.

This is exactly what happens when the people of Panem revolt against their government and its leaders. People can take just so much abuse. The kicker, of course, is that President Coin's regime ends up being no better than President Snow's regime. By eliminating Coin, the people of Panem finally achieve some true hope of liberation from oppressive power-hungry leadership. We often trade one evil for another, and as the old saying goes: "Absolute power corrupts absolutely."

In the twentieth century, the world saw revolutions in Czarist Russia; in Italy and Germany between World War I and World War II; and also revolutions in China, Cuba, and Vietnam. There were additional revolutions in Iran and South Africa, among others.

It's well beyond the scope of this book to describe all of these revolutions. For that, the reader has to turn to history texts. In general, there are some key factors that lead to outright rebellions, as in The Hunger Games series:

First, a large portion of the population is extremely frustrated and unhappy with the government. Support among all the poor and rural people is key to a successful overthrow of a repressive regime. Everyone except the leaders and their cohorts in the Capitol are poor and can be considered rural: nobody really has anything, nobody really has any power.

Second, the majority of the population—no matter what their social and economic classes—agrees that conditions are so bad that the only way to remedy current circumstances is by overthrowing the government. There's no question that this is true in The Hunger Games. As soon as one district rebels, all the districts start following suit; after District 8 revolts, the rebellion spreads rapidly to other districts. Midway through *Catching Fire*, Districts 8, 3, 4, 7, and 11 have already starting fighting against the Capitol (*Catching Fire*, 165–68). Bakers (like Peeta and his family) and engineers and inventors (like Beetee), who have higher status and better lifestyles than most people, join the revolution.

Third, the so-called elite classes vote for rebellion. This is similar to the second criterion: The vast majority of people join forces and try to overthrow the repressive government. If the intellectuals are with the cause, so much the better. In the case of The Hunger Games, it's hard to point to an intellectual class because everybody has been subjugated to such a large extent. However, there are some people who might be considered in the intellectual class—possibly Mayors; Peacekeepers who don't torture citizens; the Head Gamemaker, Plutarch Heavensbee, who is in a secret organization hell-bent on overthrowing the government (*Catching Fire*, 385); inventors such as Beetee; anyone (other than Coin and her cronies) in District 13. For Seneca Crane, Head Gamemaker before Plutarch, he had a "sentimental streak" and didn't kill Katniss during the poison berry episode, and hence, according to President Snow, the government had to kill him (*Catching Fire*, 20).

Fourth, a serious crisis paralyzes the ability of the repressive regime to use force against the people. These crises may take the form of economic collapse, no jobs, no food, too much war, corrupt leaders, an elite upper stratum that has all the money and power. Need I point out the corollaries with The Hunger Games, not to mention the current (as of February 2011) rebellions throughout the Middle East?

Finally, a major rebellion may be imminent if no other global government intervenes to help the people. Nobody from anywhere else in the world helps the repressed people of Panem. In fact, we don't know if anyone exists outside of Panem because they're never mentioned in any of the three books.

As noted in chapter 1, "The Hunger Games Trilogy," Suzanne Collins provides a couple of clues about her apocalyptic scenario. She

tells us that the government leaders feared war or complete destruction of the Earth's atmosphere (*Mockingjay,* 17). She tells us that the
seas swelled and swallowed much of the land of North America to
form a much smaller Panem, that there were "droughts" and "storms,"
and finally, a "brutal war" over any remaining food sources (*The
Hunger Games,* 18). As postulated in chapter 1, it's possible that Collins was alluding to the melting of the ice caps due to climate change.
The clue is in the swelling of the seas to the point where the continent becomes much smaller. If the entire world is flooded by the
melting of the ice in Greenland and all of Antarctica, the seas may
rise two hundred feet.[15] Without going into the entire scenario suggested in chapter 1, if we assume that the sea swells dramatically
affected all of the civilization just as it affected North America, then
we can also assume that the survivors elsewhere are busy trying to
find sustenance and stay alive just as they did in North America
after the apocalyptic event. Further, given that Collins supplies no
reason for us to believe that global satellite communications still
work or that undersea cables have survived the climate crisis, it's
safe to assume that communications with survivors on other continents are severed. Shortwave low-bandwidth radios would still
work. Ships could still sail the high seas; but, with global starvation
and meltdowns, diseases may also be rampant, which would limit
the desire to communicate via ship or any other means with other
continents. The bottom line is that Suzanne Collins does not tell us
why the apocalypse occurred, nor does she spell out what happened
to the rest of the world.

James DeFronzo, Associate Professor Emeritus at the University of
Connecticut, summarizes the five criteria needed for rebellion as: mass
discontent; elite dissent; unifying motive; state crisis; and world
permissiveness.[16] He provides global evidence that attempted
revolutions lacking one or more of these factors tend to fail.

In the United States at present, people are increasingly discontent
due to factors noted earlier in this chapter: unemployment, no hope
for jobs, losing their homes, etc. Banks have collapsed, the economy

is tanking rapidly. Republicans fling dirt at Democrats. And Democrats fling dirt at Republicans. Nobody wins. The homeless are still homeless, the starving are still starving, the uneducated are still uneducated. The cost of higher education is through the roof. The country is fighting wars on multiple fronts and at great expense, yet the government is so riddled with debt, U.S. treasury notes are actually *losing* money. There seems to be no solution to the nation's ills.

What will happen is anyone's guess.

We've witnessed the USA PATRIOT Act, the bizarre Total Information Awareness proposal, John Ashcroft's super-secret detentions, and the Guantanamo incident. (And, oh yes, some time ago, we had Nixon's "plumbers" and the Watergate Tapes, and the Joseph McCarthy Red Scare era, not to mention George W. Bush's weapons of mass destruction fiasco.)

The USA PATRIOT Act assaulted the civil rights of Americans by allowing the FBI to look at records about anyone they want without going to court first. Yes, they can view your medical records, financial records, Internet use, travel history, lending library records, and just about anything else. They can tap your phone and read your e-mail.

The Terrorism Information and Prevention System (TIPS) was a program that President George W. Bush devised that would encourage people to spy on their family, friends, and neighbors. This smacks of the Stalin era, doesn't it? Or the McCarthy era. Luckily, Congress nixed the idea.

Face it, we have very little privacy in this country. The Total Information Awareness (TIA) project can put us all under the government microscope. Its aim is to create ultra-huge databases containing all information about people. It is run by the Department of Defense Advanced Research Projects Agency (DARPA). Among its many creepy features, it works toward covertly tracking where you go and what you do—without your knowledge.

Jay Stanley and Barry Steinhardt of the American Civil Liberties Union note:

Privacy and liberty in the United States are at risk. A combination of lightning-fast technological innovation and the erosion of privacy protections threatens to transform Big Brother from an oft-cited but remote threat into a very real part of American life. We are at risk of turning into a Surveillance Society.[17]

The authors point to the extensive data mining that's already happening, as well as to the potentials of microchips embedded in our skin, and something they call brain-wave fingerprinting. Surveillance cameras *are* everywhere, watching everything we do. How different are these cameras from the ones used in *Mockingjay*? As Castor points out, the Capitol government has surveillance cameras on every street; further, the Capitol knows when and where to attack the rebels because they watch everything everywhere (*Mockingjay*, 281).

In the real world, face recognition software is used in airports. The government can trace everything we do on the Internet. They can read our e-mails, listen to our phone calls. Databases in federal agencies contain a wealth of information about citizens. The Justice Department uses ChoicePoint,[18] a data aggregator, to collect personal information about citizens.

If the banks fail, if the economy totally tanks, if people all remain unemployed, if the inequities continue or *grow*, we face criterion number one for rebellion, mass discontent.

If politicians continue to bicker, party against party with no remedies in sight, just bickering among the rich and powerful, the intellectuals will dissent as they did during the Vietnam War. We will face criterion number two, elite dissent.

If the first two happen, then we have a unifying motive.

Sadly, the government faces crises on all sides: messed-up economy; poor education for students; lack of housing; homeless people; collapse of banking and auto industries; closing of factories and production of goods in this country; and wars, wars, wars.

As for world permissiveness, what country will step up to the plate and help the United States if we collapse into civil war?

And what if that civil war happens, and a government rises that subjugates the masses with Dark Days to keep them in line so the people don't rebel again?

My personal opinion is that it will *not* happen. Misguided as I might be, I retain a belief in the backbone and strength of the United States, that we will somehow rise above the current messes and make ourselves strong again. I retain some small hope that our government and corporate leaders will put the people's interests and well-being before their own pocketbooks. Jobs, education, housing, health . . . if strong leadership with ethics and morals takes a stand and does what's right, maybe there's hope. In his inaugural address in 1961, President John F. Kennedy said, "ask not what your country can do for you—ask what you can do for your country." I don't think he had in mind the notion that our government and corporate leaders would pad their bank accounts while letting the rest of the country slope toward poverty and hunger; for if our leaders were thinking about what they could do for the country, they'd be considering its future, in short, its *children*.

In hoping for the best, perhaps I'm simply too naïve. But if I don't think this way, then I'll have constant nightmares, just as Katniss has nightmares. I don't think we will ever pit children against children in gladiator games. But I wonder what people thought before the Romans instituted the Games? Did people like me, mothers and mild souls, think such atrocities could never happen to *their* children in *their* civilized societies?

The Hunger Games series makes us think about issues like this, and for this reason, among many others, it's a very powerful fictional work.

DOOMSDAY PREDICTIONS

2000–1600 BC, Persia

People have been foretelling the end of the world, the apocalypse, since the dawn of time. Ancient prophets gathered large followings by warning that everyone was doomed, the end was near, the sky was falling. For the most part, the doomsday predictions proved false. Though if we wait long enough, perhaps they'll spin around toward truth.

The ancient prophet Zarathustra, often known by his nickname Zoroaster, hailed way back to early biblical times. This was around the time that Abram, most commonly known as Abraham, was wandering around Canaan and northern Egypt with Sarah and Lot. According to the standard Hebrew text of the Old Testament, Abraham lived between 1812 BC and 1637 BC and died at age 175. Various scholars place his birth and death at different times, but for the most part, it's agreed that Abraham lived in the first half of the second millennium BC.

Zoroaster spawned a religion, Zoroastrianism, and also appeared on the cover of a famous book by Nietzsche, *Thus Spake Zarathustra*. He was a nomad and prophet in what is now Iran, and when his people faced death at the hands (and clubs and knives) of rival tribesmen, Zoroaster begged one of his most powerful gods, Ahura Mazda, to save his kinsmen. Along with prayers and chants, Zoroaster believed that Ahura Mazda would save his people during an all-out raging annihilation war, an apocalypse, during which good (his people) would win over evil (his rivals). The post-apocalypse result would be a perfect, peaceful, harmonious world for his people.

HUNGER

STARVING IN THE DISTRICTS

HUNGER VERSUS STARVATION

Hunger grates on the people in District 12. It grates on almost everyone who doesn't live in the Capitol of Panem. Hunger is a constant theme in *The Hunger Games, Catching Fire,* and *Mockingjay.*

But "hunger" actually doesn't come close to defining what happens to Katniss Everdeen and everyone she knows and loves in District 12. It doesn't describe what happens to emaciated little Rue, who comes from the agricultural district.

The word "starvation" or possibly the phrase "starved to death" is a lot closer to the truth. We know this is true from the beginning of *The Hunger Games* when Gale holds up a loaf of bread, Katniss says she has a goat cheese from Prim, and Gale comments that now, they have "a real feast" (*The Hunger Games,* 7). If a feast consists of bread and cheese, you're not getting all that much food.

Up front, Katniss tells us that her mother "sat by, blank and unreachable, while her children turned to skin and bones" (*The Hunger Games,* 8). This reference also implies strongly that starvation is a central component of life in The Hunger Games books. In fact, hunger and other horrors are so acute for people in District 12 that Katniss vows never to have any children.

In this fictional world, food is rationed, food is a weapon. Food is withheld from everyone, then granted to the so-called lucky few who are able to kill all the other tributes in the Games. And for those holding the strings, the power, those in the Capitol who create and promote the Games for their own amusement and to dominate and control the masses, well, for them, hunger doesn't exist. The people in power have more than enough to eat. Their feasts are extravagant orgies of food, reminiscent of the overindulgence in Marie Antoinette's time. These people eat so much that they purge after meals, only because they want to eat yet more.

Is this fictional world of starvation versus overfeeding all that different from reality? Sure, we don't have a modern Hunger Games, where children kill each other on television, but we do have a dichotomy of starvation and overfeeding. Within a single country, say the United States, we have rich people attending banquets, eating in fancy restaurants, eating as much as they want of all sorts of foods; we have an obesity epidemic; we have an anorexia and corollary bulimia epidemic; and yet we also have a vast population of starving, homeless, suffering people, including many children.

HUNGER IN THE REAL WORLD

The World Hunger Education Service quotes the United Nations Food and Agriculture Organization that, as of October 2010, 925 million people worldwide are "hungry." Asia and the Pacific have 578 million malnourished and hungry people, the sub-Sahara portion of Africa has 239 million, Latin America and the Caribbean 53 million, the Near East and North Africa 37 million, and the "developed countries" have 19 million.[1] These numbers do not pinpoint starvation, but rather, malnourishment and extreme hunger. The same source states that, using stunted growth as a measure, 70 percent of "hungry" children are in Asia and 26 percent are in Africa. When mothers don't get sufficient nourishment, their babies suffer terribly, not only as infants and toddlers, but if they live to older ages, they are susceptible to mental illness and retardation, blindness, and many other problems.

These numbers are substantiated by the World Food Programme (and UNICEF), which adds that 146 million children are underweight and hungry in the world and that 10.9 million under the age of five die from hunger-related diseases.[2]

Children with *kwashiorkor* (see "The Disease of the Displaced Child" in this chapter) suffer from liver malfunctions, decreased immunity, anemia, and if not treated, eventually from shock, comas, and death. One would think that kwashiorkor would be common in young children in The Hunger Games books—that is, if they live that long.

While kwashiorkor primarily afflicts children under the age of five, a similar hunger disease called *marasmus* (see "The Disease of the Baby" in this chapter) primarily afflicts children *under the age of two*. Typically a result of insufficient breast milk or diluted/unsanitary bottle milk, marasmus causes stunted growth, emaciated bodies, loss of hair, and the type of malnutrition that can lead to mental illness, and other serious problems. Remember, during early childhood, the brain grows a lot, and if stunted by malnutrition, the results typically are disastrous. So in The Hunger Games books, a lot of children could have the bloated stomachs and emaciated bodies of the starving, could be retarded, and could die from malnutrition.

The Disease of the Displaced Child

First defined in the 1930s in Ghana—in the language of Ga—the term *kwashiorkor* means "the disease of the displaced child," whereby a child is displaced from his mother's breast, and after early weaning, grows seriously ill. It affects primarily children less than five years old. It is a severe form of protein malnutrition in children and is caused by starvation and diets deplete in meat and animal products.

One would think that a huge percentage of children in the districts would contract kwashiorkor due to their insufficient and inadequate diets, including a lack of meat. By the time most children in The Hunger Games trilogy become tributes, they would be weak, dizzy, and extremely sick. Most of them get grain as food, and few have access to meat.

The symptoms have been displayed countless times in advertisements to help the starving children of the world. The bloated stomachs, the peeling skin with white spots (called, *vitiligo*), the thinning old-man-white hair, the stunted growth, the skeletal body. Other symptoms that we don't see in photographs include diarrhea, fatigue, an enlarged and fatty liver, decreased immunity, anemia, and renal failure. If not treated, kwashiorkor leads to shock, comas, and death.

The Medical Information Service of the organization, Medicine for Africa, suggests that "close to 50% of an estimated 10 million deaths each year in developing countries, are the result of malnutrition in infants and children under the age of five."[3]

The actual numbers are hard to determine because the causes of death on official certificates may point to poisoning, infection, and other problems rather than the underlying factor of kwashiorkor. For example, children with kwashiorkor may contract and die from malaria, pneumonia, herpes infections, and gastrointestinal diseases caused by parasites, bacteria, and viruses.[4] They may die from lethal amounts of mycotoxins called *aflatoxins* that are in their food. And it doesn't take much for aflatoxins to be lethal: even tiny amounts can cause disease throughout the body and can lead to hepatitis, cirrhosis of the liver, and liver cancer. Even when treated for a year, mortality rates remain high for children diagnosed with kwashiorkor.

The Disease of the Baby

Marasmus is another manifestation of starvation and inadequate nourishment. As with kwashiorkor, a child with marasmus is incredibly emaciated and stunted, has sparse hair, and a face resembling that of an old man. Marasmus may be caused by a lack of breast milk. It may also be caused by a weak and/or unsanitary formulation of bottled infant milk. In short, it is generally attributed to a lack of overall nutrition, whereas kwashiorkor specifically refers to a lack of protein in the diet.

Generally seen in children less than two years old, marasmus causes dry, loose skin; irritability; extreme appetite; and loss of hair pigment. Kwashiorkor is more severe in that the body is no longer able to absorb nutrients, causing the child to vomit, have diarrhea, and contract infections easily.

Marasmus is the disease of the baby, while kwashiorkor is the disease of the slightly older child.

The prognosis for a child with marasmus may be better than for one with kwashiorkor, but the suffering is no less.

SADLY, HUNGRY CHILDREN have been among us forever. It's horrifying when teens and adults starve. When babies and young children starve to death, it's almost unbearable to think about.

In 1940, the Germans conquered a densely populated area of the Netherlands that imported its food. Under Nazi control, people went hungry, each consuming approximately 1,300 calories per day. In 1944, the allied forces entered the Netherlands, and to help them, the exiled Dutch government in London ordered a railroad strike in the Netherlands. In retaliation, the Nazis blocked the import of any food into the area. Going down in history as the Dutch Hunger Winter, the food embargo from October 1944 through May

1945 killed a lot of people. People were literally dying in the streets.

Because the Dutch kept such good records, baby-starvation researchers in the 1960s were able to examine hundreds of thousands of documented cases of male births during the Dutch Hunger Winter. The researchers also had access to Dutch military records for the men surviving Hunger Winter births.

The Dutch researchers concluded that infertility and newborn deaths soared due to the starvation of the mothers. For example, the period of the Dutch Hunger Winter produced only one-third of normal birth rates expected under more normal circumstances. Also, of the babies who did reach birth, a pronounced number died.

In the first trimester, malnourished mothers carry fetuses who are at great risk of having abnormal central nervous systems, and miscarriages are common. By the third trimester, any surviving fetuses are extremely low in weight, and should the babies be born, they tend to die within the first few months.

These findings are of interest when considering the people in the districts of The Hunger Games books. The same problems could be common throughout the districts, with the death of children in The Hunger Games related to far more than the reapings and the arenas. Even the mothers are at risk in The Hunger Games world because women historically have died from miscarriages, premature births, and complications due to unusual pregnancies, particularly in harsh environments without modern medical help.

Of the male babies who were born during the Dutch Hunger Winter, making it into the military in their late teens, the researchers found higher than normal occurrences of spina bifida, cerebral palsy, and hydrocephalus. However, the surviving babies were mentally competent and had normal intelligence, leading to the conclusion by the 1960s researchers that those born with brain damage had died.[5]

Later studies of the Dutch Hunger Winter in the 1970s suggested a direct correlation between prenatal/infant starvation and schizophrenia, paranoia, and psychoses. And in 1995, University Hospital

Utrecht in the Netherlands and Columbia University joined forces to study why prenatal famine results in an increased risk of schizophrenia. This research found a "spike in schizophrenia" among first trimester babies conceived during the Dutch Hunger Winter.[6]

More recent conclusions in 2010 from Leiden University working with Columbia University note that "people in their sixties who were *conceived* during the Hunger Winter of 1944–45 in the Netherlands have been found to have a different molecular setting for a gene which influences growth."[7] Hence, prenatal starvation in the first trimester can also *change the genetic material of the fetus*. This particular study points out that the genetic code doesn't change, but rather, the setting that indicates whether a gene is on or off is what changes. Specifically, the Dutch Hunger Winter survivors have fewer than normal methyl groups on their IGF2 genes. It's possible that the mutation enables the survivor to adapt rapidly to malnutrition while still in the womb.

But starvation among children hasn't been confined—not by a long shot—to the Dutch Hunger Winter. Sadly, it's been all too common throughout time.

In the past two centuries, starvation diseases such as marasmus have been at the root of many childhood deaths. According to Dr. Jacqueline Hansen, who specializes in Early Childhood and Elementary Education at Murray State University, "The rate of infant mortality, or marasmus, among orphans often has reached incredible heights. In 1915, Dr. J. H. M. Knox stated that 90 percent of American orphans died."[8] The extensive destruction of crops during the Vietnam War led to countless childhood deaths.

BBC News wrote in June 2008 that in Ethiopia, "As many as 4.5 million people are judged to need critical, emergency assistance . . . there is not enough food in the country."[9]

In Haiti today, starvation is common among infants and children; they were starving before the earthquake. As in The Hunger Games trilogy, there are hunger etiquette rules in Haiti such as: if you steal food, you might be killed, and food stolen or foraged by starving children must be shared with the community. *The New York Times* estimated in January 2010 that "two million Haitians need immediate food assistance."[10]

And we could continue with the grim statistics, the point being: In the real world, throughout history and continuing to this day, our leaders and our governments are responsible for the starvation and resulting deaths of millions of innocent children. The Hunger Games trilogy brings this problem into full focus, amplifying the real problem by acutely portraying the struggles of children who are starving to death. In our real world, do we hold leaders and governments accountable—*sufficiently accountable?*—for these deaths? Or do we continue to put up with the situation, as long as we're insulated from the horrifying realities, letting our leaders and governments continue to enact and support policies leading to starvation?

As Katniss Everdeen discovers, dumping more food on the problem may not provide a complete answer. Sure, after winning her first Games, she gets enough food to help Gale Hawthorne's family and her other friends, but the core issue remains that the evil regime in the Capitol still has control over everyone. So Katniss et al fight the Capitol *and* ultimately President Coin in *Mockingjay* because they must *put an end to the root cause*. Replacing Snow's regime with a similar one run by Coin would continue the same old problem.

Not to get on the soapbox, but seriously, how much different are President Snow and his insane Capitol supporters from many regimes throughout history and in modern times? How much different are Coin and her supporters, who want to institute a new Hunger Games at the end of *Mockingjay*?

HOW THE BODY EATS ITSELF

People like to eat, whether hungry or not, but if hungry, chemical responses zing through our bodies and brains to encourage us to find food. We can become addicted to sugar and fat in the same manner as people become addicted to alcohol and drugs. Sometimes, after eating a lot, we quickly become hungry again—although from a purely physical perspective, we can't require any more food, our bodies just want it. It's possible that this "addiction" to food results from mankind's earliest roots as foragers and hunters, when we never knew when we'd have another meal.

Casting aside for the moment the idea that people often eat too much, let's return to the unpleasant topic of starvation. As the body grows increasingly hungry and without food, the brain ceases to register the hunger as acutely as it recognizes it in the first stages of starvation. The person feels less hungry and is satisfied by increasingly smaller amounts of food.

Eventually, hunger leads to death as the body literally eats itself. It may be hideous to consider that your body may one day cannibalize you, but alas, it is true: If you starve long enough, you will be your own cannibal.

As the brain runs out of sources of glycogen, it cannibalizes the body's protein to get it. The muscles are used, and finally, the heart.

Think about newborn babies, who awaken every few hours at night because they're hungry. They're too young to produce sufficient glycogen, which is the way our bodies store sugar, and they need glycogen to think, to move their muscles, to keep their cells functioning. The calories we ingest eventually turn into glycogen in our bodies.

When the body is hungry, it uses stored calories as fuel, with approximately 85 percent of the calories coming from fat, 14 percent from protein, and the remaining 1 percent from carbohydrates that come from blood glucose or liver and muscular glycogen. If your body has 100,000 calories stored in fat, 18,000 in muscles, and 300 in glycogen, you won't last too long.

Minimally, you need glucose for your brain. But when you fast, at first the glucose level drops in your blood, which in turn, drops the insulin level circulating in your blood. As the insulin drops, your body tissues release fatty acids that travel through your blood to the liver. A hormone is released that raises your blood sugar level. Your liver converts and depletes its glycogen—still within the first day of fasting. In addition, your liver converts the glycerol that, along with fatty acids, make up the triglycerides in your body, and the lactic acid in your muscles also starts converting back into glucose.

All of the above happens within twenty-four hours of fasting. After thirty-six hours, your body relies on the use of protein to produce necessary glucose. Your muscles send amino acids to your liver and kidneys for glucose production, and your body adapts and uses less glucose, pushing the glucose produced by your muscles to your brain, where it's most needed. Your body is now eating your muscles.

At this point, your body revolts against its own cannibalization! You might have a headache and stabs of pain behind your eyes. If you continue to fast, then by the third day, most of your body's energy is now coming from converting your muscles into glucose. In addition, your liver kicks into action and turns fatty acids in your body into ketone bodies, which cells can use instead of glucose. As your body desperately tries to save its remaining protein, that is, your muscle tissues, it sends ketone bodies into your brain; and by day four, ketone bodies are supplying much of the fuel for your struggling brain.

After a week or so, you contract *ketoacidosis,* which typically is seen in people who suffer from diabetes. Too many fatty acids are in your bloodstream due to a lack of insulin. Ketone bodies are now supplying the vast majority of your brain's fuel. Your intestinal walls shrink. Your glucose level is too high, dehydrating your body, and typically by week two or three, you slip into a coma or die.

TYPICAL STARVATION TIMELINE:	HOW YOUR BODY EATS ITSELF
24 hours	Insulin level drops.
	Blood sugar rises.
	Liver depletes its glycogen.
	Muscles start converting into glucose.
36 hours	Muscles provide protein for glucose.
3 days	Most of your body's energy now coming from converting your muscles.
	Liver turns fatty acids into ketone bodies to take the place of glucose.
4 days	Ketone bodies supply much of your brain's energy.
7 days	Your body is hit by *ketoacidosis*.
	Glucose level dangerously high.
	Ketone bodies supply most of brain's energy.
	Intestinal walls shrink.
	Body dehydrates.
2–3 weeks	You are probably dead.

HUNGER ARTISTS: STARVATION ON PURPOSE

The ultimate gift is food. In *Catching Fire,* Peeta says that he and Katniss will give one month of their food winnings for the rest of their lives to each of District 11's tribute families (*Catching Fire,* 59). Nobody has ever won the Games and bestowed such a gift upon another district, and Peeta's declaration shocks and thrills all of the repressed people who hear it.

Hunger is so horrible that in the first novel, Katniss and Gale agree that they'd rather get shot in the head than starve to death (*The Hunger Games,* 17).

And yet, despite the real horrors of hunger, a lot of people do starve themselves on purpose. Some are entertainers and call themselves hunger artists. Others are anorexic, still others go on hunger strikes to prove their points. It is typically a person in the midst of plenty who opts to starve himself. It's highly unlikely that we'd find a hunger artist, for example, anywhere in the districts of Panem. Though in the Capitol, of course, there are plenty of people with anorexia and bulimia.

First, let's talk about hunger artists. These are people who starve themselves to entertain other people. In a cruel and twisted way, all of the starving people in the districts of Panem exist to entertain the people in the Capitol. The Hunger Games themselves are an entertainment platform. The starvation, suffering, mutilation, humiliation, torture, and death *of children* amuses the Capitol. Although they don't *choose* to be hunger artists and it's all against their will, people like Katniss *are* hunger artists.

The key difference between Katniss and other hunger artists, both fictional and real, is this one component: She is forced to entertain people with her hunger. But what about these other hunger artists?

In the late 1800s, Giovanni Succi performed as a hunger artist throughout Europe. He starved himself amidst cheers and adulation, and while not performing, often occupied a cell in a mental institution.

In 1922, Franz Kafka wrote his famous short story, "The Hunger Artist," in which his main character is much like Giovanni Succi: He's a professional faster who eats nothing for weeks at a time, then moves to the next town to repeat the starvation process. He's entertainment! The people love to watch him starve! Yet as with all entertainers, eventually the hunger artist is no longer popular with the masses, who have moved to their fleeting next obsession. The hunger artist withers away and right before dying, he confesses that he just never found any food worth eating. It was easy for him to starve, he says.

As recently as 2003, the magician David Blaine starved himself at length to entertain people. He lasted much longer than any typical person, who after starving himself two or three weeks, would probably die.

Thousands of fans showed up to watch Blaine finish his forty-four-day fast. It was even on television. According to BBC News, "He will spend 44 days suspended beside the London river. During that time he will apparently go without food and will only have access to water fed through a tube. Sky One showed live coverage of Blaine's entry into the box on Friday evening and will show highlights for the following 44 days, with Channel 4 showing the footage three days later."[11] An accompanying BBC diagram shows the effects of potential starvation on Blaine, including "organ failure by 6 weeks."

After emerging from the box, Blaine recuperated in a private hospital. According to CNN World, he "experienced an irregular heartbeat during his time in the box . . . caused by a lack of potassium and thinning of the heart's walls, according to a statement on his Web site."[12] He also experienced stomach cramps after emerging from the box, and he had trouble sleeping. Overall, he lost fifty-five pounds during the fast.

ANOREXIA AND BULIMIA: STARVATION ON PURPOSE

While everyone else is starving, the people in the Capitol are gorging and throwing up. They want to be thin, they want to starve down to anorexic "appeal," but they also want to eat like gluttons.

The starvation is so horrific in the districts that children often put their names in the lottery more than the required number of times so they can obtain tesserae and feed their families. Katniss tells us early in *The Hunger Games* that a tessera equals a "meager year's supply of grain and oil for one person" (*The Hunger Games,* 13).

This grain allotment is similar to the grain doles in ancient Rome except a lottery wasn't held in Rome. Instead, officials doled out grain to people from the Temple of Ceres. As in the world of The

Hunger Games, starvation and extreme hunger were common in the ancient world. Everyone relied on grain to survive.

People outside of the cities depended almost solely on the grain they grew in fields; and if a crop failed, everyone starved. But in the cities, things were even worse because the impoverished depended on imported grain and doles, and they couldn't hunt or gather wild plants in lean times. By 100 BC, Rome's population was approximately 1 million, and famine was so extreme that during grain shortages, officials would drive lowly people—slaves and criminal gladiators—out of the city.

For political reasons, the dole allotted grain to every Roman citizen once a month. Each person was *sold* thirty pounds of grain at a fixed price. Eventually, by 90 BC, Lucius Cornelius Sulla abolished the dole because for political reasons, he didn't care about the votes of all the poor citizens. After he died, again for political reasons, the dole was established once again. By 44 BC, hundreds of thousands of people were receiving free grain rations every month. But in 44 BC, Julius Caesar cracked down on the free supplies, allowing only 150,000 people to collect their monthly rations.

The phrase "Bread and Circuses," which we discuss in chapter 4, "Tributes: Gladiators in the Arena," referred to the free grain dole (the bread) along with the gladiatorial games (the circuses). While the people who live in the Capitol in The Hunger Games have empty lives with little meaning—acting as consumers of food and products and creating little value—this was also the case in developing Rome.

At sixteen, Katniss puts her name in the lottery—the reaping—twenty times, and poor eighteen-year-old Gale puts his name in forty-two times (*The Hunger Games,* 13). They put themselves at serious risk of death to get grain and oil, which barely qualifies as a fully balanced diet. As noted earlier, you have to wonder how anyone lives past a very young age with this sparse and inadequate diet. If your family is lucky to have someone like Katniss or Gale who can hunt and fish for you, maybe then you have a chance of surviving—assuming you're in a district with animals and fish. If you're in a district where you can gather fruits, berries, and vegetables, you're also lucky. But keep in mind that even in the agricultural district where Rue grows up, the very people who farm the food aren't allowed to indulge. So it's a no-win situation, and how people survive on basically grain and oil has to be a serious problem.

Anorexia is the opposite of the unwanted starvation that Katniss and her community face. People can die from anorexia, just as with starvation for any other reason. Most people with anorexia are female.

Anorexia has actually been around for longer than most people think. For example, Saint Catherine of Siena (1347–80), ritually starved herself while receiving Holy Communion almost daily. In her case, the starvation may have been a case of extreme asceticism, as she professed no interest in earthly matters such as food. She separated her body from her spirit by taking Holy Communion but nothing else. It seems she either became intensely ill due to starvation or she suffered from bulimia; whenever she swallowed anything beyond a few herbs, she forced herself to throw up.

In general, the term *anorexia mirabilis* is given to females who starved themselves on purpose during the Middle Ages. As with Saint Catherine of Siena, the condition was associated with asceticism, the desire to starve in the name of God. Other methods of hurting the body and devoting one's spirit to God included self-flagellation, sleeping on beds made out of thorns, and self-mutilation.

Saint Angela of Foligno (1248–1309) not only starved herself, but she supposedly ate scabs, lice, and pus from the bodies of sick people.[13]

Saint Veronica regularly starved herself for three days at a time, during which she would instead chew five orange seeds in honor of Jesus' five wounds.

While the Middle Ages produced a lot of women with anorexia mirabilis, the condition has also existed in modern times. For example, Alexandrina Maria da Costa (1904–55) died from anorexia mirabilis. According to the Vatican, she "fell in love with suffering" and stopped eating. For "forty days" she starved herself in honor of God.[14]

Contrast all these women who starve on purpose to Katniss Everdeen and everyone she knows and loves. According to Gale, the tesserae are a weapon that the Capitol uses to "plant hatred between the starving workers of the Seam and those who can generally count on supper and thereby ensure we will never trust one another" (*The Hunger Games,* 14). The implication is that some people in District 12 have plenty to eat while others starve, hence causing strife *inside* the community.

But at the Capitol level, the difference is far more extreme. Even en route to her first Games, Katniss experiences the pleasures of gluttony. But while she eats her lavish, full-course meal, Effie makes a stray comment about the piggish eating habits of former District 12 tributes. Katniss's anger and resentment gurgle up, and she finishes her meal like a barbarian with no manners. In a small way, she's revolting against what she sees as gross injustice. It's not much, but repressed people with no recourse can't do anything more than display small gestures of rebellion.

But what's really bizarre is when the people of the Capitol eat too much, purge the food, and then eat again. They all have bulimia. As Octavia says in *Catching Fire,* how else would they have any fun at their feasts (*Catching Fire,* 79)? This may actually be a turning point in the entire saga, because Peeta comments that he just doesn't know how much more he can stand. When repressed people suffer injustices and indignities, when they're pushed to their limits, they do eventually rebel. And it's at this point that Peeta tells Katniss that maybe they were wrong "about trying to subdue things in the districts." (*Catching Fire,* 81).

In ancient Rome, gladiatorial banquets for the spectators were orgies of gluttony and bulimia. As in The Hunger Games world, exotic and rich dishes were served in vast quantities. A Roman gladiatorial banquet might include pickled tuna, eggs, cheese, olives, wild fowl, hens, boar, gazelle, hare, antelope, and flamingo. The wealthy spectators ate with their hands and demanded that slaves clean their hands periodically so they could eat more, and yet more. People vomited so they could continue to eat more, and yet more.

We're not really sure if Marie Antoinette actually said, "Let them eat cake," but we are sure that while she ate plenty of cake, the French people starved. This is very similar to what's going on in the Capitol, that while people eat cake, the rest of the population starves. The 2006 film *Marie Antoinette,* directed by Sofia Coppola and starring Kirsten Durst, shows the dichotomy between gluttony and starvation very well.

HUNGER STRIKES AND ASCETICISM: STARVATION ON PURPOSE

In many societies, hunger strikes are viewed as noble and divinely inspired events. Think about Mahatma Gandhi, for example, who starved himself in hopes of promoting peace and salvation. Or about all the monks who starve to bring themselves closer to God.

Indeed, many of the world's religions and intellectuals suggest that starving ourselves will bring us health, happiness, and spiritual fulfillment. Buddha, Mohammed, and Jesus all fasted, as did both Plato and Socrates. Ancient physicians such as Hippocrates and Paracelsus prescribed fasting to cure a variety of maladies. And even Pythagoras fasted for forty days.

Most religions suggest that people fast on certain days each year. Cleansing of the body, we're told, helps cleanse our souls. By fasting, we ask God to forgive us for our sins; we focus on spiritual matters rather than physical ones.

BUDDHA AND FASTING

Siddhartha Gautama, the future Buddha, was born into a royal family in northern India. Deeply moved by the suffering in the world, he left his family to seek enlightenment. Using yoga, he achieved various trancelike states, but when the meditation ended, so did the trances. Then he started fasting and eventually became emaciated, but his hunger overwhelmed his asceticism, so he started eating again. Finally, while Buddha was sitting under a tree, enlightenment came to him in the form of the Four Noble Truths:

1. DUKKHA—All life is suffering. Birth, aging, sickness, separation from what and who you love, not getting what you want, sorrow, pain, grief, despair, death: everything makes you suffer, and everybody everywhere suffers.

2. DUKKHA SAMUDAYA—Suffering is caused by cravings to become (*bhava tanha*), to get rid of (*vibhava tanha*), and to have sensual pleasure (*kama tanha*). Suffering, in short, is caused by our desires.

3. DUKKHA NIRODHA—Suffering ceases when you no longer have desires and cravings.

4. DUKKHA NIRODHA GAMINI PATIPADA MAGGA—The path leading to the cessation of suffering is eightfold and consists of (a) Wisdom (*panna*): the right view and the right thought; (b) Morality (*sila*): the right speech, right action, and right livelihood; and (c) Meditation (*samadhi*): the right effort, right mindfulness, and right contemplation. In short, walking down the moderate middle path of life leads to the end of your suffering.

Over time, the Buddhist religion grew with one of its main features— asceticism, using hunger to find inner enlightenment.

OBESITY: THE OPPOSITE OF HUNGER

Before closing this chapter about hunger and The Hunger Games trilogy, we should briefly mention the opposite problem—obesity. It's actually possible that someone here and there in Katniss's world might be obese, either because they have genetic or hormonal problems or because they live in the Capitol and refuse to be bulimic.

According to the World Health Organization, one of the most significant health problems in developed countries today is obesity. More than 50 percent of adults in the United States, Mexico, Brazil, Chile, Colombia, Peru, Russia, England, Finland, and Saudi Arabia are either overweight or obese. Not only do obese people suffer while alive, they are at great risk of dying before their time.

People who suffer from a genetic disorder called Prader-Willi eat uncontrollably. Without medical help, many die from obesity-related complications by the time they're thirty years old. Some people are born without the genetic code for a hormone called *leptin*. This genetic malady can make people eat uncontrollably, but when cured with leptin injections, the weight gain ceases. In the Seam, even somebody with Prader-Willi will find nothing *to* eat uncontrollably, so they're going to suffer even more than everyone else. And the same thing holds true for the leptin genetic problem—if you have crazy hormones that make you want to overeat but you happen to live in the Seam, forget it. You're going to be even more hungry than everyone else. You are doomed!

DOOMSDAY PREDICTIONS

634 BC, Rome

Doomsday predictions were prevalent in ancient Rome as far back as the legends of Romulus, who founded the city in 753 BC. Twelve magic eagles informed Romulus that they represented the twelve decades that ancient Rome would exist. At the end of the 120 years, the city would be destroyed and the great Roman empire would collapse. The ancient Roman calendar started at the founding of Rome, with 753 BC equal to 1 AUC (*ab urbe condita*). A simple calculation put the end of the world at 120 AUC, which was 634 BC.

When 634 BC rolled around, the ancient Romans were horrified, certain they were all doomed by the imminent apocalypse. But nothing much happened that year.

Instead of instant destruction of ancient Rome, the empire slowly expired. It's widely debated when the Roman Empire fell, with many experts placing the date at AD 410, when Rome was sacked by barbarian Goth hordes.

Regardless of the final fall of Rome in AD 410, in 476 BC, Germanic chief Odoacer defeated Romulus Augustus, the last Emperor of Western Rome, over a century after the eagles predicted the Roman apocalypse.

389 BC, Rome

After Odoacer defeated Romulus Augustus in 476 BC, another apocalyptic prediction arose in the land as new prophets re-analyzed the twelve-eagle notion. These new doomsday experts decided that the original eagle prophecy was entirely wrong and that the mystical eagles represented the days in a year and had actually told Romulus that the apocalypse would occur in 365 AUC, or 389 BC. As with the earlier apocalyptic prediction that Rome would cease to exist in 634 BC, this later prophecy also proved to be false.

167 BC, Babylon

Many biblical scholars suggest that the Book of Daniel was written sometime between 168 and 164 BC when the Macabees revolted against Greek forces occupying their land. In the final part of the Book of Daniel is a fairly detailed description of the end of all time, of the resurrection of the dead, who would then go to heaven or hell. The apocalypse of all mankind would occur approximately three years after the erection of the statue of Zeus in the Jewish temple circa 167 BC.

The Book of Daniel is an early example of apocalyptic literature, with the Book of Revelation (see "Doomsday Predictions: Early AD, Holy Land") in the New Testament providing the most famous example.

4

TRIBUTES

GLADIATORS IN THE ARENA

Most fans of The Hunger Games series know that the author's reference to *Panem et Circenses* extends back to the phrase, "Bread and Circuses," in ancient Rome. In fact, Plutarch mentions in *Mockingjay* that the term has been used for thousands of years and was originally written in Latin (*Mockingjay*, 223). It's no wonder they call the country, Panem. As mentioned earlier in this book, the phrase "Bread and Circuses" refers to the free grain dole (the bread) given to the starving by the government along with the gladiatorial games (the circuses). In a Scholastic Books interview, Suzanne Collins explains that she sends "tributes into an updated version of the Roman gladiator games, which entails a ruthless government forcing people to fight to the death as popular entertainment. The world of Panem, particularly the Capitol, is loaded with Roman references."[1]

But bread plays a much larger role in the series; it's a symbol, yes, of the stuffed, fat-cat gluttony of the Capitol; yet it's also a symbol of the love that Peeta Mellark has for Katniss. Remember, when Katniss was starving and unable to feed her family, Peeta risked his mother's wrath by giving her two loaves of bread. In fact, his mother smashed something hard into his face because he wasn't feeding the loaves to the pigs quickly enough (*The Hunger Games*, 30). His first act of true generosity, kindness, and love toward Katniss was this sacrifice of the bread. It served as a foreshadowing of the deep and eventually intimate relationship they would later share. She keeps the memory of that first meeting close to her, and it reminds her always that it was Peeta's bread that first gave her hope (*The Hunger Games*, 32).

But let's return to bread and circuses, which in ancient Rome, meant a form of entertainment that instead could have been called blood and carcasses. The same holds true in the world of The Hunger Games, that the Capitol's form of entertainment boils down to a thirst for blood and carcasses.

Let's face it: There are people, too many people, who enjoy watching others suffer. Throughout history, human death has fascinated the morbid, the bloodthirsty, the power hungry, and those who need to feel superior. The Salem witch hunt was responsible for the torturous deaths of too many, as were the Crusades. How many people have been hung and beheaded throughout the ages and throughout the world? Why do people go underground to gamble on deadly dog fights and chicken fights? To this day, witnesses sit in booths to watch the electrocution of condemned criminals. There must be *some* reason why violently provocative movies, video games, and anime are so popular. The resurgence of dystopian post-apocalyptic literature itself, such as The Hunger Games series and countless zombie apocalypse novels written by countless authors, point to a current obsession with death, violence, and the ultimate destruction of everything good. Do people find relief in violence and the brutal deaths of others, whether humans and animals, because it reminds them that they are still alive and doing well? This is the classic reason given for the popularity of horror literature, that by reading about frightening things, we "get it out of our systems" and we're relieved that in our own daily lives, we're relatively fine compared to the horrors of what we've just read.

Even as Katniss battles evil and eventually overcomes the government, it's hard to say that anyone truly "wins" in the world of The Hunger Games. By the time *Mockingjay* swings down to its closing chapters, Katniss is a suicidal drug addict numb to violence and death.

Throughout history, invading nations have subjugated, enslaved, killed, and tortured those they conquered. All societies kill: in necessary and unnecessary wars; by slaughtering animals in humane and inhumane ways; by hunting; by executing criminals and other "deviants"; and by the weapon of poverty, which kills people by starvation, malnutrition, and environment.

While we delve more into these subjects later (see the upcoming chapters about torture, evil, and killer kids), for now, as we think about ancient Rome and its arenas and gladiators, we can draw direct parallels to what happens in The Hunger Games. Ancient Rome was one of the most extreme examples of a culture whose entertainment was based on human battles to the death. In their arenas, the Romans killed far more people than the Capitol does in the entire series of The Hunger Games, and they did it with efficiency and bizarre variety. Sure, the Maya and Aztecs of Mesoamerica tortured and slaughtered unbelievable numbers of people, but the key differences may be that: (1) the Maya and Aztecs killed for religious and spiritual reasons whereas the ancient Romans killed for entertainment, and (2) the Romans used *sports arenas*.

In Rome's amphitheaters and circuses, vast crowds feasted, drank, and partied while watching the gladiatorial combats, all sorts of blood shows, animal sacrifices, and even ritualized executions. Very similar, wouldn't you say, to the Hunger Games with its arenas, its deadly combat, its blood shows, and its animal-human battles? And certainly, the people in the Capitol feast, drink, and party while watching these bloodbaths. In an interview with *USA Today*, Suzanne Collins points out that had television existed in ancient Rome, the gladiators would have been pop stars. She says, "It was mass, popular entertainment. If you take away the audience, what do you have?"[2]

It's telling that the names given to people in the Capitol are *Roman* names. We have Venia, Octavia, Seneca, Plutarch, and Flavius, just to note a few. Of particular interest is the name Flavius because in reality, *the Flavians built the Colosseum,* the amphitheater and main sports-blood arena of the Romans, in AD 80. At first, it was called the Flavian Amphitheater, though it is commonly known now as the Colosseum.

Imperial Rome included many large forums for Games: In addition to the Colosseum were the Circus of Flaminius, the Theater of Marcellus, the Circus Maximus where chariot battles were held, the Theater of Pompey, and many others. Though originally, the fights were held in the Roman Forum. Spectators watched from galleries around the Forum, and by Caesar's time, underground passages enabled gladiators to emerge suddenly into the arena.

As in the Capitol of Panem, the ancient Romans enjoyed their festivals of death so much that the bloody spectacles formed a major aspect of the social lives of people from all classes. Everyone flocked to the arenas, where they gossiped during the violent and deadly shows, and they showed themselves off in hopes of "being seen" by more prominent and wealthy citizens.

People even attended the inhumane arenas in hopes of attracting lovers. Finery and show, as in The Hunger Games, dominated; as translated by George Rolfe Humphries, Ovid wrote in ancient times that:

There is another good ground, the gladiatorial shows.
. . .

Hither [women] come, to see;
Hither they come, to be seen.

[Women seeking love] Go and look at the games,
where the sands are sprinkled with crimson[3]

The eroticism associated with gladiators, the arena, and violence was enormous. It is similar to the eroticism of the Spanish matador, who slaughters bulls for public entertainment. The gladiators were so close to blood and death that they were perceived as symbols of the prohibited; in modern terms, they were certainly "bad boys" of their times, and hence, women were fascinated by them.

The ancient Romans gambled on the outcomes of the gladiatorial battles, just as they do in The Hunger Games. The Romans looked all over their Empire for victims to serve in their games, and they glorified their bloodbaths in art.

So why did the ancient Romans have no opposition to the inhumanity of their games while we, as readers of The Hunger Games series, find the violence and bloodbaths deplorable? Have people really changed that much over time? If so, why does the world still have so much violence and brutal death?

While modern society seems obsessed with violence and death in literature, film, art, and video games, we don't condone unnecessary brutality in our own lives. We read about horrors in other nations far away, but as long as the horrors don't hit too close to home, most people have learned that there's no point in doing anything other than shrugging it off. We feel impotent to do anything about the horrors in other countries. In fact, we're impotent, if you get right down to it, to fix the indignities, starvation, homelessness, and senseless violence in our own countries. Most people are disgusted, albeit horrified, by the conditions of cows, chickens, horses, and other animals, particularly those meant for human consumption. And yet, most of us feel impotent to do anything about it.

And yet, compared to the ancients, we are much more sensitive to animal rights, to the inhumane living conditions of animals intended for slaughter, the rights of those on death row to have "humane" executions, the cruelty of bullfights and rodeos, and to lab experiments on animals.

In the times of the gladiators, as Duke University Professor Matt Cartmill writes:

> No intrinsic value was attributed to the lives of beasts in ancient Greece and Rome. . . . In a world where philosophers could seriously argue that human slaves are only detached parts of their masters' bodies, and where grotesquely awful deaths were regularly meted out to human victims to amuse the arena goers, few concerned themselves with the lives of beasts."[4]

In the real arenas of Rome, the battles were much worse than in the World of The Hunger Games. For example, in AD 107, Trajan threw a twenty-three-day Games, in which *10,000 gladiators* fought to the death and men slaughtered *11,000 animals*.

It was common to beat and burn slaves to death if they were suspected of desertion, treason, or magic. Further punishments included crucifixion, and also excruciating death in the ring by wild beasts. In the latter case, a slave or criminal entered the arena naked with a chain or rope around his neck. He was tied to a post with no defense against the wild animals that then ravaged his body. The Romans sometimes used these methods on women and children as well as men.

Women were common in Nero's gladiatorial events. He thrust women of all ages and classes into the ring: slaves, foreigners, and even nobles. In AD 63, we know that Ethiopian women *and* children fought to the death in Nero's games.

There simply were no boundaries regarding the methods of torture. Professional gladiators fought against older men with disabilities. Blindfolded men fought with swords. Men fought with lassos, tridents, spears, daggers, clubs, and nets.

Considering the size and length of the Games, the number of people—men and sometimes, even women and children—violently killed in the rings, and the torture and killing of so many animals, ancient Roman games were probably the most inhumane and brutal in history. Scholars suggest that the cruelties of the Games were as horrific as the Nazi exterminations of millions of people, and that even Genghis Khan wasn't as inhumane as the ancient Romans. As one scholar put it, "No one can fail to be repelled by this aspect of callous, deep-seated sadism which pervaded Romans of all classes."[5]

As another example, in AD 80 when the Colosseum opened, Titus threw a Games in Rome lasting one hundred days, in which nine thousand wild and domestic animals were slaughtered, followed by gladiatorial combats. Next, the arena was filled with water, so men could fight each other in mock sea battles. Outside the city, additional exhibitions pitted three thousand men against each other in another mock sea battle, which was followed by a mock military battle on the ground. And by "mock," we mean that although the battles weren't really waged between opposing government forces, the men and animals were killed in brutal combat.

THE COLOSSEUM AND THE HUNGER GAMES ARENAS

The Hunger Games arenas differ from one year to the next. It's all in the hands of the Gamemakers to dictate how children will fight and die and under what conditions they will battle. When desired, the Gamemakers simply change the rules of the Games. If they want to subject tributes to monkey muttations and poison gas, they have the authority to do so. In the books, they change the rules a few times: first, to allow two tributes to win the Games, then they change the rules back to allowing only one tribute to win. It is only Katniss's ingenuity that saves both Peeta and herself.

In her first Hunger Games, Katniss is thrust into an environment similar to District 12. The arena resembles a pine forest with trees where she can sleep at night and hide, with foods she knows how to procure, with terrain she can manage to navigate.

In *Catching Fire,* the arena resembles a clock divided into wedges that possess different deadly hazards.

In all cases, the Hunger Games arenas are enclosed areas. The only way into the arena is by force, and the only way out of the arena is by death (most common, obviously) or by slaughtering all the other tributes and emerging as the winner.

The ancient Colosseum was also an enclosed arena. The only way into the Colosseum was by force (unless you were watching the Games), and the only way out of the Colosseum was by death (most common, obviously) or by somehow killing the other gladiators and emerging as the winner.

It took ten years to build the Colosseum, which was named after a colossal statue of Nero. First, the Romans drained a lake and removed 30,000 tons of earth. Then they installed solid rock and concrete foundations that ran ten to thirteen feet at the bottom and twenty-six to thirty-nine feet deep under the columns, which were made out of travertine rock. In total, there were seven concentric rings of columns, with internal columns added to support the weight of all the spectators. Marble decorated the arena as well as the thrones set aside for the senators and other officials. The battle arena was separated from the spectators' seating by a thirteen-foot-high wall. The floor of the arena where the battles were held—that is, where blood poured liberally—was thick sand. Gangways and rooms were added beneath the Colosseum, divided into four sections by two perpendicular passages. Cages beneath the arena held the wild animals, and when signaled, men hoisted the cages using lifts, opened the cages, and forced the animals along ramps through open trap doors leading into the arena.

All sorts of battle staging and equipment was hauled through the trap doors into the arena using these same animal lifts.

> This is highly reminiscent of the *Catching Fire* arena, which the Gamemakers carefully create to resemble a clock in which wedges have different hazards. Everything is designed, built, and tested with elaborate detail.

In 46 BC, Caesar threw another Games that definitely rivals the extravaganzas put on by the Gamemakers. Throughout Rome, gladiators fought on stages, athletes competed against each other, and there were horse races, military dances, plays, and fake sea battles in a pool arena built especially for the Games. These frivolities were followed by five days of gladiatorial combat featuring men versus wild animals. The finale of Caesar's Games was a battle between two armies in the Circus Maximus; the battle included five hundred men on foot, thirty men on horses, and twenty elephants.

Note the reference to Spartacus in the box titled, *"Ancient Roman Games."* A Thracian captured by the Romans and sent to their Capua gladiator school, Spartacus eventually led a revolution against Rome in 73 BC.

On a popular Hunger Games website (www.mockingjay.net), Suzanne Collins writes that "the historical figure of Spartacus really becomes more of a model for the arc of the three books, for Katniss. [Spartacus] was a gladiator who broke out of the arena and led a rebellion against an oppressive government that led to what is called the Third Servile War."[6]

For most men like Spartacus, death in the arena was a certainty. For captured prisoners of war, things couldn't have been much worse. They received no mercy at all while training for the games and certainly none while fighting in the arena. After all, the Romans thought of them as enemies, scum, worthy of nothing but the most excruciating deaths.

Spartacus was one of these men, a prisoner from Thrace, which later became known as Thracia when Emperor Claudius annexed it in AD 46. In Spartacus's time, the Thracians dwelled primarily in an area of southeast Europe that today cuts through Turkey, Greece,

Ancient Roman Games: A Timeline of Atrocities Much Worse Than The Hunger Games

ALMOST A THOUSAND YEARS OF CARNAGE

509 BC	The Romans conquered the Etruscans and founded the Roman Republic.
	The Etruscans held gladiator shows in theaters, at festivals, and at feasts. After spectators gorged on food, they were entertained by battles to the death of men, beautiful women, and children.
Fourth century BC	Lucania and Campania funeral games depicted by burial paintings show armed men fighting with spears, shields, and helmets. These funeral games were held in honor of important men who died. They were considered obligations.
	It's possible that the funeral games evolved from the ancient Greeks, who held spiritually driven funeral games complete with human sacrifices.
264–41 BC	First Punic War.
264 BC	The year the First Punic War started, three pairs of gladiators fought in the Forum Boarium funeral games for ex-consul Junius Brutus Pera.
252 BC	Circus Maximus included 142 elephants transported by Caecilius Metellus across the Straits of Messina to mainland Italy after his victory over the Carthaginians. Some records indicate that the elephants were killed in the Circus Maximus.
218–201 BC	Second Punic War.
216 BC	The year the Carthaginians defeated Rome at Cannae, 22 pairs of gladiators fought in the Forum Romanum funeral games for ex-consul Aemilius Lepidus.
186 BC	Fulvius Nobilior introduced battles between men and wild animals in the ring.
174 BC	Seventy-four pairs of gladiators fought in the four-day funeral games for Titus Flamininius's father.

169 BC	Gladiators competed against 63 wild animals *plus* 40 bears and some elephants.
167 BC	Aemilius Paullus introduced death by wild beasts into the games. Specifically, wild animals shredded and gutted non-Roman-citizen deserters from the Roman army.
149–6 BC	Third Punic War.
80 BC	Pompeii amphitheater built.
73–71 BC	Spartacus revolted. Especially strong men had been trained for decades in gladiator schools, with one of the most prominent schools situated in Capua. Men of diverse ethnicities were trained here, including Thracians, Greeks, Syrians, Gauls, Spaniards, and Macedonians. In 73 BC, 80 gladiators escaped from Capua led by 3 men: the Thracian, Spartacus; and 2 Gauls, Crixus and Oenomaus.
65 BC	Caesar hosted an extravagant gladiator event.
55 BC	Circus Maximum included man versus wild beasts.
46 BC	Caesar hosted another extravagant gladiator event, this time including group battles and several Romans from noble families.
29 BC	Statilius Taurus amphitheater built.
27 BC	Roman Empire founded by Emperor Augustus. He mandated that gladiator games would be held every year on fixed dates as well as additional dates that he would add at whim. He pit tens of thousands of men against each other and against wild animals. In his time, there were 176 official feast days, of which 10 were reserved for gladiator events, 64 for chariot races, and the rest for theater. Augustus's shows massacred 3,500 animals, including crocodiles, lions, bears, and leopards.
2 BC	Pompey killed 260 lions and 36 crocodiles in the arena.

AD 41–54	Emperor Claudius ensured that citizens received *correct allotments of grain* and held brutal gladiator battles at *lunchtime*. In The Hunger Games, not only do the impoverished receive grain allotments, but the officials eat like pigs during tribute training, and before, during, and after the Games.
AD 64	Nero's amphitheater burned down. Nero introduced women into the gladiator arena.
AD 70	Colosseum aka Flavian Amphitheater construction began.
AD 80	Colosseum opened with a huge Games lasting several weeks, in which 9,000 wild and domestic animals were slaughtered, followed by gladiatorial combats.
AD 107	Trajan's victory over the Dacians celebrated with enormous gladiator event, which included the massacre of 11,000 animals.
AD 149	Antoninus Pius staged a show that included the slaughter of rhinoceroses, tigers, lions, elephants, hyenas, hippopotamuses, and crocodiles.
AD 225	Gordianus I held a gladiatorial battle featuring the hunt and slaughter of 200 deer, 100 wild sheep, 10 elk, 200 red deer, 100 bulls, 30 wild horses, 300 ostriches, 150 bears, 30 wild donkeys, and 200 chamois.
AD 281	Circus Maximus was turned into a forest arena including 1,000 deer, 1,000 ostriches, and 100 wild boar, ibex, gazelles, and other herbivores. They were killed by tame lions that didn't provide enough deadly titillation for the public.
AD 325	Constantine started eliminating the sentencing of people to death in the arena.
AD 367	Valentinianus I banned the death of Christians in the arena.
AD 404	Gladiator games in the Colosseum ended.
AD 476	Roman Empire collapsed.

and Bulgaria. Spartacus served as an auxiliary soldier in the Roman army, but after he deserted, the Romans captured and enslaved him at the gladiatorial school.

Spartacus led a revolt of the two hundred gladiators imprisoned at the school in what would later be called the Third Servile War. Lentulus Batiates, the owner of the school, heard about the imminent uprising and segregated his gladiator prisoners. Regardless, Spartacus successfully escaped with a total of seventy-eight gladiators and a handful of household slaves and wives.

The men grabbed weapons and equipment from a cart on the Capua streets, fought the men guarding the city gate, escaped into the countryside, and headed toward the dormant Vesuvius volcano, which became their fortress.

Claudius Glaber, the Roman commander in the Vesuvius area, led his military forces up a narrow path leading toward the volcano, and they then blocked access, figuring Spartacus and his men would be trapped without food or water. However, Spartacus was waiting for troops to find him, and he'd prepared for it. He and his men had made rope ladders from the vines growing at the volcano site, and the rebel force dropped on the ladders down the cliffs and escaped Glaber's clutches. A brilliant tactician, Spartacus then led his men around the mountain and attacked Glaber's army from the rear.

At this point, Rome sent a senior officer, Publius Varinius, and thousands of troops to defeat Spartacus and his small gladiator force. But ever the brilliant military tactician, Spartacus was ready for this move by the Romans, too. He gathered thousands of escaped slaves to help his men defeat the Romans, and again, the slaves defeated the Roman troops.

Tens of thousands of slaves—not only men, but also women and children—from all over southern Italy left the farms and workshops where they were imprisoned and joined forces with Spartacus. The rebels marched to Thurii, which is now known as Terranova.

Desperate, the Romans sent Consuls Lucius Gellius and Lentulus Clodianus with four legions of men to head off and destroy the rebels.

They did manage to kill one group of rebels led by Crixus. But again, Spartacus and his forces overcame and defeated the men under both consuls. In a cruel twist of fate, Spartacus forced hundreds of Roman prisoners into gladiator battles, where they killed each other.

Spartacus moved on. The rebels defeated another Roman leader and his men, this time to the north, and then Spartacus turned back toward the south. He had originally planned to march over the Alps.

Campania fell to Spartacus, as did Lucania.

Now even more desperate, the Romans sent Marcus Licinius Crassus and another army of men after Spartacus. Crassus had served in the military and had sufficient skill to avoid an open clash against the rebels. Instead, he wore them out. He chased them for weeks, and he killed those seeking food and supplies. Spartacus was driven to the deep south, into the very toe of Italy. Crassus's plan was to trap Spartacus's forces by the sea and watch them starve to death.

Spartacus enlisted pirates to help his people escape by boat to Sicily. However, the pirates took his money and left him trapped in mainland Italy with all his men.

Trapped by Crassus, Spartacus led his exhausted men in open battle. Crassus had indeed succeeded in wearing them out.

On the banks of the River Silarus, Spartacus was killed, and with his death, the entire rebellion died.

Crassus crucified six thousand rebels on crosses that stretched all the way from Capua to Rome. He hoped to get credit for defeating Spartacus, but general Gnaeus Pompeius, commonly known as Pompey, killed five thousand rebels and took credit for ending the rebellion.

The story of Spartacus has been featured in numerous films, the most famous being 1960s *Spartacus* directed by Stanley Kubrick for Universal Pictures. It cost a fortune to make: $12 million in 1960 dollars. In 1991, the *Los Angeles Times* estimated that it cost $110 million in 1991 dollars.[7] The film starred Kirk Douglas as Spartacus and Laurence Olivier as Marcus Licinius Crassus.

Oddly, after the premiere, Kubrick commented, "I am disappointed in the film. It had everything but a good story."[8]

Spartacus was a captured auxiliary member of the Roman army.	Katniss never serves as a Peacekeeper or in any military unit related to the Capitol.
Spartacus was a gladiator, who fought in the arena to entertain the citizens and leaders of Rome.	Katniss is a tribute, a form of gladiator thrust into the arena by lottery, and she fights to entertain the citizens and leaders of the Capitol.
Spartacus leads and becomes the symbol of the rebellion of slaves in ancient Rome.	Katniss becomes the symbol of and then leads the rebellion of the Panem people against the Capitol. The people are no better than slaves. They have no freedom, and they work to provide food, products, and services to the Capitol. Some are slaves in the most traditional sense—the Avoxes, for example, who serve as domestic servants.
Spartacus forces Roman prisoners into gladiator battles.	Katniss votes at the end of *Mockingjay* to send the Capitol's children into a new Games, though her vote probably hides her true reasoning. My guess is that Katniss cast her vote expressly to keep President Coin at bay. After all, she and Haymitch exchange a glance, and then he votes with her as if understanding her true intentions: to kill Coin later. It was Coin who ultimately was responsible for dropping the bombs that killed Prim. It was Coin who wanted to quash the Capitol, just to gain power and replace one evil empire with her own.

Let's summarize the similarities between Spartacus and Katniss:

Panem and its Gamemakers are similar to the ancient Roman government in that both societies massacred people in public displays to keep everyone under control. Public punishment, in both cases, served to demonstrate the tight hold, the absolute power, that the governments held over the people. Torturous death is considered a great way to keep people obedient and subservient.

As in the world of The Hunger Games, the ancient Romans also publicly flogged disobedient citizens. These whippings occurred in the public square, or Forum. Again, The Hunger Games parallels are clear: During the first Games, Rue tells Katniss that in District 11, where crops are grown, if someone dares to eat anything in the fields, the government officials publicly whip the person in front of all the citizens (*The Hunger Games*, 202). And in the second book of the series, the Head Peacekeeper, Romulus Thread (who replaces Seneca Cray after the old Peacekeeper is killed) whips Gale to a bloody pulp in District 12's public square (*Catching Fire*, 104). Katniss is whipped, as well.

While public beatings continued to take place in the district squares in the world of The Hunger Games, in ancient Rome, things were a bit different. The flogging and execution of criminals and slaves, which at first were festivities accompanied by musicians and heralds, slowly shifted to the arena.

But in The Hunger Games, in addition to the Games, to keep people in line, District 12's Peacekeepers build a new whipping post, as well as a gallows for hanging people and a stockade (*Catching Fire,* 128). Further punishment includes massive starvation, closing the mines where people work, and burning down the Hob where people procure food and other necessary items (*Catching Fire*, 129–31).

The Circus Maximus in ancient Rome included chariot races called *ludi circenses*. Originally, the chariot races weren't particularly brutal and deadly, but over time, they evolved and both animal and human deaths became common. In The Hunger Games, the tributes aka gladiators ride in supposed glory in their chariots around the City

Circle filled with cheering fans. For the opening ceremonies in her first Game, Katniss shares a twenty-minute chariot ride with Peeta (*The Hunger Games,* 68–69).

It's interesting to note that the annual Hunger Games pit twelve couples against each other; that is, one boy and one girl from each of the twelve districts. Accordingly, at the opening ceremonies, there are twelve chariots, one for each couple. The Circus Maximus originally included twelve chariot races in a full day's program. Later, the number was increased to twenty-four.

Many gladiators in ancient Rome were professionals and well trained in all manners of fighting, including the use of weapons, just like the Careers in The Hunger Games. They fought against the beasts and common people who were ill-equipped, in most cases, to defend themselves. In The Hunger Games, winning tributes return home with prizes of housing and enough food for their families. In ancient Rome, the winners of gladiatorial battles also obtained greater freedoms and profits. However, it should be noted that Hunger Games tributes are selected by lottery, whereas the gladiators were either professionals or those imprisoned due to kidnapping, slavery, or perceived criminal activities.

The ancient Roman, Plutarch, documented the fact that the gladiators ate lavish public banquets before their battles. Ditto, in The Hunger Games, tributes eat incredibly rich meals before entering the arena.

AMERICAN GLADIATORS AND ULTIMATE FIGHTING CHAMPIONSHIPS

NBC television broadcasted a television program from 1989 through 1996 called *American Gladiators,* hosted by Hulk Hogan and Laila Ali. In this show, contestants battle each other in an arena that features "games" with names such as Assault, Gauntlet, Hit and Run, Joust, Earthquake, Pyramid, and others. Luckily, the contestants are *not* battling to the death in this arena; rather, these battles are all in fun. Hired gladiators, who work for the program, pit their strength and wits against "everyday" people who, judging by their physiques, work out a lot in the gym. The show's gladiators include action stars and movie stuntmen/women.

On television now is a program called *Ultimate Fighting Championships* (UFC). This program pits fighters against each other and allows various forms of martial arts, including boxing, jujitsu, and wrestling: *these are real fights.*

UFC is a modern version of *Pankration,* an ancient Greek Olympic fighting sport that started in 648 BC. *Pankration* athletes both wrestled and boxed, with no rules governing their fighting techniques.

Suzanne Collins is often quoted in saying that she based The Hunger Games on her father's experiences in Vietnam, on reality television programs, and on the ancient Greek story of Theseus.[9] In a recent *New York Times* interview, Collins adds that she "embraces her father's impulse to educate young people about the realities of war."[10] Oddly enough, in Greek mythology, Theseus and Heracles both wrestled and boxed against their opponents, a technique that became called *Pankration.* Today's *Pankration* is accepted in modern form by the International Federation of Associated Wrestling Styles,[11] but it is no longer part of the Olympic Games.

UFC is so violent that Senator John McCain tried to outlaw the program.[12] He contacted the governors of every state in the United States, urging them to officially ban the program. McCain succeeded in convincing thirty-six states to ban it, after which the UFC revised its rules to make things a little safer and less brutal. Eventually, UFC also revised how it marketed itself, from a "spectacle" to a "sport."

UFC remains extremely popular worldwide, with the fights now known as "exhibition matches" that are not tallied as wins or losses in professional boxing.

An interesting note about UFC: the more sponsorship a fighter receives, the more he's paid per fight. Remind you of the Hunger Games? None of the UFC competitors receives a salary, and as you might guess, winners take home more money than losers.

DOOMSDAY PREDICTIONS

Early AD, Holy Land

Setting the groundwork for The Hunger Games trilogy as well as all other apocalyptic and post-apocalyptic literature to come was the Book of Revelation. In Matthew, Jesus states that "Verily I say unto you, there be some standing here, which shall not taste of death, till they see the Son of Man coming in his kingdom," strongly implying that the apocalypse would occur within Jesus' lifetime and that at least one Apostle would still be around to see the Second Coming.

In Revelation, earth, heaven, and hell collide in one whopping huge battle between Good and Evil. The number seven, which oddly has grown to be a "lucky" number for many people, was central to Revelation and the apocalypse. Seven lamps represent seven churches, each with seven angels denoted by seven stars. Seven spirits stand before God's throne, again represented by seven lamps but also by seven horns and seven eyes. God's judgment scroll has seven seals along with a set of seven judgments. Trumpet judgments are heralded by seven angels, and when the seventh trumpet sounds, God's wrath rains down upon the earth. There are many other references to the number seven, but suffice it to say here that when Jesus opens the first four of the seven seals, that's when the Four Horsemen of the Apocalypse show up, representing conquest, war, famine, and death.

AD 93–195

AD 93, Saint Clement I preached that the end of the world was imminent. *Any second now . . .*

AD 100, Saint Ignatius wrote in prison that the end of the world was imminent. *Any second now . . .*

AD 135–156, Montanus hooked up with Maximilla and Priscilla to convince the masses that the end of the world was imminent. *Any second now . . .*

AD 195, the Sibylline Oracles predicted that the end of the world was imminent. *Any second now . . .*

AD 210, a man named Judas (not *that* Judas, but a different one with very naïve or nasty parents) toyed with the Book of Daniel and predicted that the end of the world was imminent. *Any second now . . .*

AD 365, Saint Hilary of Poitiers predicted that the end of the world was imminent. *Any second now . . .*

AD 380, the North African Christian sect called The Donatists predicted that the end of the world was imminent. *Any second now . . .*

AD 375–400, Saint Martins of Tours claimed that the Antichrist had already been born and the end of the world was imminent. *Any second now . . .*

AD 500

This was a big year for doomsday predictions.

Sextus Julius Africanus, who lived between AD 160–240, figured that God would destroy the world 6,000 years after creation. By his calculations, God created everything in 5000 BC, there were 5,531 years between the creation and resurrection, and hence, the apocalypse would happen in approximately AD 500.

Saint Hippolytus, who died in approximately AD 236, also claimed that the apocalypse was scheduled for 6,000 years after creation, or AD 500.

Saint Irenaeus, who died in AD 202, also believed that the apocalypse was slated for AD 500.

5

WEAPONS

HOW TRIBUTES SURVIVE

WEAPONS OF CHOICE IN THE HUNGER GAMES

Along with hunger, war, and rebellion, weapons are central to all three books in The Hunger Games series. We're told up front by Katniss that most people in District 12 would hunt and fish if they just had the weapons. Most only have knives. Luckily, Katniss is equipped with her father's bows and arrows (*The Hunger Games*, 5).

When tributes go to the Games, they train to use all the various weapons that might be at their disposal. Despite her prowess with the bow and arrow, Katniss worries that kids from other districts will know how to kill her "in twenty different ways" (*The Hunger Games*, 36). How can anyone possibly learn how to use a knife sufficiently to beat someone who has spent years with a knife? Is it possible to learn knife throwing within a few days of training before you're sent into the ring to compete for your life?

Aside from the Careers, who train liberally throughout life for the Games, kids from the districts train for only three days (*The Hunger Games*, 88). Yes, just three days in which to learn how to:

- Throw a knife.
- Throw a spear.
- Throw an ax.
- Use a bow and arrow.
- Swing a mace.
- Tie a knot.
- Set up snares and traps.
- Start fires.
- Make shelters.
- Fight in hand-to-hand combat.
- Identify edible plants.
- Lift weights.
- Use a slingshot.
- Climb trees.

At the beginning of the Quarter Quell Games, Katniss leaps forward and grabs a lot of weapons from around the Cornucopia. She can choose from bows and arrows, knives of all lengths, spears, tridents, axes, maces, swords, and awls. (*Catching Fire*, 269–71). If you're in a situation as deadly as the Hunger Games, you want to pick up everything you might possibly be able to use, even if you're not particularly well trained to use the items.

It's unknown to readers how starved children lacking preparation and training with weapons can succeed in remaining alive. We know that many tributes are quick witted, that some are fast runners, that others understand how to cope in the saltwater arena, that others are good with knives, etc. Each tribute possesses particular skills upon entering the Games, and they then have three days to bone up on what they don't know.

However, remember that the children are selected by *lottery*—that is, in *random* drawings. A physically weak child, a starving child, someone who is mentally ill or retarded, handicapped, extremely young, sick with anything from the flu to cancer or asthma—a vast majority of children, it seems—would be ill-equipped after three days of training and would be dead within an hour of landing inside the arena.

Keeping this issue in mind, let's look briefly at some of the Hunger Games weapons, including items such as the pyramid trap, land mines, nuclear missiles, radiation, bunker, and bombs.

THROWING A KNIFE

To excel at knife throwing, you must master a lot of techniques, such as: holding the knife, throwing it, spins and rotations, distances, and targets. Knife throwing isn't something you can master in three days, particularly when your three-day training includes so many other subjects. Maybe this is why one of the first tributes killed in *The Hunger Games* dies with a knife in his back (*The Hunger Games*, 150). Much later, Katniss is injured by a knife thrown by Clove, but she doesn't die. Perhaps Katniss is lucky. Her forehead is sliced open, and Clove moves in for the kill, revealing an "impressive array" of knives in her jacket (*The Hunger Games*, 285). However, luck comes into play in the form of Thresh. If not for Thresh and his rock, Katniss probably would have died by the knife right then (*The Hunger Games*, 286).

First, it should be pointed out that there are many types of knives, and each requires a different set of techniques. Most likely, Clove's huge array of knives includes most or all of the types described in this chapter. By the way, we'll assume that ordinary kitchen knives and diving knives, which are used underwater, are not part of the Hunger Games weaponry cache. We'll focus on the knives used for hunting, fighting, and overall survival and talk a little about some of the more common types.

A *hunting knife* is used when "dressing game," which is the common euphemism for "carving up animals." This type of knife may have a mildly curved blade, an extremely curved blade, or a clipped blade. A subcategory of the hunting knife is the skinning knife, which as you might guess from its name, is used for stripping animal hide; these have short razor-sharp blades sometimes tipped with a barbed hook—known as the "gut hook"—for eviscerating animals. We're told in *Mockingjay* that to feed eight hundred people in the Seam, Gale is equipped with only one hunting knife, two sets of bows and arrows, and a fishing net (*Mockingjay*, 7). We don't know what kind of hunting knife he has, and while reading, we assume it's a general hunting knife as opposed to one specifically designed for skinning animals.

A *survival knife* is sturdy and often has a hollow grip with an O-ring seal to keep out water. Modern survival knives can be quite elaborate, containing a lot of equipment in the hollow grips: pommels for pounding, thin lines for fishing and making snares, plastic ties, barbed fish hooks, bandages, matches, and other items. It is most likely that the tributes competing in the Games use survival knives of varying types. These knives can be used to hack brush; cut wood; and kill, skin, and gut animals.

Survival knives are typically used in combat, for example, by the major military forces around the world. The U.S. Marine Corps and U.S. Navy issue KA-BAR knives[1] to all soldiers. It weighs about one pound, has a seven-inch blade, is made of steel, and has a leather-like or synthetic handle. As with all knives, the survival knife comes in many flavors, and it's a fair guess that Clove has several of them.

A *utility knife* is a fancy way of saying "pocketknife" or "box cutter."

Along with several blades, it might contain pliers and other tools. Used when installing kitchens, carpets, and other home furnishings, and when opening cartons, it's common in factories and warehouses.

A *stockman's knife* is a fancy way of saying "switchblade." This is a folding knife with at least three blades: a clip, a normal, and a spey.

An *electrician's knife* is insulated to protect from electric shock. This would come in useful when Peeta thrusts his knife into the "invisible barrier" around the four-to-five o'clock wedge (*Catching Fire,* 344).

A *kukri* is a fighting and utility knife with a deep curve.

A *machete* is larger than a knife and shorter than a sword, and it's heavy so it can slash though brush.

A *butterfly knife* opens and closes as you spin it in your hand.

A *dagger knife* is short and used for stabbing rather than slicing meat.

A *fillet knife* is used with fish and ranges between one-half and one foot long.

A *throwing knife* can be almost any of the knives described above—if you're desperate enough and only have a dagger, for example, you might want to throw it. But there are knives that people use specifically for throwing at targets. Typically, they're made of one piece of steel and have no handles. The knife has a blade and a grip.

Throwing knives also come in other shapes such as stars, a staple of spy movies. But the knives thrown in the Hunger Games are probably survival knives and ordinary throwing knives.

INTERNATIONAL KNIFE THROWERS HALL OF FAME

The International Knife Throwers Hall of Fame opened in 2003 in Austin, Texas. An interesting tidbit is that the actual Hall of Fame building is four miles west of "Slaughter Lane."

To determine the champions, events are held for adults, youth (twelve to fifteen years old), and juniors (eleven years and younger).

These are the rules of the knife throwing event, as posted on the Web site of the Hall of Fame:

> Throwers throw four rounds of three knives from each of five distances, for a total of 60 knives. Each round consists of three knives from a minimum distance of 2 meters; three knives from a minimum distance of 3 meters; three knives from a minimum distance of 4 meters; three knives from a minimum distance of 5 meters; and three knives from a minimum distance of 6 meters."[2]

THROWING A SPEAR

Unfortunately for any Avox trying to run away from Capitol pursuers, spears are a likely form of death. Remember in *The Hunger Games* when Katniss tells Peeta about the time she and Gale watched a spear kill a boy from a hovercraft. The vile Capitol pursuers then hauled the dead body into the hovercraft via the cable attached to the spear (*The Hunger Games,* 82).

Spears are also part of the Games themselves, and tributes can opt to learn how to throw a spear during the pre-game training. In fact, Katniss watches a boy from District 2 practicing his spear-throwing techniques from fifteen yards away from a dummy (*The Hunger Games,* 95). One of her earlier fears during her first Games is that she'll be killed by spears or clubs (*The Hunger Games,* 149). And even later, Peeta hoists a spear over her, but then stops as he sees that he's about to kill Katniss (*The Hunger Games,* 193). Maybe worst of all, poor Rue dies by spear in *The Hunger Games.* This is a poignant scene, with Rue screaming Katniss's name right before a boy from District 1 kills her. Katniss can't make it to her friend on time, and when she reaches the body, she sees that the spear is embedded up to its shaft in Rue's stomach (*The Hunger Games,* 233). The weight of the scene is heavy because as readers, we know how much Rue means to Katniss, we know that she identifies Rue with her little sister Prim. Even more poignant is the fact that her first kill is the boy from District 1. She begins to wonder if she's what I call a "killer kid" in chapter 8, "Killer Kids." Has she been programmed and desensitized to killing? Is the taking of a human life really all that different from that of an animal's life? At this point, Katniss feels terrible about killing other children. At this point, she realizes that they have names and families and friends, just as she does. Finnick, we learn, is also good with a spear, particularly with a trident, which is a type of spear used in his fishing district (*Catching Fire*, 209).

A spear, of course, is a pole that has a shaft and a sharpened point. Spears are often made of wood, which might be the case in the Games—we don't know—but they can also be formed out of bamboo, obsidian, bronze, or iron. Typically, the sharpened point is shaped like a triangle.

Wooden spears have been in use for at least 400,000 years. Neanderthals made stone spear heads 300,000 years ago. Early humans constructed complex spear heads from stone more than 200,000 years ago. Spears were a popular form of weapon during the Stone Age, but fell a bit out of favor once firearms were discovered.

It's interesting to note that the *pan troglodytes verus* subspecies of chimpanzees know how to create and use spears. The chimps strip the bark off straight tree limbs and remove any branches, then they use their teeth to sharpen one end. They use the resulting spears to hunt and kill galagos.

LEGENDARY SPEARS

- *Poseidon's three-pronged spear, or trident, given to him by Cyclops.* According to Greek mythology, Poseidon created water using his trident, and by slamming the earth with the spear, created tidal waves, storms at sea, and tsunamis.
- *Trishula Spear of Hindu god Shiva.* This god always holds a trident in his right hand, and it represents Sattva, Rajas, and Tamas, the three Gunas through which Shiva rules the world.

- *Gungnir Spear of Norse god Odin.* This magical spear always hit its target. Wagner's opera *Siegfried* immortalizes the Gungnir Spear of Odin, whereby the spear is from Yggdrasil, the tree of everything in the world.
- *Holy Lance, the spear that pierced the side of Jesus' body when he was crucified.* This is also known as the Holy Spear, the Spear of Christ, and the Lance of Longinus, among others. As the story goes, to make sure Jesus was dead, a Roman soldier named Longinus thrust the spear into his side.
- *Octane Serpent Spear of Zhang Fei during China's Three Kingdoms period.*

Among the vast number of spears worldwide are simple wooden spears from Western Australia; barbed fancy spears from Hawaii; bone-barbed spears from the Solomon Islands; Roman javelins; iron-bladed spears with colored hair on the shaft from the Naga people of Asam; barbed, iron-bladed spears of the Mobati people of Zaire. Sizes vary, as do the types of spear points.

THROWING AN AX

The techniques for throwing an ax are similar to those of throwing knives and spears. But as you may have guessed, they differ in some ways. As mentioned in earlier sections, the tributes do have the option of training with axes before they compete in the Games. When Haymitch was in the Games, a girl tried to kill him with an ax, which flew over a cliff, bounced off a force field, returned to the playing field, and killed *her* (*Catching Fire,* 202). If not for this ax and Haymitch's intelligent move—he ducked, knowing the ax would hit the force field and return—he would have died. And it's this clue from Haymitch's earlier Games that helps save Katniss later. In one of the many blood-drenched scenes in The Hunger Games trilogy, Johanna drives an ax into Cashmere's chest while Finnick saves

Peeta from Brutus's spear but yields to Enobaria's knife, which slices into his leg (*Catching Fire*, 333).

As noted earlier, weapons such as knives, spears, and axes are central to The Hunger Games. And as with these other tools, axes have been used since the dawn of time. The earliest known axes had stone heads with wooden handles. Later, axes were made from cooper, bronze, iron, and steel. Modern axes tend to have steel heads and wooden handles.

FOLKLORE ABOUT AXES

Since the late Neolithic time period, axes have had spiritual significance for many people. For example, axes have been found that clearly weren't used in fights or wars. These axes were probably early gifts to the gods. Female priests used double axes in religious ceremonies in Minoan, Crete.

For the early Romans, axes were symbols of execution, and later, axes symbolized Fascist Italy during Mussolini's time.

In folklore, people thought stone axes were thunderbolts that guarded them against lightning. To protect their crops from bad weather, people often put steel axes in their fields.

The most common form of the ax as a weapon is probably the standard battle ax. Compared to a spear, knife, or sword, the battle ax can cleave into armor more readily.

Other forms of the ax as a weapon include the tomahawks used by Native Americans; the Japanese *ono*—the Japanese word for ax—which was typically four feet long with a huge steel blade and was used by shei warrior monks; and the Slovak shepherd valaka, which looks like a walking stick. Throwing axes, specifically, tend to be smaller than other fighting axes, and if made exclusively from metal, can inflict a great deal of damage.

USING A BOW AND ARROW

Bows and arrows . . . the fighting, hunting, and pleasure choice of Katniss Everdeen. If not for her prowess with bows and arrows, her family wouldn't survive the starvation, she wouldn't survive the Games, and most of her friends would be dead, as well.

Her weapon of choice, the bows and arrows are illegal, and while she hides them in the woods, she tells us how rare they are, how the officials would have "publicly executed" her father "for inciting a rebellion" had they found them (*The Hunger Games,* 5).

The bow and arrow even help save her mother from the deep depression she's been suffering since losing her husband in a mine explosion. Katniss, her mother, and Prim have been starving and without meat for months, and when Katniss makes her first kill with her father's bow and arrows, it awakens something in her mother, a glimmer of hope. The meat, a rabbit, may have reminded her mother of life before her husband died. Unfortunately, when someone is depressed, it takes more than a memory wisp to break free, and Katniss's mother sinks quickly back into deep depression anyway (*The Hunger Games,* 51).

In the most basic terms, a bow is made up of a pair of curved flexible limbs that are connected by string. The draw weight of a bow is a measure of its power, the force required to hold the string stationary when you draw the string completely back. When choosing a bow, keep in mind that the draw weight is a measure of how much weight is required to actually draw the bow back. Hence, the archer's strength is a prime factor in determining an appropriate draw weight for his bow. A larger draw weight means the bow is more powerful, which in turn, means the arrows can go farther and faster.

Also, the actual size of the archer makes a difference: If your arms are long, you can draw the bow back further, and the arrows are going to fly farther and faster. If you have to hold the bow high in order to gain leverage and aim, then the bow is too heavy for you. If your muscles shake when you draw the strings back, then the bow is too heavy for you.

Shooting arrows in the wild, say while hunting or aiming at other tributes, is different from shooting at a practice range. For one thing, drawing the bow smoothly becomes increasingly difficult as you become tired from running and hunting; and also as you become more tense or cold. If in a hunt to the death, as in the Hunger Games, the exhaustion and stress coupled with the use of a bow not fitted to your strength, weight, and body measurements could result in your death. In addition, if using a bow and arrows for a lengthy amount of time, you could very well suffer from chronic tendonitis and bursitis: overuse injuries that afflict archers using bows with the correct draw weight. With an incorrect draw weight, these shoulder and elbow injuries intensify. How Katniss copes with these issues in the Games and the Quarter Quell is truly amazing.

The draw length of a bow is determined by the length of the archer's arms and width of her shoulders. It is the distance between the grip and the string when you hold the bow at full draw. Arrows are often shorter or longer than the draw length.

The basic parts of a bow are:

- The nock, which is a groove where the string is attached to the bow.
- The upper limb.
- The arrow pass.
- The grip, where the archer holds the bow.
- The lower limb.
- The bowstring.
- The belly, which is the side of the bow facing the archer.
- The back, which is the side of the bow facing the target.

The bow can also come with different profiles, among them:

- Curved. This type of bow is cheaper than most recurved bows, and the same bow can be fitted to archers who are right or left handed. For beginners, this is the most common bow used today.
- Double curved.
- Asymmetric.
- B-shaped.
- Four curved.
- Triangular.
- Joined angular.
- Compound. These include pulleys and cams, and are often used by modern hunters. As far as we know, Katniss's bow doesn't have pulleys and cams, stabilizer inserts, sight windows, and so forth, so hers is not the type of bow used by most hunters today.

Simple bows are made from one type of material, most commonly wood. Backed bows are made from one type of material plus a backing of resilient material for strength. Quite often, the resilient material is made from another type of wood or from sinew. Laminated bows are made from three or more types of material, though typically all are different woods. Composite bows are made from three layers of different materials, such as wood, sinew, and horn. Modern recurved bows might have wood cores coated by carbon and fiberglass laminates.

Bow strings are made from all sorts of materials: sinew, flax, hemp, cotton, ramie, silk, etc.

At the training center for the Games, Katniss encounters a wide variety of bows made from all sorts of materials, some so exotic she doesn't know what they are. The arrows are perfect. But the practice range is nothing for her, offering only human silhouettes and bull's-eyes.

The bows are different from the ones to which she's accustomed, and at first, her practice is way off target because of the tension in the bow. However after a lot of practice, her aim is dead-on again (*The Hunger Games*, 101). This makes a lot of sense because in reality, the elasticity of the bow directly affects the projection of the arrows. When you pull back the strings of the bow, potential energy is stored within the bow itself. When you release the bow, the string is released, as well, and the potential energy is transformed into projectile motion.

In the actual Games, a tribute would have to use any bows she finds, and it would be impossible to train with them or get accustomed to them before using them in a life-threatening situation. If someone is short, then a bow might weigh too much or be too big to hold. If someone is tall, then a bow might be too small for a good grip and release. If someone doesn't have sufficient muscles in her arms, shoulders, and back, she may not be able to use a larger or heavier bow. So Katniss is actually quite lucky during both the Hunger Games and the Quarter Quell to find bows that fit her size and physical abilities.

For tributes without Katniss's experience with the bow and arrows, the Games can prove deadly. Remember Glimmer? She tries to kill Katniss with arrows, but she doesn't have much skill (*The Hunger Games*, 182).

By 16000 BC, ancient people were binding flint points to split shafts using sinew. They were also binding feathers to the shafts. So people have used arrows for hunting and protection since very early times. As for bows, we've found fragments dating back to approximately 8000 BC, but these were lost during World War II. Fragments dating to 6000 BC still exist, however, from Denmark.

Cave paintings show people using bows between 10000 and 5000 BC. The earliest bows we know about were made of wood and came in varying shapes and sizes. For example, the flat bow found in Holmegaard, Denmark dating back to approximately 6000 BC is straight with pointed ends. From the late Stone Age, circa 2000–1500 BC, an oak bow found in peat in Viborg, Denmark is slightly curved with pointed ends. An early Egyptian bow, made from acacia wood, dates to 1400 BC and has a double convex shape.

Like bows, arrows come in many sizes and shapes. In general, the parts of the arrow are:

- Head or point.
- Shaft.
- Crest.
- Index feather or vane.
- Fletching or feather.
- Nock.

Most of the common arrowhead shapes were developed during the Stone Age:

- Lozenge.
- Barbed.
- Swallowtail.
- Leaf.
- Triangular.
- Chisel.

The shape of an arrow's shaft is important to its projection toward the target. The shaft must be flexible, but not *too* flexible. If too stiff, it will swerve sideways in flight and miss the target. And if not stiff enough, it will continue to bend in flight and slow down.

Also important is the type of arrow you use. Wooden arrows are the most common. Fiberglass arrows break easily but can be fitted to the archer's draw length and weight. Aluminum arrows are durable and can use different arrow tips, but they're expensive. Carbon and aluminum-carbon arrows are very expensive but quick in flight.

The nock of an arrow is critical to the performance of an archer in hitting her target. Typically, it's a tiny piece of plastic that is pushed into the end of the shaft or glued directly onto the shaft. It must fit snugly on the string but be loose enough to enable the arrow to fly when you release it.

If the nook is at all crooked, you might aim perfectly but still miss your target. A slightly misaligned nook is all it takes to push an arrow sideways and make it fly way off target.

Fletching refers to the feathers or plastic vanes on the bow. Most feather fletching is made from the primary wings of a turkey. While vanes might be more durable and quiet than feathers, the latter is much more effective when using a bow that doesn't fit you perfectly. Feathers compress and enable a smoother aim at your target, whereas plastic vanes don't compress and might flicker off target as you shoot. Feathers are also lighter and provide a faster initial speed to the arrow. So in the case of the Games, it would be to Katniss's advantage to use feather bows rather than plastic vanes.

The fletching size is also important, and today, it's common to see arrows with three 5-inch feather or plastic vanes. To make the arrows lighter, some hunters use three 4-inch fletches. But as with everything related to archery, the fletching size is also affected by the arrowheads.

Perhaps the most interesting aspects of bows and arrows in the trilogy are found in the third book, *Mockingjay*. When preparing for outright military combat, Katniss uses weapons that are loaded with "scopes and gadgetry" (*Mockingjay*, 68).

Scopes attach to bows and enable more precise aim at the target. As with everything else having to do with bows and arrows, the scopes come in many types. For example, a laser scope projects a red dot onto the target, so you can pinpoint exactly where you want to hit before you release the arrow.

For beginners, scopes are useful to reduce the anxiety caused by killing creatures. They enable you to focus on the red dot rather than the animal. Sad, but true.

It's unlikely that Katniss would prefer all the gadgetry to what she's accustomed to using. Sometimes, if you have to think too much about what to twiddle and fuss with, you lose focus on your prime agenda, which is killing your target quickly. If an animal is racing away through a thicket, for example, it makes more sense to do what Katniss has always done: shift position quickly, aim, and shoot—without overthinking the situation.

Scopes and Gadgets: A Partial List

Fiber optic scope	This is the most common type of scope on a bow. It channels light into the tip of a pin, and from there, emits a bright dot (usually red) onto the target. The scope includes a pin guard to protect the fibers.
Single-pin scopes	For close-range shooting a fixed single-pin scope may suffice. But for shooting at variable and longer distances, movable single-pin scopes make more sense. Here, the hunter can adjust her "sight" to the correct distance while pinpointing her target.
Multiple-pin scopes	Most pin scopes have four-to-five pins that you can set in increments of approximately ten yards. When the distances shift constantly between you and the target, these multiple "sights" enable you to stalk and kill prey with increased precision. But using this type of scope also requires that you pause and frame your target within the correct pins in your configuration, and then shoot. If battling to the death in a Hunger Games arena, good luck!
Dot scopes	Most of these scopes are electronic and illegal in some US states. They rely on batteries, which can die during the hunt. Also, a dot scope requires a heavy mounting bracket, so it's not particularly useful when you're running from killers and shooting tributes to save your own neck. The dot sight looks like a fancy, old-fashioned camera device, with a long, protruding "lens" and several focus knobs and handles. The red target dot is displayed inside the scope itself.

Rifle-Bar scopes	This device has a rear "sight" as well as a front "sight" that's on a foot-long steel bar. You have to adjust the "sights" for various distances, so this probably isn't a great choice when using archery in battles to the death.
Crosshair scopes	A very common type of scope, the crosshair enables hunters to target their hits accurately without missing a beat. An added "peep sight" lets the hunter view the target although the vertical string of the crosshair scope might be obstructing her view.
Laser scopes	Laser scopes are electronic and illegal in some US states. Similar to a dot scope, the laser variety projects the red dot onto the target rather than displaying the dot inside the scope itself. If too far from a target, the red dot will not display accurately where you want it. The beam's strength is highly dependent on distance.
Mechanical release aids	Most archers today use mechanical release aids, which grip the string at one point, thus enabling each arrow to fly from the identical place on the string. You squeeze a trigger on the mechanism to shoot the arrow. As with everything else, there are many types of mechanical release aids, among them, finger held, concho, and wrist strap.
Shooting gloves	These are typically made out of leather and have slots for three of your fingers. Also included is a leather strap to secure the glove to your wrist.
Finger tabs and spacers	A finger tab is typically a small leather pad secured to your middle finger with a tiny ring. A finger spacer is often used with a finger tab. You place the tab between your fingers and the string.
Arrow rests	This device holds the nocked arrow in place and is considered vital by many archers. It helps keep the arrow aligned correctly at the moment you release it.

Nock sets	These are placed at the nock point of the string. They consist of either extra thread wrapped around the nock point or a couple of metal rings. Nock sets help prevent the arrow from slipping.
String silencers	As the name implies, a string silencer dampens the vibration noises of your string. Typically, you attach a rubber strip about six inches from the end of the string. You knot the strip in place, then use a knife or scissors to shear the strip into threads.
Kisser buttons	This is a plastic disk inserted on the string to help with accurate target sighting. The kisser button touches the archer's mouth at the same place every time she shoots an arrow.
Wrist slings	Typically made from leather or another strong material, the wrist sling attaches to the bow directly under the grip and loops over your wrist. Its purpose is to help ensure that you don't drop the bow after releasing the arrow.

Even someone skilled with basic archery equipment would have a hard time with the sophisticated and unusual equipment described in the above "Scopes and Gadgets: A Partial List" box. These additional mechanisms and techniques require practice at varying distances and reaction speeds.

Added to the sophistication of the bows and arrows in *Mockingjay* is the fact that *the bow recognizes Katniss's voice.* The "Mockingjay" bow reminds her of a flying blackbird, and the bow seems to be responsive: *it vibrates.* When Katniss says "good night" to the bow, it turns off its special abilities (*Mockingjay,* 69–70).

Voice recognition software is common today to convert spoken words into digital text. It often comes with the ability to recognize a speaker's voice. While modern voice recognition software learns the attributes of a particular person's vocal sounds and can recognize what that person is saying in many cases, it's very weak in understanding what other people say.

When first using a voice recognition system, you must speak to it until it learns to recognize your voice. Sophisticated algorithms are used to create the software because everyone's voice differs based on the shapes and sizes of our mouths and vocal chords.

One of the first real applications of Hidden Markov Models was speech recognition software in the 1970s. These models analyze each vocal signal as a static, or stationary, item; for example, a few millisecond utterance might be stored as a discrete item. In extremely simple terms, each utterance (possibly a phoneme) then has a unique statistical output distribution. Again, this is a very simplistic view of how Katniss's bow might work.

Instead, the bow may recognize her voice using other algorithms or possibly—though unlikely—a simple neural network. Pattern matching algorithms, decision trees, and other audio techniques are possible. But most likely, the bow employs a Hidden Markov Model.

The arrows are also unlike anything Katniss has seen before. They explode, they are "razor sharp," they cause fires. But with a simple "good night" to the bow, these features turn off (*Mockingjay,* 70).

Anyone who has seen *Rambo* remembers exploding arrows, which are also common in a large number of comic books and action films. But probably nobody can beat the Green Arrow from DC Comics, who uses all sorts of crazy arrows, such as ones containing:

- Corrosive acids.
- Atomic warheads.
- Cryonic devices that freeze targets on impact.
- Grappling hooks.
- Ice cutters.
- Explosives that detonate on impact.
- Firecrackers.
- Fire extinguishers.

- Handcuffs.
- Harpoons.
- Boxing gloves.
- Balloons.
- Antlers.
- Buzz saws.
- Boomerangs.
- Drills.
- Nets that unfurl and ensnare targets upon impact.
- Tumbleweeds.
- Tear gas.
- Umbrellas.
- Smokescreens.
- Peppermint sticks.
- Parachutes.
- Ropes.
- Safe crackers.
- Reflectors.
- Rain.
- Stunners.
- And many more.

A final comment about the bow and arrow:

Archery is so central to who Katniss is and how she thinks that the bow and arrow is almost an extension of her own body. She uses the weapon without thinking—she's so quick that she can fluidly decide to shoot, then immediately aim and hit the target. Without the bow and arrow, it would be hard to think of Katniss as the same person, wouldn't it?

For example, when the Gamemakers drool over feasting on a

roasted pig, in a grand show of rebellious behavior, she shoots an arrow into the pig's mouth (*The Hunger Games,* 102). What a great moment in the book! Absolutely superb! This act shows Katniss at her best: how angry she is about the Games, in general; about the repressive nature of the Capitol on the citizens of Panem; about the frustrations of her terrible life; about how she is probably going to fight the Capitol if given half a chance. This one scene foreshadows everything to come, particularly the ultimate rebellion in *Mockingjay.* It's a great example of excellent plotting and beautiful character development by the author, Suzanne Collins.

SWINGING A MACE

We're told that in one year of the Hunger Games, tributes had only "horrible spiked maces" as weapons (*The Hunger Games,* 39). And as mentioned earlier, while training for the Games, tributes learn how to swing maces to protect themselves and kill their competitors (*The Hunger Games,* 92). Indeed, this all comes in very handy because Katniss does find maces among the many types of weapons in the Quarter Quell's Cornucopia (*Catching Fire,* 271).

Anyone familiar with fighting-type video games knows about spiked maces. Remember *Dynasty Warriors 2*?

A mace is basically a club with a heavy ball on one end. The ball is made from stone, copper, steel, iron, or bronze, and typically has flanges, knobs, or spikes on it to inflict more damage. Maces used by people on foot—such as tributes in the Hunger Games—range from two to three feet long. Developed in about 12000 BC to kill humans, they are rarely used today. As humans learned to wear leather armor to absorb the blows of weapons, the first maces made from wood and studded with stones became less popular. But along came copper and bronze, and the maces became much more dangerous.

EARLY MACES

The early Egyptians used maces extensively as did the people of Canaan. The Egyptians eventually replaced the stone heads, which easily shattered during warfare, with copper cones. The warriors fighting for Ramses II against the Hittites used maces with bronze heads.

The ancient Romans avoided the use of maces, most likely because of armor. Also, the Roman infantry used tight formations in battle, making weapons such as short swords and spears more useful.

During the Middle Ages, armor and chain mail protected warriors from the blows of sharp weapons such as swords, spears, and arrows. Nonetheless, maces made from solid metal, particularly those with flanges, still inflicted serious injury on opponents.

Many peasants and makeshift armies used little more than maces, poles, and axes. And the Italian mercenary armies from the fourteenth century on also relied on maces as their main weapons.

Maces with pear-shaped heads were common in medieval Russia and Poland. Flanges probably came into use in twelfth-century Russia and then spread throughout Europe. The most popular mace in eastern Europe at that time had six flanges and was powerful enough to crack most armor.

Even the Inca warriors used maces with metal and stone heads. The Aztecs attached sharp stone blades to wooden clubs, a form of mace.

In Africa, the Zulu mace, also called a "knobkerrie," is made entirely from wood, both the shaft portion and the head.

USING A SLINGSHOT

One of the most heartbreaking characters in The Hunger Games trilogy is twelve-year-old Rue from District 11, who reminds Katniss of her little sister, Prim. Rue is so tiny and fragile that she looks much younger. Katniss becomes very close to Rue during the Games and, as mentioned earlier in this book, one of the saddest part of the trilogy is when Rue dies. Among Rue's gifts is the ability to hit targets accurately using a slingshot (*The Hunger Games,* 99).

We all know that a slingshot is basically a length of cord or other material that is used to throw objects such as stones. The most common way of using a slingshot is to make an overhand throw. You can also use an underhand throw, which is similar to pitching a softball; and even sideways throws, in which you swing the slingshot around your body before releasing the stone.

PYRAMID TRAPS AND LAND MINES

In the first book, Foxface dashes toward the pyramid, hopping over barrels and otherwise avoiding what might be killer landmines and other hazardous obstacles. The Careers have purposely set things up so someone like Foxface will think she can grab their supplies without being killed. When Katniss shoots an arrow at an apple sack, all the land mines in the area explode (*The Hunger Games,* 220).

Land mines are common in warfare. They include a casing, a main charge, a booster charge, a detonator, and a firing mechanism. They are triggered by all sorts of things: pressure, such as being struck by an arrow; but also sounds, vibrations, and even magnetism in some cases.

THE DARK DAYS, BOMBS, NUCLEAR MISSILES, AND RADIATION

The Dark Days in the world of The Hunger Games may have referred to nuclear warfare after the possible melting of the ice caps. My theory about The Hunger Games apocalypse is in chapter 1. There's no way to really determine the cause of the apocalypse, but we do know that District 12 "is pretty much the end of the line" and that

District 13 was leveled by "toxic bombs" (*The Hunger Games*, 83). As with many "end-of-the-world" scenarios, the survivors in District 13 hide underground, but in their case, the subterranean hideout is more than a mere bomb shelter: it's a labyrinth of sophisticated machinery, agriculture, medical facilities, housing, and endless elevators to endless levels.

This concept mirrors the 1950s bomb shelter mania, in which government, schools, and families had basement facilities and underground bunkers in case nuclear war broke out. It also mirrors the underground post-apocalypse cities featured in many anime and post-apocalypse films.

After World War II, the United States created the Federal Civil Defense Administration to help people get ready for possible nuclear war. Survival literature called for suburbanites to build fallout (aka bomb) shelters. At its best, a bomb shelter had shielding from radiation and was built from concrete with walls at least twelve inches thick. Most of the fallout shelters probably wouldn't have helped much during a massive nuclear attack.

POST-APOCALYPTIC ANIME: A PARTIAL LIST

Anime and video games are replete with post-apocalypse scenarios. Here's a partial list, but there are plenty more. It's possible to view dystopian post-apocalyptic anime twenty-four hours a day for months and still not see everything available.

1. AKIRA. Post-apocalyptic Tokyo gang wars eventually lead the hero Tetsuo to the military, where he's transformed into a machine-flesh human.

2. EVANGELION. The Second Impact destroys Tokyo, turning it into a battleground of Angels, and several young teenagers turn into machine-flesh humans who must save humanity from the Angels.

3. APOCALYPSE ZERO. Set in post-apocalyptic Tokyo, a sister and brother battle it out to either save humanity or destroy it.

4. HOKUTO NO KEN: RAOH GAIDEN TEN NO HAOH. Nuclear war destroys most of humanity, and warriors use martial arts to survive.

5. DEMON CITY SHINJUKU. A boy must defeat demons in post-apocalyptic Tokyo in order to bring peace to the ravished world.

6. ICE. A space station falls onto Earth and kills all men. The surviving women battle bioterrorism and seek to discover the truth about ICE, a technology that might enable them to bear male babies again.

7. TOKYO UNDERGROUND. Ordinary high school freshmen encounter an underground city where Elemental Users control water, fire, magnetism, and other fundamental forces of nature.

8. CHROME SHELLED REGIOS. Filth Monsters rage in a post-apocalyptic world that houses a mobile city inside a dome.

9. RAHXEPHON. Aliens battle an average boy controlling a mechadroid in a post-apocalyptic world for the fate of humanity.

10. SHINZO. Genetically engineered Enterrans attack their creators, humanity, and the few survivors are housed in a sanctuary.

11. FINAL FANTASY: THE SPIRITS WITHIN. Monsters known as Phantoms invade the planet and kill almost all human life. A few cities are sprinkled around the Earth with barriers keeping them from each other.

12. GIGAMESH. A terrorist attack wipes out the planet, and a brother and sister learn that their father was the terrorist.

13. GENESIS SURVIVOR GAIARTH. After a massive war, humanity is almost wiped off the face of the Earth, with the survivors sprinkled across a barren post-apocalyptic landscape. Robots and machine-flesh creatures duke it out.

14. Many, many more.

In The Hunger Games trilogy, we're told that District 13's elaborate underground city was basically in place before the apocalypse.

Fearing war or complete destruction of the Earth's atmosphere, the government leaders planned to race to their underground city and leave the people above to cope and die (*Mockingjay,* 17).

In the real world, Camp David (in the United States) reportedly includes a bomb shelter built by President Eisenhower. British Prime Minister Harold Macmillan saw the shelter in 1959 and wrote that it was a "Presidential Command Post in the event of atomic war. It holds fifty of the President's staff in one place and one hundred and fifty Defence staff in another. The fortress is underneath the innocent looking huts in which we lived, hewn out of the rock. It cost 10 million dollars."[3] In addition, recent articles point to a secret bomb shelter for the U.S. Congress. Built to protect both houses of Congress and supporting staff, it was beneath the five-star luxury Greenbrier Resort in White Sulphur Springs, West Virginia. Twenty-five ton steel and concrete doors secured the shelter from nuclear radiation.[4]

Most likely, the United States has secret underground facilities to protect government leaders. And it would be naïve to think that other nations haven't done the same thing.

Perhaps if the nukes fly, we'll all be dead. The only surviving humans will be a handful of government leaders. Now, there's a cheery thought.

Bombs and missiles are standard weapons in the hands of the Capitol. It's nothing for hoverplanes to pop into view and bomb an entire district into oblivion (*Catching Fire,* 145). Suzanne Collins brilliantly weaves personal horror and empathy into the narrative to make the bombings and destruction more pronounced. For example, it's hard not to feel bad for Twill, whose husband was killed by a bomb, and Bonnie, who lost her entire family.

A non-nuclear bomb is no laughing matter. Dropped from a warplane, a single bomb can burst in the sky and then rain dozens of bombs upon a location—for the sake of the world of The Hunger Games, this might be a district, and for the sake of the real world, it could be anywhere at anytime. Inside each bomb is a fuse that is timed to detonate the actual explosion, which may include chemical and biological agents. The following appeared in *Popular Science* magazine way back in May 1945:[5] "New chemicals and new mechanisms have been brought together in new *fire bombs*." Old technology, folks, but enough to destroy entire districts in The Hunger Games.

The worst things that could happen to Katniss are to: (a) lose her family and loved ones, and (b) lose her home, that is, District 12. She does lose Prim, which acutely hurts the reader, and she does lose her home at the end of the Quarter Quells when the Capitol drops *fire bombs* on District 12 (*Catching Fire*, 391).

To keep things simple, we'll define bombs as munitions dropped by warplanes aka hoverplanes. The aerial bombs, or fire bombs, in the World War II era were dropped on both battlefields and cities, and included in these bombs were napalm and nuclear devices. Typical aerial bombs have streamlined shapes, stabilizing fins, fuzes (as opposed to fuses), and detonators to light the fuzes. Modern bombs can be "smart," meaning they hone in on targets with great precision; they are built with extra features such as electronic sensors, control systems, batteries, and adjustable fins.

Types of Bombs

Explosive bombs	Includes demolition bombs that destroy structures, fragmentation bombs that kill people, and general purpose bombs that do both. Also includes incendiary bombs, which are extremely deadly, as well as fuel air explosives and anti-armor bombs that are dropped in clusters with incendiary and fragmentation bombs. (Incendiary bombs are the most likely candidates for the fire bombs in The Hunger Games.)
Biological bombs	Includes pathogenic organisms.
Chemical bombs	Includes killer chemicals in the form of gas, smoke, and/or fire.
Guided bombs	Pinpoints targets, "smart" bombs.
Nuclear bombs	The granddaddy of all bombs, includes fission or fusion.

As the war erupts in the third novel of the series, the Capitol sends squads of bombers, hoping to wipe out the rebellion. Somehow, Katniss manages to hit one of these bomber hoverplanes with an arrow, and the hoverplane erupts in flames (*Mockingjay,* 96). It's great entertainment but possibly farfetched that someone could shoot an arrow from the ground, hit a plane, and cause an explosion; but we buy into it because the story is good and we want to believe that Katniss is the ultimate heroine, who can do anything with her bow and arrows.

Nuclear development continues in District 13, which supposedly is why the Capitol has allowed that district to survive at all (*Catching Fire,* 146–47). As mentioned above, the post-apocalypse nuclear fears are similar to the mood of the United States and Soviet Union in the 1950s.

In 1949, President Harry Truman told the citizens of the United States that the Soviet Union had atomic bomb technology and had actually exploded its first bomb. People started worrying about a full-scale nuclear war between the two "superpowers." Throughout the 1950s, this fear escalated with the development of the hydrogen bomb by both "superpowers." A 1957 report determined that the Soviets would soon have nuclear superiority, which further increased the fear of a nuclear holocaust. As late as 1961, President Kennedy asked that $100 million be set aside for the construction of U.S. bomb shelters.

Both District 13, the makers of nuclear weapons, and the Capitol—the evil empire—are at an impasse: If one shoots its nukes at the other, retaliation is inevitable. Hence, the Capitol keeps its arsenal somewhere "out west" and leaves District 13 to its underground lifestyle (*Mockingjay,* 17).

These nukes are just like the ones we have in reality: If used, according to President Coin, they would kill everyone either upon impact or by flooding the environment with deadly radiation (*Mockingjay,* 138). Powerful bunker missiles—either nuclear or otherwise—would plunge into the deep underground city of District 13 and then explode (*Mockingjay,* 147).

Nuclear explosive devices rely on fission or fusion. In the first case, uranium or plutonium atoms split into lighter atoms; a free neutron from one atom fuses with a uranium atom; the fusion causes the uranium atom to split into two lighter atoms; and two neutrons plus thirty-two Pico watts of energy are released. The two free neutrons then collide with more atoms, and the process repeats in a chain reaction. In this manner, more than 36 million million watts of energy can explode from one pound of U-235.

In the case of a fusion bomb—a hydrogen or thermonuclear device—atoms are fused rather than split. For example, with deuterium fusion, in the heat of an initial fission explosion, two deuterium atoms collide then fuse with one atom of Helium-3, releasing one neutron and energy. A resulting chain reaction causes a massive explosion. With deuterium and tritium fusion, one deuterium atom collides with one tritium atom, fusing into a Helium-4 atom and releasing one neutron and energy. And then, the chain reaction takes over.

A hydrogen or thermonuclear bomb uses a core containing lithium and deuterium that is surrounded by U-235 or plutonium. This shell is then surrounded by U-238, a much more inert form of uranium than U-235. After the initial fission reaction, the deuterium and tritium undergo fusion and release neutrons and energy that make the U-238 undergo fission. In essence, this type of bomb combines fission and fusion in a sequence of events: fission, fusion, fission.

Clearly, we're supplying only the basics about bombs and nuclear devices. It's beyond the scope of this book to really explore these topics in detail. Suffice it to say that bombs, both aerial and nuclear, as well as missiles are commonly used in the battles between the government and the people in The Hunger Games.

In large part, the rebels' destruction of the Capitol and its government is due to the bombing of District 2's Nut, a fortress mountain that is home to the evil empire's military. The Nut has evil empire computers, weapons, barracks, and entry and exit paths for the bomb and missile-packed hoverplanes, but the actual nukes are kept elsewhere on the edge of the Capitol (*Mockingjay*, 192).

If you remember the James Bond movie, *You Only Live Twice*, then you also remember Ernst Stavro Blofeld's mountain fortress. Hell-bent on triggering nuclear war between the United States and Soviet Union, Blofeld kidnaps spaceships and astronauts from both countries and blames the other countries for the crimes. His giant rocket base is in an inactive volcano in a remote section of Japan. Inside the mountain is a vast secret base, complete with evil empire computers, weapons, barracks, and entry and exit paths for outerspace rockets and space stations.

There are some differences between Blofeld's fortress and the Nut, of course. For one thing, the Capitol doesn't kidnap space ships and astronauts. For another, the Capitol keeps its missiles and planes on the edge of the Capitol rather than in the Nut.

While reading *Mockingjay*, I kept wondering about a few things. First, nuclear weapons deteriorate over time and must be maintained and replenished. Also required—for replenishment purposes—is a nuclear reactor, which cannot be underground. I never quite understood how District 13, "the maker of nuclear weapons," was able to maintain and replenish its nukes. The people of District 13 aren't allowed above ground, so where's the nuclear reactor?

Assuming District 13 does indeed have access to a reactor and can hence make nukes, then as Katniss puts it very early into the third book (*Mockingjay*, 81), and I also wondered while reading: Why doesn't District 13 help everyone else? Better yet, given how easily they blow up the Nut in *Mockingjay*, after finishing the book (and reading it three times), I wondered why District 13 didn't blow up the Nut years ago. We're told that during the Dark Days, the Capitol and District 13 *both* had nuclear weapons, so the Capitol agreed to leave District 13 alone if all the people stayed underground. The Capitol then hid the fact that District 13 existed from all the other districts (*Mockingjay*, 17). But if it's so easy *now* (in Katniss's time) to take the warplane-hovercrafts to the Nut and bomb it, then why hadn't District 13 done this a very long time ago? Somehow, Boggs's explanation

(*Mockingjay*, 81) felt "off" to me, that District 13 *would* have launched nuclear missiles but they feared the end of all human life and they simply weren't ready to attack the Capitol yet. It's no different in Katniss's time that a nuclear war could end all human life. And it hardly seems reasonable that District 13 was "barely surviving" given their complex technologies (updated Capitol hovercrafts, power generation, heat, food, water purification, high-tech body armor and shoes, missile launchers, armored vehicles, and much more). Surely, District 13 could have filtered help to one district, then another, and so on down the line, making their way to the Capitol—decades ago.

Even after reading *Mockingjay* three times, I remained perplexed by this aspect of the series. The first time I read *Mockingjay*, I thought perhaps that District 13 was in cahoots with the Capitol, and hence, didn't filter its weapons to the other districts earlier.

I also wondered how an underground society trains its warplane-hovercraft pilots. It would be pretty hard to fly a bomber with accuracy for the first time if you've lived underground during your entire life.

These are nitpicking points, of course. As a whole, the series stands as a remarkable literary achievement. *The Hunger Games* is brilliant; *Catching Fire* has some remarkable technical imagery and poignant moments; and *Mockingjay* is a gruesome violence-fest that winds down to a bittersweet ending. The rebellion had to occur somehow during Katniss's time, or we wouldn't have a satisfying end to her story. In the end, readers must always suspend disbelief while reading science fiction and fantasy. If there are loose ends that feel disjointed or somewhat illogical, we tell ourselves that the story was a good ride, the novels were beautifully written, we loved certain characters, and the books had depth and emotional impact. What more do we want?

DOOMSDAY PREDICTIONS

AD 793, Spain

Bishop Elipandus of Toledo wrote about an Easter Eve doomsday panic, in which Beatus of Liebana proclaimed that the world would end that very night. People were frantic and fasted all night, believing death would take them at any moment. By dawn, everyone realized they were still alive, the world had not ended, and they could now eat, drink, and make merry again.

AD 806–992

AD 806, Bishop Gregory of Tours calculated that the end of the world would occur between AD 799 and 806. *Any second now . . .*

AD 848, Thiota, a female prophet, was certain that the end of the world would occur in 848. *Any second now . . .*

AD 950, Adso of Montier insisted to King Otto of Germany that the end of the world was imminent, that the Antichrist would rise and destroy the Frankish kings. Europe flew into an apocalyptic frenzy.

AD 970, the geeks of all geeks, the Lotharingians crunched a bunch of numbers and determined that March 25, 970 was exactly the day that marked the end of all time.

AD 992, Benard of Thuringia calculated that the end of the world would occur in 992. *Any second now . . .*

6

TORTURE AND EXECUTION

WHAT A WAY TO GO

Aside from the torture of starvation (chapter 3) and the gladiatorial arena (chapter 4) with its full array of monstrous weapons (chapter 5), the Peacekeepers, Mayors, and other Capitol officials dish out plenty of other excruciating tortures. They use torture, of course, to intimidate people, deter possible uprisings, and to punish supposed traitors.

Given that torture tends to shock people into downward spirals of fear and terror, it's no surprise that Peeta basically loses his mind and Katniss suffers from constant nightmares. The two are so intertwined that her nightmares whip into frenzies of torture scenes in which Peeta is being mutilated, beaten, burned, drowned, and shocked with electricity (*Mockingjay*, 9). Suzanne Collins has said that her own father suffered from terrible nightmares after returning from Vietnam and that as a child she heard him "crying out" at night.[1] In large part, it's Peeta's change from a happy-go-lucky, delightful, loving, giving boy into a terrified zombie-like drone that pushes Katniss *toward* him. She empathizes with him and feels responsible, if only out of friendship, to help him, but given that he can't distinguish reality from whatever's swirling in his mind, and given that he's convinced she's an enemy who needs to die, it's a battle for her to help him. Still, her nightmares persist. We see the true beauty of her character in light of her deeply rooted kindness, loyalty, and genuine concern. Had Peeta simply remained a happy-go-lucky, delightful, loving, giving boy, then the reader wouldn't see Katniss with the same depth.

Some of the methods of inflicting pain and executing victims that the Capitol uses to exerts its power over citizens are:

- Mutilating and cutting off body parts.
- Beatings and whippings.
- Drowning.
- Electric shocks.
- Burning.
- Hangings.
- Hijacking and psychological—torture by fear.

We'll examine each method as used by the leaders of Panem and then touch on fear as it relates to torture.

MUTILATING AND CUTTING OFF BODY PARTS

The most obvious example of this form of torture is in the form of Avoxes, supposed traitors whose tongues have been cut out so they can't talk. Given that this torture is introduced early in The Hunger Games series, it makes a huge impact on the reader, who isn't expecting anything quite this horrific in a young adult novel. Of course, the tortures and violence only get worse as the story continues, but we're not yet used to reading these gruesome aspects this early in the series. Katniss and Peeta first encounter an Avox when they run into Lavinia in the Capitol (*The Hunger Games*, 78). Later, two Avoxes wait on Katniss, and she realizes that one, Darius, is from District 12 and once saved Gale (*Catching Fire*, 218). This makes Darius's mutilation hurt Katniss even more than the impact of Lavinia. When they clasp hands briefly beneath a banquet table, the reader knows that she feels his pain and wishes she could save him; but we also know that the author is probably foreshadowing his ultimate death at the hands of the Capitol.

Sadly for poor Darius, the foreshadowing is right on the mark. Peeta eventually watches government officers torture both Darius and his companion Avox, Lavinia, to death using a variety of techniques: electric shocks and beatings, which we'll talk about later in this chapter; and cutting off body parts (*Mockingjay*, 274). We're not told which body parts the torturers slice off, nor are we told the types of instruments they use. In sparse fashion, we're told that it took days to torture Darius to death, so we can only assume the worst.

As you might imagine, having your tongue ripped out of your mouth would be excruciating. In ancient times, torturers used tools called mouth openers and tongue tearers to punish those accused of heresy and blasphemy. The mouth opener had three horizontal pieces held in place by two vertical poles. A large screw was inserted into a hole in the topmost horizontal piece, and it descended into the middle pieces. On the bottommost and middle pieces were two plates that jutted out and sloped down.

First, the torturer tied up the victim so he couldn't struggle, then he pushed the mouth opener's plates between the victim's lips. The sloping of the plates kept the mouth very wide open, with the tongue clearly exposed. By twisting the screw, the torturer could widen the distance between the two plates, thus forcing the mouth open as widely as he wanted.

With the victim's tongue sticking through the device, the torturer picked up his tongue tearer, which looked like very sharp shears with pointed ends. The two handles of the shears were held together by another large screw. The torturer clipped off the tongue at its root, and if needing more force to slice through the solid back muscle, he cranked the screw tighter.

King Louis IX of France put a twist on the tongue-ripping torture. He ordered that his officers slice and shred the tongues and then pierce the still-attached tongues with hot irons.

As for the severing of other body parts, as mentioned, we don't know what form this torture took in *Mockingjay*, and it's beyond the scope of this book to delve into the vast array of possible methods.

BEATINGS AND WHIPPINGS

Poor Darius and Lavinia are also beaten during their ultimate torture by the Capitol. But beatings and whippings are common in Panem and are doled out liberally by the Peacekeepers and other officials. For example, according to Rue, if anyone is caught eating crops in the agriculture district, they're whipped in public (*The Hunger Games*, 202). And Gale is whipped so badly that "his back is a raw, bloody slab of meat" (*Catching Fire*, 105). As was done in medieval times, the method in Panem is to tie the victim's wrists to posts—typically in the public squares—and then whip the naked flesh until the victim passes out from pain.

Beatings are a common form of punishment. Not only do we still read about deadly beatings taking place around the world today, by everyone from mobs to police to the military, we've all read accounts of floggings throughout history.

In England teachers used to routinely cane students for all sorts of activities, anything ranging from violence and theft down to lascivious thoughts and behaviors. It's anyone's guess how authorities figure out what anyone is thinking, but in authoritarian environments, it really doesn't matter.

In the Middle Ages, people whipped children after forcing them to watch public executions. The reason? Same as with the rulers of Panem: Look what will happen to you if you get out of line! But it didn't stop there; men whipped their wives, people publicly whipped prostitutes, and beggars were routinely whipped, as well.

Whippings have even been used as self-punishment by religious zealots. The Dionysian cult in Greece and the cult of Isis in Egypt both used whippings as part of their religious fervor. Dionysus, Greek god of wine, music, and ecstasy, was worshipped not only in the Greek Dionysian cult, but also by the ancient Minoan civilization on the island of Crete. The cult was an unconventional form of religion and included dancing, music, intoxication, and trances.

Isis was the Egyptian goddess of motherhood and fertility, as well as a protector of the dead. She was worshipped not only in Egypt, but later in Rome, Greece, and elsewhere around the world.

In the Middle Ages, the European Flagellants whipped themselves and each other in hopes of achieving God's good favor. Although the Catholic Church viewed them as heretics—though not because they whipped themselves—it also considered self-flagellation as a form of penance.

In Perugia, Italy in the 1300s, thousands of people were Flagellants and marched in huge processions while whipping themselves. This group was so extreme that they believed that anyone who did *not* whip himself worshipped Satan.

The Flagellant movement spread all over Italy until major cities each had some ten thousand people in their processions.

DROWNING

Anyone of reading age has probably heard about waterboarding. Torture using water has been around for as long as humans and water have coexisted. Who *hasn't* seen a movie in which some poor fool has his head dunked in a toilet until he finally confesses a sin or provides critical information?

In The Hunger Games trilogy, Haymitch tells Katniss that Johanna was drenched in water and then tortured with electricity (*Mockingjay,* 253). And while Katniss worries that officials might drown Peeta (*Mockingjay,* 9), luckily, it doesn't happen. Perhaps the closest thing to water torture in the three novels is the tidal wave that slams down the man-made foothills in *Catching Fire.* In an interesting parallel to Johanna's torture by water and electricity, Beetee sets things up so any dampness from the tidal wave will interact with his high-voltage wire and electrocute any tributes who are standing too close (*Catching Fire,* 359–60).

ELECTRIC SHOCKS

We've mentioned a few cases of electric shocks already: Darius, Lavinia, Johanna, and Beetee's method. Given that criminals are still executed in electric chairs, it might be worthwhile to delve into this topic briefly. Just what happens when a victim is hit by electric current? How is someone tortured by electric shocks?

Electric current damages the heart and nervous system, and it causes muscle contractions. The higher the current, the more harmful the effects.

One method of electric shock torture is to put electrodes on the victim's body and wrap wires around his fingers, toes, and possibly even his tongue. Then the torturer uses something like a cattle prod on the victim to apply the voltage.

Just sending ordinary household current through a person's chest for less than a second can cause ventricular fibrillation, a condition that is considered—under normal circumstances as opposed to during torture—a medical emergency. The reason is that the heart muscle cells are contracting abnormally and are no longer pumping blood throughout the body. If the heart continues to contract abnormally, this arrhythmia may quickly result in cardiac arrest. Using an electrode, for example, to shoot significantly lower current through the chest also can induce ventricular fibrillation.

Shooting electric current over the chest also can damage the victim's nervous system. The person may lose control of his body, and his organs may start to malfunction. And then, cardiac arrest may take hold.

The resistance of our skin to electricity drops dramatically when wet. This means that Johanna, for example, who is soaked when they torture her with electric shocks, is going to suffer damage a lot more quickly than she would with dry skin.

Ohm's Law states that current is equal to voltage divided by resistance. This means that the amount of electric current in a body is equal to the voltage shot through him at two separate points divided by the electrical resistance of his body at those same points. With increased voltage, electrons will flow more quickly through the body. If your body has decreased resistance to the flow of electric current—for example, if your skin is wet—the electron flow will slow down.

Given that a milliamp is equal to $1/1000$th of an amp, these are general approximations for the effects of electric shocks on the human body:[2]

Effect of Electric Shocks on the Body	Men	Women
Pain.	62 mA DC 9 mA of 60 Hz AC	41 mA DC 6 mA of 60 HZ AC
Severe pain.	76 mA DC 16 mA of 60 Hz AC	51 mA DC 10.5 mA of 60 Hz AC
Intensely severe pain and breathing difficulties.	90 mA DC 23 mA of 60 Hz AC	60 mA DC 15 mA of 60 Hz AC
Ventricular fibrillation within seconds.	500 mA DC 100 mA of 60 Hz AC	500 mA DC 100 mA of 60 Hz AC

As for using electricity to kill criminals "quickly and painlessly," we turn to the electric chair. It all began when dentist Albert Southwick saw a drunk man touch the terminal of a generator, and he got the idea that death by electrocution was a humane way to go. Remember, he was a *dentist*; hence, the use of *the chair*.

New York Governor David Hill adopted Southwick's idea of an electric chair, and eventually made electrocution the state's method of capital punishment. Engineers Harold P. Brown and Arthur Kennelly created the first actual electric chair. Thomas Edison, the famous inventor of the light bulb, is often credited with the development of the electric chair, but this is because both Brown and Kennelly worked for him. The first experiments electrocuted animals for six months, and in 1889, the Electric Execution Law was passed, making it legal to kill people with electricity.

In 1890, the first electric chair in New York executed William Kemmler. The first electric shock was 1,300 volts for seventeen seconds. Kemmler didn't die. After the generator recharged, a second shock of 2,000 volts lasting more than a minute polished him off. The inventor of alternating current, George Westinghouse, who was against the use of the chair, was horrified that it took so long to kill the man.

Controversy surrounds the use of the electric chair as an instrument of death. There are those who oppose it, saying it takes too long to put a man down, that it causes too much suffering. For example, in 1985 in Indiana, William Vandiver was exposed to five electric shocks over the course of seventeen minutes before he finally died.

We can only conclude that electrocution is inhumane. And this includes the use of electric shocks, as with the torturers of Panem.

BURNING

One of the most horrible methods of torture and execution in The Hunger Games series occurs in *Mockingjay*. Keep in mind, once again, that we're bypassing the atrocities of the arenas and the starvation itself because those topics were covered in earlier chapters. There's very little in terms of torture that could possibly eclipse what happens in the Games. Except perhaps this one example.

All of the children, including Prim, are trapped inside a concrete barricade, when a hovercraft drops silver parachutes down to them. Because parachutes usually contain food, medicine, and other good things, the children scramble to open them, but after the hovercrafts steer clear, the packages explode. Not only have the perpetrators burned children to death, they've used the sadistic method of having the children open their own packages of death. It's the depth of cruelty to tempt children with much-needed food and medicine, not to mention with other gifts, only to murder them.

Many of the children die as they're tortured by flames on the ground. Because the explosives wrench off body parts and burn whatever's left, this is not a painless death.

HANGINGS

The threat of losing one's head is always close for the citizens of District 12. If children escape the Games, they might be whipped and beaten, or worse, they might be hung in the gallows or strapped to the stockades and stoned to death. To get even with Katniss, new Peacekeepers show up in *Catching Fire* and erect new whipping posts, stockades, and a gallows for public torture and execution (*Catching Fire,* 128).

The gallows, as we all know, hang a man by a rope around his neck. Execution by hanging is still common around the world, with death caused either by breaking the victim's neck or strangulation. In the United States, hanging was a common method of execution until approximately 1890, with the Delaware government performing the last official hanging in 1996.

As sanctioned by the government, the correctional officers weigh the condemned prisoner, then practice hanging a sandbag that weighs the same amount. Based on the practice drops, the rope length is adjusted; if too long, the victim will be decapitated, and if too short, he will strangle to death over the course of possibly forty-five minutes or more. The rope itself is boiled and stretched before the actual hanging takes place. In addition, the knot is waxed so the rope will slide easily through it, hence providing quicker tightening around the neck. After blindfolding the victim, the correctional officer places the noose around his neck, then someone opens the trap door beneath the victim's feet, and . . . that's it for the guy. In theory, his neck should break because the gallows has been calibrated with the sandbag for his weight. However, this is *infrequently* the case. More typical is strangulation by the rope.

THE STOCKADE

There are two types of stockades, and given that Katniss mentions that several have been erected in District 12's public square, it's a fair guess that people will be punished using both types.

The first, also known as a "pillory," has parallel wooden boards that are hinged on one side, and includes a central hole for the victim's neck and two holes to restrain his wrists. After forcing the victim to put his neck and wrists in place, the torturer fastens the boards, and then the poor guy rots in place.

The stocks are similar to the pillory, but in this case, the parallel boards have two holes in which to place the victim's ankles. The poor guy lies on his back with his legs up and his knees bent so his ankles will fit securely in the stocks. Then he rots in place.

In history, crowds mercilessly pummeled, battered, beat, and even tickled victims. Crimes leading to the stockades included cheating on taxes, perjury, insubordination, writing poems deriding the church, and similar acts.

It seems unlikely that the citizens of District 12 would pummel, batter, beat, and tickle their family, friends, and neighbors who are subjected to the stockades.

Or does it?

When you consider that the people allow the government to take their children off to gladiatorial to-the-death combats, then it's not really farfetched at all to think that they might brutalize their own neighbors if "forced" by the government.

HIJACKING AND PSYCHOLOGICAL TORTURE BY FEAR

Torture dehumanizes its victims. Think about Peeta, who is so dehumanized that he thinks Katniss is the enemy and tries to strangle her in *Mockingjay*. Psychological fear takes hold and dominates until a person cracks under the weight. Suzanne Collins uses psychological torture and fear very skillfully to bring her characters alive for us; we feel their pain, their torment, their terror. Her antagonists, the government leaders and their minions, not only use physical torture, but the most extreme forms of psychological torture upon the people; and in seeing how the protagonists, such as Katniss and Peeta, deal with that torture is what makes them so alive to readers.

In a stroke of genius, Suzanne Collins comes up with a new method of psychological/fear torture. She calls it *hijacking*. Her character, Beetee, explains that "it's a type of fear conditioning" and uses tracker jacker venom, which Katniss knows "targets the part of the brain that houses fear" (*Mockingjay*, 180).

Fear is typically thought of as a feeling of anxiety caused by the possible or real presence of danger. As with any emotion, such as obsession, jealousy, and love, fear comes in many shades of gray. Mild fear might refer to a general feeling of uneasiness or apprehension. An example is the fear we feel if someone makes an unkind comment that makes us worry about his loyalty and friendship. But severe fear, as triggered by tracker jacker venom, is a whole other thing. Here, the victim—such as Peeta—cannot remember what is real and what is not real. When he remembers something, the venom changes the memory as he's thinking about it, and the brain gets confused and stores the revised false memory instead of the real one (*Mockingjay*, 181).

Could this really work? Is it possible to create a venom or other potion that actually changes our memories?

According to scientists, this is a real possibility.

When we experience fear, our body reacts in certain ways. Our heart rate increases, sending blood pumping through our veins, as our body makes sure that our muscles have enough oxygen to face danger. Our blood pressure rises as we grow fearful. In a stress situation, our body shuts down any unnecessary systems, including our digestive system. We therefore produce less saliva—a digestive fluid—and our mouth turns dry.

When we are scared, certain primitive traits prepare us for action. Blood vessels near the skin tighten so as to reduce bleeding if injured. The pupils of our eyes dilate to focus on any movement. The hairs on our skin stand up, making us more sensitive to movement. The more scared we are, the more noticeable the symptoms.

Neuroscientists believe that the seeds of fear lie in a part of the brain called the amygdalae, which is derived from the Greek "amygdala," meaning almond. Each amygdala is an almond-shaped group of neurons located in the medial temporal lobes in humans and other complex vertebrates. The temporal lobes are in the cerebrum at the sides of the brain. The amygdalae encompass nuclei such as the cortical nucleus; the centromedial nucleus; and the basolateral complex, which can be divided further into basal, lateral, and accessory basal nuclei.

In neuroanatomy, a nucleus refers to a structure composed primarily of gray matter that acts as a transit point for electrical signals in one neural subsystem. Gray matter consists of unmyelinated neurons, where myelin is a phospholipid layer of electrical insulation surrounding the axons of neurons. The myelin layer, or sheath, enables impulses to propagate more quickly, almost "hopping" down the fibers, whereas in unmyelinated fibers, impulses move as waves.

So the gray matter is made of nerve cell bodies and short axons and dendrites that do not have myelin sheaths. It basically processes information from sensory organs and motor stimuli.

The amygdalae perform vital roles in our memories of emotional reactions and in our processing of fear and aggression. They are part of the limbic system, which is the portion of the brain that integrates our emotional states with our memories of physical sensations, influences our motivation to do things, and instills fear in us.

When we are frightened, the amygdalae transmit impulses to the hypothalamus, which links the nervous system to the endocrine system through the pituitary gland. The hypothalamus regulates various metabolic and autonomic processes, such as body temperature, thirst, and hunger. When the hypothalamus receives impulses from the amygdalae, it activates the sympathetic nervous system, which in turn, triggers the sympatho-adrenal response, commonly known as "fight or flight" response. Acetylcholine is secreted, along with adrenaline. As mentioned earlier, our heart beat may increase, blood vessels may become constricted. Our pupils may dilate, we may sweat, our blood pressure may rise.

Along with transmissions to the hypothalamus, the amygdalae also send impulses to the reticular nucleus for increased reflexes. It transmits signals to the nuclei of the facial and trigeminal nerves so our faces display fear. And along with all of these sensations, our emotions rise and flutter. In short, we are in a state of terror.

When we are frightened, sensory input enters the amygdalae and forms associations with memories of being frightened of these specific types of sensory input. The association between frightening events and the sensory stimuli may be directly affected by the potential of the involved synapses to react quickly due to what's known as "long-term potentiation."[3]

Long-term potentiation refers to the prolonged enhancement of the efficiency of the synapse between neurons. Scientists believe that long-term potentiation contributes to synaptic plasticity, or the ability of the synapse between neurons to change in strength over time. It is a foundation of learning and memory.

Columbia University scientist and 2000 Nobel Prize winner Eric Kandel has discovered two genes that can be used to inhibit the amygdalae from learning how to fear things. In May 2006, a summary of his work at the Howard Hughes Medical Institute stated:

> Fear in mice, monkeys, and people is mediated by the amygdala, a structure that lies deep within the cerebral cortex. To develop a molecular approach to learned fear in the mouse, we identified two genes as being highly expressed both in the lateral nucleus of the amygdala—the nucleus where associations for Pavlovian learned fear are formed— and in the regions that convey fearful auditory information to the lateral nucleus.["4]

One gene is GRP, and the other is stathmin, an inhibitor of microtubule formation that is highly expressed in the amygdalae. Deficits in either the GRP receptor or stathmin cause mice to be more aggressive, bold, lacking in fear.

Studies involving humans and the GRP gene are still in the future. However, scientists are already discussing the possibility of fear serum that would be given to children to banish all fears and phobias from their minds. Whether such youngsters would grow to be superior or inferior to normal humans is a matter for much debate. Fear is an important defense mechanism in all animals. A man or woman without fear might be the possible next step forward in human evolution. Or the next step back.

Even more chilling, scientists report that it may soon be possible to delete "single, specific memories while leaving other memories intact."[5] In the lab, they discovered that they could inject an "amnesia drug" into someone *while the person was remembering a specific thing.* The drug revised the memory, and in some cases, totally erased it.

Professor Karim Nader, an amnesia drug researcher from McGill

University, is quoted as saying, "When you remember old memories they can become 'unstored' and then have to be 'restored.'" Nader goes on to explain that this is the point when scientists give the person the amnesia drug—while the memory was being saved back into the brain's long-term storage.[6]

According to Professor Joseph LeDoux, Principal Director of the Center for the Neuroscience of Fear and Anxiety:

> Each time you form a memory, "your brain begins to form that memory in a temporary way that can be interfered with if nothing else happens. So you have to convert a temporary memory into a long-term memory in order to have that memory at some time in the future . . . instead of giving the protein synthesis inhibitor after learning and blocking consolidation, you give it after the retrieval of a previously consolidated memory . . ."[7]

This is the method used by the tracker jacker venom in The Hunger Games series. It is what happens to Peeta courtesy of the government. And it's all very real.

DOOMSDAY PREDICTIONS

AD 999–1033

Another grand time for all doomsday prophets! New Year's Eve AD 999 stretching through the first day of AD 1000: One can only imagine the self-flogging, the starvation, the shrieking and praying, and the packed churches.

The apocalyptic hysteria continued until approximately AD 1033 because, when Jesus didn't return in AD 1000, mystics decided the end of the world would come on the thousandth anniversary of the crucifixion, AD 1033.

7

THE NATURE
OF EVIL

PRESIDENT SNOW AND HIS CRONIES

What kind of society forces its children to mutilate, torture, and kill each other for entertainment purposes? What kind of society starves its own people? Enslaves them, whips and beats them, hangs and beheads them in public squares? Are the leaders of Panem *truly* evil? Or are they just doing what they think is necessary in "times of war"?

As for the children in the arena, we take it as a given that they are *not* truly evil; rather, they're forced into gladiator roles by their elders, they really have no choice. But the effects of what they are forced to do—the mutilation, torture, and killing of other children—may harden them and make it *appear* that they are evil. If forced to kill for long enough, can children become *killer kids*? The next chapter, appropriately titled "Killer Kids," touches on this subject. For now, we look at the nature of evil itself. What makes the adults in The Hunger Games trilogy so despicable?

And there's no doubt that they *are* despicable. Some seventy-five years after the Dark Days, they're still holding Hunger Games and Quarter Quells. Surely, the excuse that they must torture and execute people during "times of war" is invalid in their case. They're so afraid of an uprising, as discussed in chapter 2, "Repressive Regimes and Rebellions," that they make hell a way of life. But does this make them evil?

I would argue that the adult leaders of Panem in The Hunger Games are indeed evil, as evil as can be. Hunger Games evil isn't at all the same as "zombie apocalypse" evil or other forms of fantasy horror evil that exist on a separate plane from people. Modern horror monsters can be in the form of human-eating zombies, blood-sucking vampires, killer werewolves, giant octopus-shark creatures from alien worlds, that sort of thing. But Hunger Games monsters are human beings. President Snow certainly can't use the excuse that a huge wasp-vampire creature from outer space made him torture and execute children. He doesn't claim that Satan made him do it. There is no supernatural basis for President Snow's evil. He is responsible for all of his deplorable deeds and actions.

Those who follow him, the so-called Peacekeepers and the Gamemakers, as well as the citizens who dwell in the Capitol, are also responsible for their bad behavior. They eat and they party, they have plastic surgery and fuss over their fashions and appearances, they actively participate in getting the children ready for the Hunger Games. They're portrayed, in some cases, as fairly loving and fun people, not truly despicable, but they turn away from what they're doing and do not take responsibility for their own misconduct. Perhaps they can justify their bad actions with the types of excuses that Nazi citizens used in World War II, that their leaders make them ignore the killings and torture; but as noted earlier, the Dark Days were some seventy-five years ago—that is, World War X is not currently going on—so the followers can't whine that they are acting in "time of war" any more than the leaders can whine about it. No. All of these adults are responsible for what they do to the children in The Hunger Games Series. Even Katniss's mother, *who is not evil at all,* fails to protect her children.

The heroes are the children themselves, who eventually save the people of Panem from the adults. Of course, Haymitch and other adults do help the children and contribute to the rebellion in *Mockingjay,* but Katniss and the other kids are the ones who really get the job done.

People have always lived with conflicts, aggression, and territorial disputes. From the earliest times, some 6,000 years ago, we banded into units to survive the forces of nature, because after all, the power of several outweighed the power of one. Later, the power of many replaced the power of several.

As humans banded into larger tribes, then into states and countries, our struggles with nature were joined by our struggles against each other. Wars over territory, food, mates—all the attributes of survival in the animal world—took hold, and mankind fought itself in massacre after massacre. Rules, regulations, and laws were created in an attempt to govern our actions, and every alliance has had its military and police forces.

The notion of *evil* has its roots in ancient religious sources; as examples, the Old and New Testaments use the word hundreds of times but includes under the *evil* umbrella all sorts of immoral behaviors and bad actions. Evil in the Bible includes minor items such as touching crawling creatures.

In the Old Testament, evils abound in the Ten Commandments, in Deuteronomy, and Leviticus. For example, Deuteronomy 22:21 declares that a female's promiscuous behavior is so "evil" that people should stone her to death. Chapter 7 lists abundant evils of the soul, including selfish behaviors, lust for objects rather than spiritual pursuits, coveting what other people have, and so forth. Leviticus focuses on religious laws related to everything imaginable: sacrifices, diet, childbirth, shaving, self harm, sorcery, strangers, hate, etc.

In the New Testament, Paul's Epistle to the Galatians describes his age as "evil" (1:4–5) basically because mankind performs evil deeds. He warns that "if you bite and devour one another, take care that you are not consumed by one another (5:15)."[1] He warns against "deeds of the flesh" such as immorality, impurity, sensuality, idolatry, sorcery, enmities, strife, jealousy, outbursts of anger, disputes, dissensions, factions, envying, drunkenness, and carousing (5:19–21).

The Koran identifies similar behaviors as evil, and Zoroaster suggested that people are controlled by a god of light and good as well as a god of darkness and evil.

Theological arguments that try to reconcile the existence of evil in our world with the assumption of a peaceful, benevolent God are called a "theodicy." The word comes from the Greek words, "justifying God," and was first used in an essay in 1710 by the German philosopher, Gottfried Leibniz. A typical theodicy hinges on the argument that evil is the result of God letting people have free will. If mankind didn't have the choice of doing good or evil, then people wouldn't be any different from machines.

THE FINE LINE BETWEEN ANGELS AND DEMONS

Religions are stocked with images of angels and demons, and also with angels who become demons; hence suggesting that there is a fine line between the two. The implication is that, given our free will, we can fall either way.

Consider Lucifer, the light bearer, the angel who fell from grace and became Satan. According to biblical accounts, his crime was to challenge God's authority, and for this crime, he and his fallen angels were sent to Hell forever. Once good, he is now evil.

As with all evil governments, Satan has Beelzebub to do a lot of his dirty work. Beelzebub decides that the evil forces should corrupt people and make them evil, too; so Satan corrupts Adam and Eve, and

they nibble on the apple, which in their time was a grievous sin with dire consequences.

Possibly, these religious ideas about evil come from the fact that in ancient times, people lived in small tribes that had to fight constantly for survival. Giving birth to and nurturing boys became essential to the success of one tribe over others. During combat, if one tribe had, say, twice the number of warriors than another, then that tribe would probably win the battle. Hence, in early religious sources, crimes relating to all sorts of things that might injure or otherwise hurt the chance of a tribe to survive would be pegged as evil. Rules (or "evils") regarding cleanliness and diet also contributed to the potential of a tribe to survive. The smaller the chance for infection and potentially deadly illness, the greater the chance for survival.

Definitions of evil vary from time to time, from culture to culture, and from individual to individual; that is, some people think it's evil to hit a child, while others reserve the term evil for greater crimes such as torturing and murdering a child. It's hard to know where to draw the line.

Noted scholar Susan Neiman suggested in her best-selling book, *Evil in Modern Thought,* that perhaps a reasonable way to define evil is that it "shatters our trust in the world."[2] In his best-selling book, *The Death of Satan: How Americans Have Lost the Sense of Evil,* Andrew Delbanco further defines the term as expressed during a 2001 PBS interview:

> [T]here are human beings who are able, by convincing themselves that there's some higher good, some higher ideal to which their lives should be dedicated, that the pain and suffering of other individuals doesn't matter, it doesn't have to do with them . . . That they're expendable, that it's a cost that's worth making in the pursuit of these objectives. So evil for me is the absence of the imaginative sympathy for other human beings.[3]

Delbanco's definition clearly places the government leaders of The Hunger Games into the category of evil. The pain and suffering of other people, albeit children, doesn't matter to them; in fact, *they promote the pain and suffering of children*. Other people, albeit children, are expendable, in the pursuit of the higher ideal of quashing any remote chance of rebellion.

Harking back to the need of ancient tribes to survive, more modern group survival mechanisms include Delbanco's definition. If all members of a group adhere to the leaders' values and methods of control, the better the chance that the group itself will survive. People justify evil actions in the group by telling themselves that they are willing to do anything that is necessary to defend and strengthen the community.

The group survival reasoning is a form of evil in which moral virtues and idealism support violent actions. This so-called idealistic evil pushes terrorists to kill both other people and themselves without remorse. Their inner strength spurs terrorists to commit relentless and merciless atrocities.

But before modern terrorism, severe brutality was common among groups that considered themselves idealistically superior to those around them. One obvious example is the Crusades, which divinely sanctioned torture, mutilation, and murder involving millions of people. The Pope called for Christians to gain control of the Holy Land from the heathens, and the Crusaders brutalized people while considering themselves good men with high morals, serving their Church and God.

During the First Crusade, Arabs from the town of Aleppo tried to defend themselves, but they failed miserably against the onslaught of the armored knights. After beating down the resistance, the Crusaders hacked off the heads of the Aleppo men and catapulted the heads into the town of Antioch, hoping the citizens in that walled city would not resist them.

Also, during the First Crusade, the knights took Jerusalem, massacred the Muslim citizens, then burned alive Jews in their synagogue.

While modern people rarely think of the Crusaders as good and just men who treated unarmed citizens decently (and that is quite an understatement), the word *crusade* is still used when talking about organized movements whose purpose is the greater good. We have crusades against terrorists, drugs, crime, and so forth.

Murder fits most definitions of evil. Murder of children is almost universally accepted as evil. The perpetrators of the murders—for example, President Snow and his cronies—clearly plan and intend to torture and kill children in the most excruciating and horrific ways possible. They know and delight in the fact that the children will suffer immensely. They have no shame. It is this excessive use of suffering that makes the leaders evil. They could choose to limit freedoms without torture and death, but they choose instead to commit· evil acts that go over and beyond what is required to maintain control of the people. It's interesting to note that the Anglo–Saxon roots of the word *evil* were "over" or "beyond."

Scientific laws do not define evil with mathematical precision or experimental proof. As mentioned earlier, there are a thousand gray shades of evil, ranging from murder to theft to bullying to innocent comments that make someone commit suicide. However, if we look at evil as not being supernatural, but the result of a wide range of human behaviors, both intentional and innocent, then we can examine it in a more scientific manner.

Recent explanations for the behavior of serial killers usually revolve around extra Y chromosomes or insanity. It's been suggested by scientists that a genotype of XYY causes men to fly into fits of anger, into rages, into acts of great violence. Insanity, as we all know, is often used as a defense for violent crime. Yet, not only serial killers murder people. Seemingly normal people commit acts of evil every day.

As for being born evil, it seems unlikely. Some scholars claim that there are scientific roots in the evil mind, that a newborn baby with a perverse twist in his DNA will grow up to commit atrocious crimes; that no matter how much this baby is loved from the moment of birth, it won't matter.

But then, there's the theory that evil people are born with what researchers call criminal or risk genes.

In 2002, a group of scientists working for the Institute of Psychiatry in London claimed that they had discovered "the criminal gene." According to the scientists, the particular gene was strongly linked to criminal and antisocial behavior. Children from poor circumstances were nine times more likely to act unlawfully when compared to other children living in similar circumstances if they had a particular variation of the gene.[4]

Needless to say, not everyone agreed with the findings of the Institute of Psychiatry. Especially when Nuffield Council on Bioethics located in London declared that a criminal's genetic makeup should be taken into account during his trial and his sentencing.[5] Politicians on the right immediately suspected a plot to pardon criminals for the most unforgivable sins using the argument that such acts were a result of genetics not intent.

Rising like tidal waves from both sides of the political spectrum came dire warnings of early twentieth-century eugenic programs, which championed sterilizing criminals so that their traits would be wiped out of future generations. These stories were quickly followed with talk of Nazi genetic experiments in the 1930s, forced sterilizations of specific groups, and the possible existence of an "alcoholic" gene that turned ordinary Englishmen into drunkards. No one wanted to be categorized by their genetic code. Nor did either political party want criminals set free due to a mix-up in their genetic code. At present, there's no agreement on whether the criminal gene actually influences behavior or not. The argument has moved out of the scientific community into politics and it's doubtful any resolution to the question will be soon found. Evil remains a matter of behavior, not genetics.

Several personality disorders—psychopathic, sadistic, antisocial, and schizoid—have been linked to violent crimes. If a person can't empathize with and have compassion for other people, then he's most likely to commit violent crimes against them. The brain becomes *wired* for violence. The perpetrator becomes addicted to the high he gets from his atrocious crimes.

Psychopaths empathize with but lack compassion for other people. Schizoids are aloof and lack both compassion and empathy. Many of these people don't fit into ordinary society and have immense trouble forming emotional bonds. And if someone has psychopathic, sadistic, antisocial, and schizoid traits, then he will probably commit evil acts.

However, these killers are not mentally ill, and in fact, they most definitely know what they're doing and they enjoy it. To be insane, a person must be unable to distinguish right from wrong, he must be unable to assist in his own defense.

PSYCHOTICS VERSUS PSYCHOPATHS

A psychopath is quite different from someone who is psychotic.

The psychotic person suffers from severe mental disorders that are probably caused by biological factors. For example, schizophrenics can be confused, they have delusions and hallucinations. They tend to be withdrawn, depressed, and anxious.

The psychopathic person, as defined by doctors, has a disorder of character or personality. These people are lucid, they do not hear voices or see things that don't exist. They can be quite charming. They do not suffer from increased angst, depression, or insecurities. Many simply lack any compassion or empathy for their victims.

Evolutionary psychologists tell us that our minds evolved long ago to help us survive. We learned how to recognize each other's faces, how to recognize and cope with cheating, how to choose mates, and how to talk to each other. Various groups of neurons might handle something like language and be located in one area of the brain—in the case of language, it is located in the area known as Broca's area. Other groups of neurons might not be located in the same area. In this way of looking at the brain, small modules of neurons feed information to larger modules. Even smaller modules feed information to the small modules, and so forth, until at the lowest level, an individual neuron fires during specific events.

A neuron fires electrochemically, meaning that chemicals produce electric signals. When chemicals in our bodies have an electric charge, they are termed ions, and ions in the nervous system include sodium and potassium, each with one positive charge; calcium with two positive charges; and chloride with one negative charge. Neurons are surrounded by a semi-permeable membrane that lets some ions pass through while blocking other ions.

When the neuron is not firing, the inside of the cell is negative compared to everything immediately surrounding the cell. The ions keep trying to pass from the inside of the neuron to the outside, and vice-versa, with the membrane controlling the balance. For example, when the neuron is not firing, potassium ions pass easily through the membrane, and for every two potassium ions the membrane allows to enter the neuron, it allows three sodium ions to leave. Basically, there are more sodium ions outside the neuron and more potassium ions inside it. At rest, when the neuron is not firing, the difference in voltage between the inside and outside of the neuron is approximately -70 millivolts, meaning that the inside of the neuron is 70 millivolts less than the outside.

When a neuron sends information down an axon away from the cell body, neuroscientists say that there is an action potential or that a spike has occurred. The action potential is created by a depolarizing current, which creates electrical activity. An event, or stimulus, occurs that moves the resting potential of -70 millivolts toward 0 millivolts. The stimulus causes the sodium channels to open in the neuron, and because there are more sodium ions outside the neuron than inside, sodium ions flood into the neuron. Because sodium ions have a positive charge, the neuron becomes more positive and depolarized. When depolarization shifts downward to approximately -55 millivolts, the neuron fires an action potential, which is known as the threshold. If the neuron never reaches its threshold, it won't fire.

The potassium channels open after the sodium channels, and when they do, potassium moves out of the cell, reversing the depolarization. The sodium channels start closing, and the action potential reverses, moving back toward -70 millivolts.

So what does this have to do with evil tendencies and obsessions? It explains what's happening inside the brain to cause experiences, behaviors, actions, thoughts, and possibly, the psychopathic, schizoid, antisocial, and sadistic acts we call evil. *Scientific American* reported in 2003 that evidence indicates that, when people think they are seeing aliens, ghosts, and demons, or when they think that they are floating on the ceiling, what's really happening is a firing of neurons inside their brains, imposing upon them the fiction that they're seeing things or floating. It's all induced inside the body, specifically by the neuronal connections in the brain.[6]

There's plenty of scientific evidence to support this notion. For example, neuroscientist Olaf Blanke provokes out-of-body experiences in people by stimulating the right angular gyrus in the temporal lobe.[7] Neuroscientist Michael Persinger subjects patterns of magnetic fields to patients' temporal lobes to induce all sorts of supernatural and out-of-body experiences. He forces the neuron firing patterns to become abnormal and unstable, with the result that patients have abnormal psychological states. With six hundred patients studied now, he says that these abnormal and unstable neuronal events could occur naturally during times of great stress, when we fast, when we're flying at high altitudes, and when our blood sugar changes dramatically.[8]

Of course, we're talking about possible underlying reasons for psychotic behavior rather than psychopathic behavior. Remember, psychopaths don't hear voices or see ghosts. However, it remains possible that men such as David Parker Ray and President Snow are evil because their brains have abnormal and unstable neuronal firing patterns. They are very much connected to the real world, meaning insanity defenses wouldn't play out very well for them. However, they both have serious personality disorders that could be based on neuronal malfunctions.

It's likely that, as with most human behavior, psychopathic behavior results from a combination of biological traits and social environment. And then there's that gray area: How extreme does the behavior have to be for a person to be called psychopathic?

President Snow, for example, exhibits all the behaviors associated with psychopathic criminals.

Psychopathic Traits, President Snow, and His Gamemakers

Personality Traits and Behaviors Associated with Psychopaths	President Snow and Gamemakers
Egomaniac.	Yes
No compassion for others.	Yes
No empathy for others.	Yes
No remorse.	Yes
No feelings of guilt.	Yes
Meticulously plans tortures and killings.	Yes
Manipulative.	Yes
Chronic liar.	Yes
Superficially charming and personable.	Yes
Inflated sense of self-worth.	Yes
Very good at faking intimacy and compassion.	Yes
Callous.	Yes
Accepts no responsibilities for his actions.	Yes
Control freak.	Yes
Sadistic—enjoys humiliating and hurting other people.	Yes
Sexually promiscuous or selling others for sexual purposes	Yes
Preys on others.	Yes

For the moment, set aside the arguments about what defines evil versus good, whether our biological wiring determines evil versus good, and whether social environments are the main factors. It doesn't matter how we define evil. It doesn't matter if a man grew up in a tent, a trailer, a penthouse, a country estate, whatever. It doesn't matter if he was born to a prince or a pauper. Regardless, we are left with one sad fact: People like President Snow are simply *bad people*. You might say that they're *evil*. And when you study all the literature, you realize that scientists really don't know why.

DOOMSDAY PREDICTIONS

AD 1186–1524

AD 1186, John of Toledo determined that a planetary alignment would occur on September 23, 1186, causing the world to end. *Any second now . . .*

AD 1260, Joachim of Fiore declared that the entire world would be destroyed between AD 1200 and 1260. *Any second now . . .*

AD 1284, Pope Innocent III taught that the world would end 666 years after Islam began, corresponding to AD 1284. *Any second now . . .*

AD 1346, no doomsday discussion can be complete without mentioning the Flagellants and the Black Death. Believing that the end of the world was imminent . . . yes, any second now . . . the Flagellants whipped and spiked people into bloody pulps to absolve them of their sins.

AD 1367, Militz of Kromeriz proclaimed that the Antichrist was already alive and would make himself known between AD 1363 and 1367, and that the end of the world would occur between AD 1365 and 1367. The precision of these prophecies, as well as many that came before Militz, are all quite remarkable, don't you think?

AD 1378, Arnold of Villanova declared that the world would end in 1378.

AD 1420, Martinek Hausha declared that the world would end by

February 14, 1420. Another precise calculation that didn't amount to much.

AD 1516, the Fifth Lateran Council banned apocalyptic prophecies and all end-of-world doomsday scenarios. Needless to say, given future events, their proclamation didn't take hold. Shortly after . . .

AD 1524, London astrologers created widespread apocalyptic terror by proclaiming that the end of the world would start by a flood in London on February 1. Tens of thousands of people fled. However, as these things tend to go, not a single drop of rain fell in London that day.

AD 1524, astrologer Johannes Stoeffler foretold that February 20 would mark the end of the world instead of February 1. It must have also been the year of global ocean terror because Stoeffler also claimed that a flood would bring about the apocalypse.

KILLER KIDS

HOW RESPONSIBLE ARE THEY?

T he awful thing is that if I can forget they're people, it will be no different at all [from killing animals]." So thinks Katniss in *The Hunger Games* (40).

This statement occurs very early in the three-book series, and in many ways, it is a premonition of what is to come. In times of war, as discussed a bit in the previous chapter, soldiers may start to view the enemy as nothing more than objects. They are the "others," no more human than a bug. In times of religious combat, such as during the Crusades or anywhere in the world today where terrorism occurs, the killers tend to forget that they are indeed murdering *human beings*. Children on one side of a border are no different from those on the other side: Both are living, breathing, thinking human beings. But as soldiers, crusaders, and terrorists grow more accustomed to acts of cruelty and killing, they slide into automatic pilot mode, and killing humans becomes no different from killing animals.

Katniss's evolution into a killing machine takes time. At first, she kills animals so her family won't starve. Her first solo hunt results in supplying a rabbit to her hungry mother and sister (*The Hunger Games,* 51). She's killing for the same reason animals hunt in the wild: to survive. She doesn't know it at the time, but soon, she'll be forced to hunt and kill humans for the same reason: to survive.

In her first Hunger Games, she must kill other children in order to save her own life. The first person she kills—ever, in her entire life—is a boy who spears her friend Rue. After shooting an arrow into the boy's neck, she wonders why she even cares about his death (*The Hunger Games,* 243). She has already evolved from a girl who had to learn how to hunt animals for food to someone capable of murder. And while, yes, eventually she would have to kill the boy anyway to become the winning tribute, she kills him without thinking in a cold act of retaliation. She's angry that Rue is dead, and she wants him to pay.

Somehow, the reader empathizes with her and is pleased when she kills the boy who took poor Rue's life. Even we, the readers who are not in combat at all, understand why Katniss has killed another person. In fact, we identify so strongly with Katniss that we want her to emerge from the Games as the victor, and we know this means she must kill multiple children. We see Rue's murderer as "evil" and we see no reason why Katniss shouldn't do away with him and save her own neck.

Even after her cold act of retribution, she identifies with the dead boy and those who mourn for him. She is not a killer at heart. Not yet.

By the time Katniss is in the thick of battle in the second book, she thinks like a killer: "I make a silent promise to return and finish [Beetee] off if I can," (*Catching Fire,* 383). And by the time she leads the revolution in the third book, she blames herself for the hideous deaths of a lot of her companions, and worse, she is directly responsible for killing an "unarmed citizen" (*Mockingjay,* 323).

How do people like Katniss and Peeta become killer kids? What makes a sweet, innocent child turn to murder?

Clearly, Katniss and Peeta must kill in order to remain alive. But Katniss herself comments more than once that she's become a killing machine, a killer, someone who actually mows down an unarmed woman. At what point does a *child* shift from killing for survival to killing *out of habit*?

We've all seen photos of children holding machines guns with caps pulled low over their too-old eyes. The pictures are jarring because we don't associate the innocence of children with the evil of mass murder. Who puts deadly weapons into the hands of their young and sends them out to slay victims? Well, we know the Capitol and their Gamemakers do it, but in the real world, leaders have been doing the same thing since the dawn of time. The gladiator ring, while prevalent for a century in ancient Rome, is another matter (see chapter 4, "Tributes: Gladiators in the Arena"). But sending kids out to torture and murder is such a global phenomenon that it's almost chillingly common.

There's something profoundly disturbing about the idea of killer kids, whether in Hunger Games arenas, in the ancient gladiator battles, or in adult warfare. Humanitarians claim that it should be a war crime for adults to enlist children in warfare. They argue that innocent, vulnerable children are manipulated and lured into service and given light-weight weapons that turn them into killing machines. While this is true to some extent, it's not entirely true. Take Katniss Everdeen as a fictional example of what is also true in the real world. In *Mockingjay,* Katniss leads a rebellion because it is the only recourse the people have to find freedom. Though she resists the role for a long time, in the end, she takes on the leadership. A posse of adult generals doesn't show up in her town, kidnap her, and brainwash her to bear light-weight weapons and slaughter hundreds of innocent people. She rebels and fights against the posse of adults who have enslaved and tortured her people since the Dark Days.

In the nineteenth century in North America, Native American Cheyenne boys went to war for their tribes at approximately the age of fourteen. But when you consider the atrocities against the Cheyennes—for example, Lt. Col. George Armstrong Custer and his troops in 1868 killed more than a hundred Cheyenne women and children during the Battle of Washita River—it's not a stretch to understand why warrior-trained Cheyenne boys would fight back. In 1875, the Cheyennes along with the Sioux and the Lakota killed Custer and many of his soldiers in the Battle of the Little Bighorn.

In the Sudan, Dinka boys received military spears between the ages of sixteen and eighteen.[1] Fighting has been a constant for the Dinka tribe, and a decade ago, reports estimated that warfare had displaced 4 million people in Sudan and forced another half a million to emigrate to neighboring countries.[2]

During the eighteenth and nineteenth centuries in the Amazon, girls were inducted into warfare at the age of nine. In fact, the Amazon Dahomeys were an *all-female* group of warriors some 4,000–6,000 strong. Known as the Mino, or Our Mothers, the girls received rigorous training and a robust supply of weapons, including guns, rifles, knives, and clubs. A common means of death by a Mino was decapitation. Many girls enrolled in the Mino by choice, though others were forced into service by their husbands or fathers.

Western societies have also sent their children to war for centuries. In the middle ages, the British military included a lot of boys, and by the late nineteenth century, British institutions systematically recruited them. In 1803, the Duke of York founded the Royal Military Asylum to train boys as soldiers who might be able to lead others in battle. In 1765, Britain created the Royal Hibernium Military School from an orphanage to train twelve-year-old boys to serve as rank-and-file soldiers. In fact, these young Hibernium boys fought for the British during the American Revolution.

In the United States during the Civil War, boys routinely fought and died. Conservative estimates place the number of young boys battling for both the Union and Confederacy at approximately

250,000–420,000.[3] Parents inducted them into service, as did schools. Many of them volunteered. Avery Brown enrolled in the military at the age of eight, lying on the recruitment paper that he was twelve, old enough to serve! Joseph John Clem enrolled at the age of ten, and his weapons of choice were a musket and a gun. Often called the "boys' war," the boy soldiers in the Civil War accounted for as much as 20 percent of all recruits.[4]

Rather than consider it a crime that the boys served in war, the public at large considered their deaths noble; they were admired and respected.

Only in modern times do we see the rising abhorrence by the public of sending children to war. This is, in large part, a reason why The Hunger Games trilogy strikes such a chord with readers. The modern reader thinks, *How can they send these boy and girls into battle? This is inhumane and against everything that's right!* But in reality, we've been doing it forever.

During the industrial revolution, it became more common to think of children as innocent youth who must be educated and protected, isolated from adults, and allowed to enjoy their childhoods for as long as possible. Formal schooling took hold and started replacing apprenticeship as the primary tool of education. Of course, many kids never made it through the formal education process. Many were orphans, many were poor. They were needed in coal mines, on farms, in factories, so they became warriors of another fashion: fighting the industrial revolution rather than a bloodbath war.

And along with the formal education came military disciplinary structure. To this day, military training is considered virtuous, and parents send their sons into the military to teach them discipline and morals and to provide structure to their lives. During the industrial revolution, uniforms and regimentation seeped into the schools, and off the children went to become officers and soldiers.

During World War I, the practice of enlisting boys continued. There were age restrictions, but still, it wasn't all that uncommon to find young boys fighting alongside men on the front lines.

In modern times, throughout the world, some people still view warrior children as honorable and moral, to be admired and respected.

Killer kids are on the rise because the techniques of global warfare are changing. In 1996, Graça Machel wrote a landmark publication, *Impact of Armed Conflict on Children*,[5] for the United Nations about this problem. The widow of Samora Machel, leader of the Mozambique guerrilla war against Portugal and first president of Mozambique, Graça Machel served as a guerrilla fighter in Tanzania and also fought against Portugal. She also served as minister of education for Mozambique and is famous worldwide as the wife of Nelson Mandela. In her report, she states that modern warfare has abandoned all standards of conduct due to the fact that globalization and revolution have decimated traditional societies. The breakdown in what was once normal societal structures has been exacerbated by governmental collapses, internal feuding, financial inequities, and the dissolution of services that are essential to life; among other factors. As everything normal collapses around people, civilians become warriors, and violence escalates. According to Machel, the horrors of modern combat that are now taken as givens include ethnic cleansing, genocide, and the use of children in military combat.

As mentioned above, many children are forced into battle, such as in The Hunger Games trilogy. If they don't fight, they and/or their families are tortured and sometimes killed. To alienate new recruits, adults force the children to kill family members, neighbors, and friends. According to Amnesty International:

> Worldwide, hundreds of thousands of children under 18 have been affected by armed conflict. They are recruited into government armed forces, paramilitaries, civil militia and a variety of other armed groups. Often they are abducted at school, on the streets or at home. Others enlist "voluntarily," usually because they see few alternatives. Yet international

law prohibits the participation in armed conflict of children aged under 18.[6]

The figures are staggering. According to Peter W. Singer of the Brookings Institution, *before the war in Iraq*:

> Although there is global consensus against the morality of sending children into battle, this terrible practice is now a regular facet of contemporary warfare. There are some 300,000 children under the age of 18 (both boys and girls) presently serving as combatants around the globe, fighting in approximately 75% of the world's conflicts.[7]

The United Nations wrote in 2000 that more than fifty countries were actively recruiting children into military service that year, and further, that the youngest known soldiers were only seven years old. Possibly even more grim, in the 1990s according to the United Nations, *2 million children were killed in armed combat; 4 to 5 million were disabled; 12 million were left homeless; and a staggering 10 million were "psychologically traumatized."*[8]

Unfortunately, the use of killer kids isn't confined to fictional worlds. What brings it close and up front in the world of The Hunger Games is that we feel the atrocities in a very personal way—from the viewpoint of Katniss. We may be shocked by the real-world statistics, but the impact hits home when we read Katniss's story.

Let's look at a few real-world examples of child soldiers. First, there's the war in Iraq, where children are regularly recruited into military service. Saddam Hussein's government enlisted and trained thousands of children as young as ten years old. According to Singer:

> A common means for totalitarian regimes to maintain control is to set their country on a constant war footing and militarize society. This justifies heavy hierarchic control and helps divert internal tensions towards external foes. The recruitment,

training, and indoctrination of children also offers the regime the opportunity to deepen its reach into Iraqi society.[9]

Remind you of anything, say, the Capitol and its leaders in The Hunger Games? It's common practice for totalitarian regimes to keep civilians under control by maintaining an environment of constant threat of war. Sure, the Dark Days were seventy-five years ago and well into the past, but to maintain its grip on the population, the government saturates its propaganda with the idea that war could erupt again at any time. In addition, they prohibit districts from communicating with each other. They pit children against each other in the Hunger Games to maintain even tighter control over the people.

But Iraq is just one of hundreds of examples of child soldiers. Another obvious example is the Darfur civil war in Sudan.

According to The Guardian in 2008, "Thousands of child refugees from Darfur, some as young as nine, are being abducted and sold to warring militias as child soldiers."[10] Further, the report says that "the UN estimated last year that between 7,000 and 10,000 child soldiers had been forcibly recruited in Chad, where more than 250,000 refugees from Darfur are in camps."[11] As of February 2010, 2.7 million people were homeless due to the war,[12] which began in 2003 when the Sudan Liberation Army and the Justice and Equality Movement attacked the Sudanese government for oppressing black Africans in favor of Arabs.

And there's Rwanda, where unspeakable acts of mass murder were inflicted on the Tutsis by the Hutus. Estimates place the number of murdered civilians—during a one-hundred-day period of attempted genocide—at 800,000. When Hutu Rwandan President Juvénal Habyarimana was killed after his airplane was shot down, violence spread and escalated throughout Rwanda. Within hours, the Hutus sent killers all over the country to slaughter all Tutsis and any Hutu who didn't conform to the military mindset.

Were child soldiers involved? Of course. A United Nations study concluded that "Rwanda's army and government helped recruit fighters, including children, to support the Democratic Republic of Congo's rebel leader Laurent Nkunda . . ."[13]

In Sierra Leone, 10,000 children fought during a civil war that lasted ten years. In this case, the Revolutionary United Front was determined to decimate the civilian population so they created havoc and then took over the diamond fields. The government attacked its own people. Most of the civilians were murdered with machetes and knives.

But as mentioned above, despite the grim reality of the situation, children aren't *always* forced into battle. Quite often, they volunteer for service out of duty to their families, communities, and governments. They believe in the cause.

Consider the Basij, a volunteer army founded by the Ayatollah Khomeini in 1975. People, including children and women, join the Basij for benefits and out of loyalty. The Student Basij is comprised of children who are in middle school and high school. They feel that they are holy martyrs, and during the Iran–Iraq War, tens of thousands of the Basij sacrificed their lives on the battlefield for the cause. Children and teenagers formed a battlefront line that moved constantly toward the enemy forces. As bullets, canons, and land mines mowed them down, more children and teenagers moved forward in additional suicidal lines. According to some reports, the Ayatollah Khomeini once said that "a country with twenty million youths must have twenty million riflemen or a military with twenty million soldiers; such a country will never be destroyed."[14] And after the election of President Mahmoud Ahmadinejad in 2005, the government used the Basij to suppress possible rebellion. The same thing was done during the elections in 2009. In December 2009, thousands of middle and high school children fought to suppress student demonstrations—*yes, thousands of child soldiers battled other children on the streets of their own cities.*[15]

How different are the Career Tributes, really, from the Basij and other children dedicated to fighting to the death for spiritual and political reasons? The Careers are volunteers in the Hunger Games, and train "throughout their lives" for the event. According to Katniss, they "project arrogance and brutality" and "head straight for the deadliest-looking weapons" (*The Hunger Games*, 94–95). Just as the Basij fight together, the Careers fight in packs against other tributes in the Games.

Katniss, of course, is not a Career Tribute. She's forced into the Hunger Games like the Darfur children were forced into battle. She has no choice.

But later, as she hardens to acts of violence and murder, she becomes more of a volunteer. When she accepts the mantle of Mockingjay and leads the rebellion against the evil Capitol, her mindset is more in the mode of the Basij than that of the naïve Katniss we saw in both *The Hunger Games* and *Catching Fire*. By the time she's in charge of Squad 451, she wants to be on the front lines.

Earlier, during her first Games, she is almost killed by Thresh, but gets out of it by explaining how she sang to Rue as the little girl died (*The Hunger Games*, 288). Poor Thresh is stricken, as most kids would be, with grief over the loss of Rue and also by gratitude to the girl who loved her as a sister. In a tragic error of judgment (for Thresh, certainly not for Katniss), he lets Katniss go out of respect for what she did for Rue. This seems highly unlikely, to be honest, but we can only assume that Thresh holds little value in his own life, that he's traumatized, and possibly, that he's not too sharp.

Later, Katniss is relieved to learn that Thresh has been killed by another tribute. Now, she won't be burdened by the dilemma of what to do should the two of them be forced to fight for their lives (*The Hunger Games*, 307). Had she faced the identical dilemma in *Mockingjay*, after she'd hardened more to the thought of killing people, she might not have reacted in the same way. Instead, she might have had no qualms whatsoever about killing Thresh. But we'll never know because he dies in *The Hunger Games*.

Even Peeta sees how Katniss is changing over time. (Obviously, he changes quite a bit, as well, but in other ways—for details, see chapter 12, "Medicines and Poisons," and chapter 13, "Muttations and

Other Hybrids.") Sometimes, they work together, as in killing Cato during their first Games (*The Hunger Games,* 340). Here, she's working *with* him, not against him, and she's killing with great regret and only because she has no choice if she's to survive. He's doing the same thing.

Sometimes, she thinks he's out to kill her (*The Hunger Games,* 143), but then he begs her to kill him so she may live (*The Hunger Games,* 343), which totally confuses her. She swings back and forth about Peeta, whether she trusts him, and whether she loves or fears him. It's common for people to swing back and forth, wondering about their boyfriends, girlfriends, and spouses. Love? Hate? The most passionate teenage lovers often end up breaking up for reasons they don't even understand. And it's not limited to teenagers. Adults who have been married for a long time and have children together break up far too frequently, as well, and they rarely understand the true reasons, either. Luckily, most of us don't have to thrust our romances into the horrors of a killing arena, where we have to wonder whether our potential mates are out to kill us or save us.

By the end of *Catching Fire,* Katniss kills other tributes, hoping their deaths will save Peeta (*Catching Fire,* 377). No wonder poor Peeta's confused. It's tough to understand why he is so kind to her in face of her often brutal treatment of him. How many guys hang in there, trying to win a girl's heart, when she keeps stringing him along, wondering if she's in love with somebody else? How many guys would put up with it—making their intentions to marry and love forever clear, making their utter devotion clear, while the girl isn't sure how she feels about some *other* guy? Toss the entire killing concept into the mix, and it's explosive. Does she want to kill him? This goes *far* beyond the question, *Will she ever love him?* But on the other hand, Peeta subjects Katniss to far more complex emotions: after all, he ends up thinking she's a nonhuman mutt who should be killed (*Mockingjay,* 190)! No wonder poor Katniss is confused. He sums things up well when he tells her, "These last couple of years must have been exhausting for you. Trying to decide whether to kill me or not" (*Mockingjay,* 270).

Eventually, Boggs wants Katniss to kill Peeta (*Mockingjay,* 280). Luckily, she still has enough self-control and remains Katniss of *The Hunger Games* at heart. She remains moral and decent.

Nonetheless, one of her conditions for taking on the role of Mockingjay is that she gets to kill President Snow (*Mockingjay,* 38). At this point, the reader figures she's now a killing machine as contrasted to the earlier Katniss we saw in *The Hunger Games.*

When in charge of Squad 451, not only does she want to be on the front lines, she's determined to kill Snow (*Mockingjay,* 256). Much to the shock of the reader, she votes "yes" for the symbolic Hunger Games that will pit Capitol children against each other. As mentioned earlier in this book, Katniss probably votes "yes" as a ploy to push President Coin into thinking that she is on her side. This way, Coin will be easier for Katniss to assassinate. Katniss may be a killing machine at this point, but she retains her core personality: She does not really advocate another Hunger Games. Rather, she wants to get rid of Coin, who is as deplorable as Snow.

Given the same circumstances, many of us might do the same thing.

War and battle do crazy things to people. We've all heard about post-traumatic stress syndrome, for example, in which battle-weary soldiers become depressed, can't sleep, can't function, and don't think normally anymore. They are transformed by war into people who barely resemble the soldiers who left home before the battle.

Clearly, Katniss's suicidal tendencies and drug addiction as *Mockingjay* winds down are evidence of something akin to post-traumatic stress syndrome. She's lost the will to live. She's lost the ability to view herself as anything more than a terrible person. She takes drugs to zone herself out so she doesn't have to remember who she's killed and what she's done. Contrasted to her innate bravery and determination—she is a very strong person—she cannot live through war without breaking down in the end. She's traumatized to the point of total numbness.

Her behavior is very common for child soldiers, as described by the United Nations:

> Child soldiers are among the saddest victims of conflict: they rarely emerge from military service with a sense of their own worth and identity. Worse, they often experience violence that leaves them physically or psychologically scarred. Facing a difficult adolescence, many turn to drugs, alcohol and anti-social behaviour.[16]

Consider Haymitch, who becomes an alcoholic after winning his Games. He can't live with himself and he's lost everyone close to him, so he drowns his memories, guilt, and misery in liquor.

Consider Peeta, who is psychologically scarred, not only due to the horrors of the Games, but also because he's been poisoned to become mentally ill. The Capitol steals his memories and replaces them with his worst fears along with outright falsehoods.

DOOMSDAY PREDICTIONS

AD **1525–1600**

AD 1525, Thomas Müntzer preached all over Germany and Switzerland that the end of the world was imminent, so the peasants should revolt and kill everyone who was rich, powerful, or otherwise in control. Along with some 8,000 peasants, Müntzer went up against swords, cannon-balls, and burly military men. It was indeed the end of the world for Müntzer. He was tortured and beheaded.

AD 1528, Hans Hut and tens of thousands of followers predicted that the end of the world would occur on May 27, 1528. He died in prison.

AD 1532, Viennese bishop Frederic Nausea (yes, that was his real name, I'm not making it up) proclaimed that the world would end in 1532. His reason? People kept telling him about the strangest things— bloody crosses alongside comets streaming across the sky, multiple suns, bread falling from heaven—and he believed it all.

AD 1533, Michael Stifel, a math geek, went wild with his calculations and determined that the world would end in October.

AD 1534, Jan Matthys, who took control of the town of Munster, claimed that the world would end on Easter and only Munster would survive. When the apocalypse didn't come, all the Catholics and Lutherans he had tormented came back to town and killed him.

AD 1555, Pierre d'Ailly wrote in AD 1400 that 6,845 years had passed since creation, and the end of the world would come in the 7,000th year.

AD 1583, astrologer Richard Harvey calculated that the apocalypse would occur at noon on April 28, 1583. He wasn't alone with this prediction. As with all other precise doomsday calculations, it only goes to show that you should always check your math.

AD 1584, astrologer Cyprian Leowitz calculated that the apocalypse would occur this year.

AD 1600, Martin Luther claimed that the world would end by the year 1600.

HYPE OVER SUBSTANCE

A MIRROR OF MODERN TIMES

Peeta doesn't know what's real versus what's just in his head. He's been shot up with tracker jacker poison. But quite often, throughout The Hunger Games series as well as in real life, the line between real and not real blurs and blends to the point where people don't know the *truth*. Modern public relations departments wouldn't exist if the truth were mandatory. Advertising companies would fold. The government would simply collapse. Let's face it, the world *runs* on hype. And for many of us, we can't tell the difference between most hype and real substance.

How many people watch reality television programs? Is the "reality" true to life, or is it fictionalized? Let's look at a few news reports and viewing numbers:

- "During the [*Keeping Up with the Kardashians*] season 4 premiere, the reality TV show's often exaggerated drama managed to drag 4.1 million people in front of their television sets."[1]

- "*Kourtney & Kim Take New York* pulled in 3 million viewers on Sunday night, beating *Kourtney & Khloe's* old record from last season, which premiered to 2.6 million viewers."[2]

PRESS PAUSE. These reality television viewing numbers come from spin artists, people who write about celebrities. So how real are the numbers? Do we know for sure?

- "The [*Jersey Shore*] series returned Thursday night to 8.4 million viewers."[3]

- "[*Jersey Shore*] delivered 8.6 million viewers . . . last night."[4]

PRESS PAUSE. These reality television viewing numbers come from *Entertainment Weekly,* widely known for reporting accurate viewing numbers. But again, these guys are spin artists, too, the ultimate in entertainment publicity and news. The *Jersey Shore* numbers, by the way, have been reported at 8.9 million viewers and more.

NEXT UP ARE *The Real Housewives of Beverly Hills* (a TV press release reports 3.7+ million viewers,[5] January 14, 2011) who follow in the footsteps of the insanely successful *The Real Housewives of New York City* (2.64 million viewers, as reported on June 5, 2010).[6] Perhaps viewers are more interested in cat fights among celebrity wives more than they're interested in squabbling among wealthy Manhattanites. And yes, there are *The Real Housewives of New Jersey* (3.2 million viewers, as reported on July 15, 2010)[7] and *Atlanta* (3.5 million viewers, as reported on February 2, 2011),[8] as well; and they're not in Beverly Hills with film celebrity wives, so why are they so popular? Lest we forget them, we also watch *The Real Housewives of Orange County* (2+ million viewers, as reported on January 27, 2011),[9] and even *The Real Housewives of D.C.* (1.6 million viewers, as reported on August 9, 2010).[10]

And don't forget about *The Millionaire Matchmaker* with its 1.3 million viewers.[11] Plus *Project Runway, Rock of Love, A Shot of Love with Tila Tequila, America's Next Top Model, The Bachelor* and *The Bachelorette, Celebrity Rehab, The Girls Next Door, The Hills, Laguna Beach, Hogan Knows Best, The Janice Dickinson Modeling Agency, The Fifth Wheel, Shear Genius, The Surreal Life,* and those old favorites, *Queer Eye for the Straight Guy, Newlyweds: Nick and Jessica, The Osbournes, The Simple Life,* and *Flavor of Love.*

If we dig even farther back, we can list a slew of original reality shows in *The Real World* series: These programs took place everywhere from New Orleans to Las Vegas to Key West to Hollywood to . . . well, name a city and there probably was a *Real World* show there.

What fascinates us, why are we glued to reality TV shows? And what do they have in common with *The Hunger Games?* (Astute readers are now thinking, "*What?* No mention of *Survivor?*" Trust me, we're going to talk about *Survivor* in this chapter.) Here's a sampling:

Reality Television Program	Squabbling and In-fighting	Romantic Intrigue
The Hunger Games	Careers versus everyone else. Groups of tributes battling other groups, then splintering into individual fights because only one tribute can survive the Games.	Katniss and Peeta. Katniss and Gale. Katniss's wedding gown. The supposed enduring love that supposedly makes Katniss and Peeta decide to die together. President Snow and Caesar's public fascination with Katniss and Peeta's love affair.
Keeping Up with the Kardashians	The official tagline[12] is: "A tempest of siblings, business, and fame engulf Olympic decathlete Bruce Jenner and paparazzi fave Kim Kardashian as their huge Hollywood families collide."	Plenty of it. We have Scott Disick, supposedly with a very hot temper, possibly engaged to Kourtney. We have Kim's romance with Reggie Bush, Gabriel Aubry, Kris Humphries, and more. We have Khloe and Lamar Odom, who married after a one-month romance. Tabloids speculate that the marriage is bogus, created for the sake of better reality television drama.
The Real Housewives of Orange Country	Housewives gang up on each other constantly.	We have everything from older single mothers to miserably married career women to trophy wives. And everything in between.
Rock of Love	Heather versus Lacey. Heather versus Daisy.	Each season, one lucky girl supposedly won Bret Michaels's heart.

Fashion and Style	"Big" Personalities and Drama (aka knowing how to entertain the audience, people who seem "bigger than life")	"Underdogs" We Root for and Want to Win
Before competing to the death, tributes are scrubbed, stripped of hair, and styled to the hilt at the Remake Center. Katniss meets her stylist Cinna early in *The Hunger Games* (63). Also on her fashion and style team are Flavius, Venia, and Octavia. Katniss knows that "the best-looking tributes" get more sponsors (*The Hunger Games*, 58).	Katniss knows that she must play to the audience in order to win sponsors and stay alive. Her theatrical costumes, complete with fire, attract audience share. Her not-so-fake ("Is it real?" as Peeta asks) or fake ("Is it not real?") romance with Peeta also plays to the audience.	Sponsors root for and give lifesaving gifts to their favorite tributes. People root for the underdogs, such as Rue. People immediately are touched by Katniss, who steps in to save her little sister, Prim.
Entire Web sites are devoted to Kim Kardashian's fashions, makeup, hair, and trendsetting styles.	Everyone on the show is a celebrity: sports stars, Olympic athletes, *Playboy* models.	Audiences feel sorry for characters who are exploited, as in the recent episode where we're led to believe Kim appears nude without her approval.
The housewives have fashion shows and buy thousand-dollar dresses in their living rooms.	Housewives seem chosen to conflict with each other. Each personality is "big" and they're all dramatically different from each other. On the program, the housewives get free vacations, spa outings, etc. simply because they are television celebrities.	Were we really supposed to feel sorry for the trophy wife? When her old hubby died, was her grief real, or not real?
Trashy outfits galore. Tattoos, mini-bikinis, strippers!	Heather versus Lacey. Heather versus Daisy. Lacey Conner from the first season is now performing with the Lords of Acid.	We always root for our favorite girls to win Bret's heart!

What's real? What's not real? This is what Peeta wonders during the reality series he and Katniss are forced to star in, and this is what audiences wonder about reality programs that are actually on our televisions. The main difference is that the actors and actresses know what's real and what's fake; whereas in *The Hunger Games,* apart from Peeta and Katniss's romance, there's not much "acting"—all the players are fighting to the death. Most of us take it for granted at this point that reality shows are pre-staged to ramp up the drama and gossip, that what we think is real actually is fake.

Regarding *The Hills,* actor Brody Jenner was once quoted as saying, "The thing is, as you saw on the end—what's real and what's fake, you don't know . . . Our relationship [Jenner and costar Kristin Cavallari], the entire time could have been fake . . . That's one of the questions: What was real and what was fake?"[13]

In *The Osbournes,* Jack kills one of the family's dogs, setting off speculation in all the gossip rags and among fans about whether the death was real or not.

Writes *Newsday,* "[T]he *Real Housewives* series has never been about 'real' anything. The cast for a show like this, by definition, consists of exhibitionists."[14]

As for the *Kardashians,* Rashad McCants, who briefly dated Khloe, told gossip columnists that the show is "completely fake."[15] In January 2011, Piers Morgan at CNN interviewed Kim and Kourtney about "what's real . . . and what's not."[16] The sisters discussed Botox, plastic surgery, girdle-type underwear, and breast implants. It's not a typo, folks: yes, this interview aired on CNN.

Flavor of Love star Flavor Flav has been quoted as saying his show was completely fake. Posts one reality gossip Web site, "It's obvious that people will wonder if the show is real or not since at least two seasons of Flavor of Love were pronounced pointless by Flavor Flav himself!"[17]

The Real World was one of the first reality shows, and it was immensely popular. Series spinoffs were featured in close to twenty cities. Viewers and gossip columnists have long pronounced the popular series as totally fake. One example: "From the casting to the editing to the dorm-style bedrooms to the sponsorship clubs and restaurants that provide free food in exchange for airtime, even without scratching the surface there's not any debate as to how deeply and completely the manipulations go."[18]

Anyone who has watched reality television shows—and if you haven't watched any, you're in quite a minority—has guessed by now that the shows are primarily scripted and fabricated. Their prime purpose is to titillate audiences and promote speculation. Their goal is to entertain. Period.

The Hunger Games is a blend of various reality shows: *Survivor* plus *American Gladiator* plus any of the programs listed in the above table. Just as with real shows such as *Survivor, American Gladiator, Rock of Love, Flavor of Love, The Bachelor,* and *The Bachelorette,* "contestants" are eliminated until only one is left.

Much worse, of course, is the fact that in *The Hunger Games* reality television series, the combat is all *too* real. After submitting to the whims of stylists and fashionistas, the tributes are interviewed by Caesar Flickerman, a bizarre character who reminds the reader of a snake-oil salesman crossed with a Ken doll crossed with a punk rocker crossed with a public relations slime crossed with the announcer of the old Miss America pageant. Dressed to the hilt, fed at banquets, tributes are interviewed as if they're about to perform on *American Idol.* And just like the winners and runners up on shows such as *American Idol,* just like Susan Boyle in Britain, the tributes become television celebrities.

Everything is so trumped up that television crews simulate battles for audience consumption, Peeta and Katniss pretend to be engaged to increase their audience popularity, sponsors are essential to winning the Games (just like television sponsors are critical to winning the ratings games in the real world). And as for the fashions, is it any wonder that people are emulating Katniss's style sense? To name one example in our real world, Jessica Simpson has been earning billions of dollars on her styles; her celebrity status has made her a very rich and successful woman in the fashion industry.

Is it any wonder that the people in the Capitol are obsessed with style rather than substance? *Aren't we—in the real world—also obsessed more with style than substance?*

It is this celebrity-and-fashion obsession that fuels the tabloids, that drove paparazzi to follow Princess Diana and hound her literally to death. Many people are obsessed with the latest royal wedding, even in the United States where we supposedly don't have royalty. Between the paparazzi and the gossip rags, we're all lost in an illusion of reality as presented by celebrities and public relations specialists. Tila Tequila became famous just for being famous. And Paris Hilton is famous because of her celebrity status; she didn't raise to her current level of fame because she won an Academy Award or won a Pulitzer Prize. People like to see what she's wearing, and like Jessica Simpson, Paris Hilton has her own fashion line that does quite well. Mary Kate and Ashley Olson, who did rise to stardom due to their childhood acting abilities, are known for being on best-dressed lists *and* worst-dressed lists. They've made fortunes selling clothing, perfumes, fashion dolls, and cosmetics. Young girls buy their items due to their celebrity status.

It's hard to forget the focus on Sarah Palin's clothing and hair expenses during her 2008 United States vice presidential campaign. *Style over substance*: The Republican National Committee spent $150,000 on clothing for Palin and her family, and the Federal Election Commission ruled that it was okay. Overall, she spent $290,000 on clothing, hair, and makeup during a two-month campaign period. So important was style that she spent $42,000 on a hair stylist and $68,000 on a makeup artist.

In the meantime, Palin was bombed by the press for saying nothing of substance. For example, gossip columns bore headlines such as "Sarah Palin Lays into Obama, Uses Crib Notes, Says Nothing of

Substance"[19] and legitimate hard news sources bore headlines such as "Biden on Palin's Speech: Style but No Substance."[20]

What about Hillary Clinton, the other woman at the forefront of the 2008 campaign? Though she delivered substance in her speeches and is well-known as former President Clinton's wife, Hillary Clinton's fashions and style sense were also analyzed by the press. *Glamour* magazine featured a story about Clinton's *pantsuits*: "Hillary Clinton Pulls a Pantsuit Out for the DNC: The Woman Knows What Works."[21] *The Guardian* posed the question, "She's hoping to become the most powerful woman in the world—so why does Hillary Clinton wear such uninspiring clothes?"[22]

First Lady Michelle Obama has a stylist, and her clothing has been analyzed by none other than *Vogue.* In fact, Michelle Obama's style sense and clothing have made headlines around the world, been features of magazine covers, and have prompted *The Huffington Post* to publish stories with titles such as "More Details on Michelle's New Wardrobe Advisor," "Diane von Furstenberg 'So Embarrassed' by Michelle Obama State Dinner Dress Flap," "Michelle Obama Goes Curly on Thursday," "First Lady Arrives Home in Questionable Pants," and many more.[23] Daniel Mendelsohn writes in *The New York Review of Books* that "The popularity of First Lady fashion and style often supersedes any true importance about the President's wife and what she accomplishes. The most recent example, of course, is Michelle Obama. Books have already been written about her fashion sense."[24]

Michelle Obama follows in the footsteps of former First Lady Jackie Kennedy Onassis, lauded for decades as America's style icon. How many people remember anything of actual substance that Jackie Kennedy did as opposed to remembering her stylish and elegant image? How many people remember something that Michelle Obama has done to change the world for the better? Here's what *USA Today* wrote about the subject:

> From her sleeveless dresses and her embrace of the arts to the way she mothers her girls and presents herself abroad,

Obama has been favorably compared to Kennedy in ways that no other first lady has in the nearly five decades since a stunned nation reluctantly closed the door on the era known as Camelot.[25]

So why should we be surprised that the tributes are subjected to the same fashion, style, hair, and other trivial scrutiny? Why should we be surprised that people don't care about the evil inflicted upon the tributes instead of what they are wearing? The Hunger Games trilogy reflects our current society's obsession with style over substance, and as with all great speculative fiction, the series pushes the point to the extreme.

So focused are the people of the Capitol on style that tributes from District 12 have been forced to wear near-naked costumes as well as nothing *but* black powder to symbolize coal. Katniss's first outfit is a unitard, shiny boots, and a fluttering cape with a matching hat. She must smile, wave at the crowds as if she's the Queen of England in her chariot, and if she's lucky, sponsors will remember the fire associated with her cape and headdress (*The Hunger Games,* 69–71).

Meantime, the citizens of the Capitol get plenty of plastic surgery, dye their hair (and bodies) strange colors, and look freakish. Sadly, in our real world, both male and female newscasters get plastic surgery and dye their hair just to remain employed, and up close, a lot of them look freakish, too. Our celebrities are even worse: plastic surgery is a given, and without the touchups, air brushing, and other artistic flourishes, not to mention the softening by various camera lenses, they can look beyond freakish.

In *Catching Fire* (48–49), Flavius comments that he wishes he could perform "alterations" on Katniss; and by this, he's referring to plastic surgery. Octavia and Venia both agree that with plastic surgery, Katniss would look much better.

According to the American Society of Plastic Surgeons (ASPS), as of February 7, 2011—in the midst of a major economic depression—*13.1 million cosmetic surgeries were performed in 2010.*

In addition, surgeons performed *more than 5.3 million reconstructive plastic surgeries in 2010.* So if you think the people in the Capitol are crazy in The Hunger Games for having so many bizarre cosmetic procedures, consider our real society and its bizarre practices in an era when people are starving, homeless, and permanently unemployed. Says Dr. Phillip Haeck, President of the ASPS, ". . . as the aging population continues to grow, people are investing in plastic surgery procedures to help stay competitive in the workplace."[26] He cites the top five requested plastic surgeries: breast enlargement aka boob jobs (yes, I'm sure gigantic breasts will land that lucrative job for a sixty-year-old woman whereas her normal breasts would cost her valuable income); nose jobs (yes, I'm sure a fifty-year-old man will lose a potential job at McDonald's to another old guy who "invested" in a Michael Jackson nose); eyelid surgery (puffy lids obviously tell potential employers at Walmart that you're an alcoholic); liposuction (if you're not bone thin, all potential employers will think you must be a lazy slob); and tummy tucks (God help you if that potential employer makes you show your belly flab during the interview!).

In addition, many millions of people get botulinum toxin injections, fat injections in their face to make them look younger, brow lifts, removal of spider veins, thigh lifts, arm lifts, body lifts, body contouring, breast lifts, chin surgeries, hair replacements, and permanent makeup. In a body lift, the surgeon removes fat and skin all over the body to try to emulate muscle tone and youth. People are willing to undergo plastic surgery procedures even given the horrific medical risks such as scarring, bleeding, infections, blood clots, skin discolorations and permanent swelling, long-lasting pain, pulmonary and cardiac problems, and more. Most people do not experience these post-plastic surgery problems, but still . . . the fact that so many millions are willing to take these risks to look physically more attractive is a frightening glimpse at the psyche of today's society.

In the Capitol's case, things go far beyond plastic surgery. These people implant claws and whiskers, cut patterns into their skin, dye their skin, and more. *And yet, how weird is this, really?* In our real world, surgeons implant pigments beneath the skin to add permanent color to our flesh. If you have the money and you want it badly enough, you can have dyed skin just like the strange people in the Capitol. Just hold still while the surgeon sticks a needle into your face (or other body parts) hundreds of times per minute until finally, you look "terrific." Don't want to waste time applying blush to your cheeks, but think you need blush to get a job? Thousands of needle jabs will give you a permanent blush. Think your eyebrows are too thick or dark to win that coveted position for ten dollars an hour with no benefits? Thousands of needle jabs will "paint" permanently colored eyebrows on your face.

Katniss initially thinks of her prep team—Flavius, Venia, Octavia, and Cinna the stylist—as "total idiots." She later learns to like her crew, seeing them as real people who are caught in a society of weirdness; and when they're killed, she's devastated. This is true of a lot of people in our own world. Just because someone undergoes some of the plastic surgery procedures described above doesn't make him or her less of a person. We are all caught in a society of weirdness.

Soon, it will become routine for people to alter our DNA as often as we now undergo plastic surgeries, wear tinted contact lenses, and take antidepressive drugs. Gene products will provide lovely, soft skin without blemishes; and will alter our personalities based on who we want to be rather than who we really are. According to Dr. Henry I. Miller, a Senior Research Fellow at Stanford University, we will routinely use genetic therapies to enhance our physical and mental capabilities. He points out that in the future genetic therapy for achieving favorable physical and mental attributes will be as ordinary as going to a counselor or psychiatrist, taking psychiatric medications or antidepressants, or getting drug treatments for baldness, obesity, and age spots.[27]

In addition to style and fashion, the tributes also learn how to walk as if they're on a fashion show runway, how to smile and make eye contact, and much more. In reality, entire television programs center around people competing on the runway: Not only do we have *America's Next Top Model,* we also have *RuPaul's Drag Race* and many other shows devoted to models and runways.

Readers might be tuned into the Scott Westerfeld *Uglies* books, in which all teenagers get plastic surgery. Again, it's style over substance: Everyone must conform to defined beauty standards. The heroine of the series, Tally, wants to become a Pretty, yet all the Pretties receive lobotomies during the plastic surgery. The Uglies series is faintly reminiscent of *The Stepford Wives,* in which husbands make their wives into robotic yet beautiful drones. Pretty is all that matters.

It's only fitting that we close this chapter, which explores reality television programs, with a discussion of *Survivor.* In the United States, the program launched in 2000, and it was so popular that it spawned reality television as a staple of programming. The show has taken place all over the world: Nicaragua, Fiji, China, Borneo, Australia, Africa, Thailand, The Amazon, Samoa, Gabon, Brazil, etc.

The Hunger Games is an extreme version of Survivor. Suzanne Collins has pushed *Survivor* into the horror of dystopian post-apocalyptic fiction, where she pits competitors against each other for prizes worth a lot more than merchandise and cash.

Just as everyone in the Capitol can't wait for the Games, apparently people in the real world are obsessed in the same way with *Survivor.* Rating have been through the roof, ranging from 10 million to *52 million viewers.*

In the real *Survivor* program, tribes of strangers are stranded in a game locale that varies from season to season. The competitors must find water, food, and shelter, just as in the Hunger Games. They pair off and compete against each other so they won't be eliminated from the game. One person wins each *Survivor* game and is designated the Sole Survivor. He also gets a million dollars, just as the Sole Survivor of the Hunger Games get a free mansion and food for life. While the Gamemakers often change the rules of the Hunger Games, so do the gamemakers of *Survivor.* The point is to keep the program entertaining, because after all, if the competitors always used the same strategies to win, nobody would watch the show.

What about style versus substance? Is *Survivor* real or fake? According to MSNBC, it's mostly real; however, the show does actively hire models and actors for programs. On *Survivor Fiji*, "everyone except one person . . . was recruited."[28]

DOOMSDAY PREDICTIONS

AD **1603–1800**

By now, you realize that throughout history, hundreds if not thousands of doomsayers rose up and convinced the masses that "we are all going to die . . . any second now." The list is extensive, and I'm only providing you with a barebones look at the various apocalyptic prophecies. There are plenty more.

At this point, I'll skip a lot of the predictions and try to shift us over the next five "Doomsday" boxes to the current time.

AD 1603, Tomasso Campanella, a Dominican Monk, said the sun and Earth would collide in 1603.

AD 1623, more geeky math as Eustachius Polyssel calculated that the world would end in 1623.

AD 1624, another London flood was supposed to cause the end of the world this year. It didn't.

AD 1654, Helisaeus Roeslin claimed the world would end in a blaze of fire in 1654.

AD 1657, according to the Fifth Monarchy Men of England, the apocalypse was set for sometime between AD 1655 and 1657.

AD 1662, North America, cleric Michael Wigglesworth wrote a long poem, "The Day of Doom," in which he claimed the world was going to end. *Any second now . . .*

AD 1666, a must-mention date if only for the fact that 666 is three-quarters of it. This year came after a civil war in England and the plague and also happened to host the Great London Fire.

AD 1688, John Napier, the mathematician who discovered

logarithms much to the distress of many teenagers throughout time, also made some doomsday calculations. The first figured 1688 to be the end of the world.

More more more more more. Seriously, I could fill up an entire book with Doomsday Predictions. Let's close this box with John Napier's second doomsday prediction of AD 1700; with Jacques Bernoulli's prediction of AD 1719 due to a comet; with another London flood terror predicted by William Whitson for AD 1736; and with William Bell's theory that the world would end by earthquake in AD 1761.

10

THESEUS AND THE MINOTAUR

PARALLELS

I n a famous interview with Scholastic, Suzanne Collins tells us that the ancient Greek myth of Theseus and the Minotaur served as a "significant influence" on The Hunger Games series. According to the author, she views Katniss as "a futuristic Theseus."[1]

So who was Theseus, and how does Katniss resemble him?

According to mythology, Theseus was the son of King Aegeus of ancient Athens, and of Aethra, daughter of King Pittheus of Troezen. At first, Aegeus wasn't aware that Theseus was his son because Pittheus and Aethra hid the fact from him. In fact, as the story goes, Aethra claimed that Poseidon was really Theseus's father.

Aegeus's wife, the sorceress Medea, bore the king a son named Medus. In the meantime, Aethra led her son, Theseus, to a rock, where Aegeus had hidden his sword and sandals.

When Theseus grew older, he traveled to Athens to meet his human father, Aegeus. Medea didn't want any competition against her own son, Medus, for the throne, so she sent Theseus on what she hoped was a doomed quest to capture the savage Marathonian Bull. Expecting Theseus to die, Medea was shocked when Theseus captured the bull. She persuaded Aegeus to poison the boy with tainted wine. But in the nick of time, Aegeus recognized Theseus's sword as the very one he hid near Aethra's home. He realized that Theseus was of his own flesh and blood. So he knocked the goblet of poison wine from the boy's lips, and he banished Medea and Medus from Athens.

Aegeus, in the meantime, was at war with his brother, King Minos of Crete. The people of Crete suffered from war and hunger, and as a result, Minos demanded every year for nine years, seven boys and seven girls be sacrificed to the Minotaur.

Fighting over the throne with his brothers, Minos had resorted to desperate measures. He had prayed to Poseidon for a white bull as a sign of Poseidon's approval to rule Crete. He promised to then slay the bull in honor of the Greek gods. But when Minos saw the beautiful bull, he couldn't bring himself to kill it. Bad idea. You don't mess with the gods. Poseidon was furious with Minos, and worked his magic on Minos's wife, Pasipha, who fell in love with the bull. Alas, as is the case in stories of the ancient gods, Pasipha had a child with the white bull. It wasn't a boy. It wasn't a girl. It was the Minotaur: a monster with a man's body but the head and tail of a bull.

Minos ordered the architect Daedalus to create a huge labyrinth in which to imprison the Minotaur. And then, every year for nine years, he cast seven boys and seven girls from Athens into the labyrinth, where the monster would feast upon them.

Hoping to end the sacrifices, Theseus volunteered to be one of the young men who had to battle the monster for his life. Suzanne Collins points out that, in this regard—because Theseus volunteered to fight the Minotaur—Katniss is a "futuristic Theseus." He sailed to Crete, where Minos's daughter Ariadne helped him defeat the Minotaur.

In the meantime, Aegeus assumed that the Minotaur had killed Theseus, and he threw himself off the Acropolis into what later became known as the Aegean Sea.

Suzanne Collins describes in her Scholastic interview how struck she was, even as a young girl, by "the ruthlessness of this message. 'Mess with us and we'll do something worse than kill you. We'll kill your children.'"[2]

Let's summarize:

Theseus is the son of a king—or possibly a god—and a king's daughter.	Katniss is the daughter of a coal miner and a healer.
Medea sends Theseus on what she hopes is a doomed quest to capture the Marathonian Bull.	Katniss does not have an evil stepmother like the sorceress Medea. She is not sent on a quest to capture a bull.
Medea wants Aegeus to poison Theseus with tainted wine.	Katniss's father does not try to give her poison wine.
Poseidon is furious with Minos and makes his wife Pasipha fall in love with the bull. She and the bull have a child, the Minotaur.	There are no gods or bulls giving birth with humans in The Hunger Games, though many of the muttations merge human and beast.
Minos orders the architect Daedalus to create a huge labyrinth in which to imprison the Minotaur. And then, every year for nine years, he casts seven boys and seven girls into the labyrinth, where the monster feasts upon them.	The labyrinth is akin to the arenas of the Hunger Games. Katniss and the other tributes must find their way through mazelike arenas to survive. Every year, the government casts an equal number of boys and girls into the arena, where they die.
Hoping to end the sacrifices, Theseus volunteers to be one of the young men who must battle the monster for his life.	Hoping to thwart the sacrifice of her sister Prim, Katniss volunteers to take her place as a tribute in the Games.

Aegeus assumes that the Minotaur has killed Theseus, and he throws himself off the Acropolis into the sea.	Everyone worries that the tribute they personally know will be killed at any moment in the Games.
The King of Athens does not get along with his brother Minos, who rules Crete. Minos demands that Athens send sacrificial "tributes" to Crete every year.	The Capitol demands that the districts send sacrificial tributes to the Capitol every year.

DOOMSDAY PREDICTIONS

AD 1856–1900

AD 1856, many people considered the Crimean War of 1853–56 to be Armageddon. If Russia took Palestine, then all would be lost.

Bypass hundreds of additional doomsday predictions and fast forward to AD 1870, when Irvin Moore's The Final Destiny of Man, predicted that in 1870, Jerusalem would become the capitol of the world and the apocalypse would occur.

AD 1891, Mormon founder Joseph Smith predicted in AD 1835 that the apocalypse would occur in 1891.

AD 1900, another landmark doomsday year, in which Father Pierre Lachèze marked us for total obliteration and one hundred members of the Brothers and Sisters of the Russian Red Death killed themselves before the apocalypse could take them.

11

SURVIVAL INSTINCTS AND STRATEGIES
DOES KATNISS KNOW WHAT SHE'S DOING?

From the beginning of The Hunger Games series, we know that Katniss Everdeen operates in survival mode on a daily basis. Her survival instincts and strategies are well honed from many years of practice. Her need to survive against all odds is the basis of the entire trilogy, and author Suzanne Collins roots this idea firmly in our minds right away. We know the series will be fraught with horror, action, adventure, tragedy, misery, and strife.

The first few pages of *The Hunger Games* build Katniss as a girl we like: She's kind; she loves her mother and sister. However, these opening pages also show another side of Katniss's life: We're told that her mother doesn't look quite as "beaten-down" when she's asleep, and we're told that Katniss tried to drown her sister's cat,

Buttercup, when it was just a kitten. We know immediately that there's a dark side to the life of our kind girl.

Suzanne Collins jacks up the hints of upcoming horror by page four, as the tone mingles the lightness of youth and kindness with the darkness of impending trouble that we sense is beyond anything with which we might be familiar. Here, the author tells us that Katniss feeds entrails to Buttercup, that she hunts for the family's food; that today, she must once again face the reaping.

Survival instincts and strategies will be paramount to Katniss, this is very clear when we learn that she lives in District 12, the Seam, where downtrodden coal miners can barely feed their families, where even the Meadow is "scruffy," where barbed wire fences surround everyone, and usually the fences are electrified.

This is a place that needs basics such as electricity, food, work, and modern conveniences. We get the feeling that Katniss is living in medieval times, yet we're also distinctly aware that these are not medieval times at all; rather, people are executed by Peacekeepers for basically any reason at all. Everyone's starving all the time, even the people who govern.

Over the course of all three novels—*The Hunger Games, Catching Fire,* and *Mockingjay*—Katniss uses almost every survival technique known to mankind. Hers is a dystopian post-apocalyptic society, where children are selected by lottery tickets to compete to the death in an arena reminiscent of the ancient Roman Colosseum. They battle in front of the entire population of the world as they know it; they battle on reality television. The series is like a gore-filled video game in which Katniss has no choice but to kill in hopes of saving her own skin. While battling in the arenas of *The Hunger Games* and *Catching Fire,* she receives "gifts" and ponies up health points, just as she would as the heroine of a video game. But unlike a video game, Katniss suffers real losses: her friends, her sister, her own sanity are all on the line. The physical suffering is far more acute than in any video game. The emotional pain is simply unprecedented for video games, and for this reason, quality fiction still affects us in ways that video games do not.

Suzanne Collins has been widely quoted as stating that one of her main inspirations for the series came from her father's experiences fighting in Vietnam. It's clear that the author knows a lot about combat and survival techniques in early and primitive societies, as well.

Katniss has frequent nightmares, which are common in post-traumatic stress syndrome. She trains constantly for battle. She wears camouflage. She knows how to find and conserve water, food, weapons, and medical supplies. She knows how to barter for what she wants and needs. She knows how to find shelter so she can sleep without being killed. These are all aspects of real survival strategies.

And if all else fails, she's even equipped with poison berries so she can commit suicide. Not exactly a way to *survive,* but suicide is often used in espionage and warfare to protect the overall group.

WATER

Let's start with water, a critical resource for anyone lost in the wilds or thrust into a combat arena. Katniss clearly knows how to squeeze water from her environment, and when she needs tips, Haymitch is there to help her. His last advice to her before she first heads into the arena is to "find a source of water" (*The Hunger Games,* 139).

Now let's look at real techniques for obtaining water where there is none and compare what Katniss does to how it's actually done.

Obviously, you can wear camouflage, create makeshift weapons, hide behind trees, rocks, in caves, and so forth. You can improvise a lot when you're in the wild, but you can't improvise *water.* If you have a chemistry lab, you might be able to do it, but in the wild, you have to know how to find and leech water from all sort of environments.

Most of us depend on power grids and water that's piped into our homes, restaurants, offices, malls, and airports. If the grid goes down, the water towers are depleted very quickly, and before you know it, people must seek water from natural sources.

Similarly, if using a well, which many people still do, if it runs dry or becomes polluted or otherwise unsuitable, natural sources must be found. Quickly.

We do have lakes, ponds, and rivers. We can collect rainwater. But how do we purify the water so we don't get sick? Can it be done in the wild?

Sure it can.

With a source of springwater, you're in good shape should doomsday come. As in the arena of the Hunger Games, in a post-apocalyptic world, people will kill to access and control the water supply.

In the real world, if using an *unknown* source of water, the supply could be heavily contaminated with pesticides, bacteria, and other dangerous pollutants. We see no evidence of heavily polluted water in The Hunger Games series, so purification of drinking water is not a huge issue; though in *Mockingjay*, District 13 does purify its underground water sources.

Well water typically requires pumps, which in turn, require grid power. If the power fails, the water pressure drops, and you're dry. There are ways around this problem, such as using a photovoltaic sun-driven method of pumping well water, but installation is probably prohibitive for most people.

If necessary, most of us could collect rainwater in buckets and use it for bathing and washing clothes and dishes. If collected directly from the sky—that is, without letting it drip off the roof or down a pipe—we can drink the water, too. We've all done it as children by tipping our heads in a storm and letting the drops flow into our mouths. But rain collected from spouts could be dangerous, as it might contain coliform bacteria and other hazards.

It's wise to purify all water before drinking it regardless of whether it comes from a spring, a well, or a rainstorm. If in a populated area or someplace with farms, it's wise to distill or otherwise treat water for pesticides and herbicides. Unfortunately, most methods of purification, including boiling, treating with chlorine solutions, and filtering don't kill chemical toxins.

Purification should at least remove particulate matter, which you can do by pouring water through several layers of cloth. If at all possible, you should chlorinate the water or use iodine, then filter it more finely. The sizes of microorganisms vary, so for example, if using a filter (like most cloth) that traps particles that are 1.0–4.0 microns big, protozoa such a *Giardia* and *Cryposporidium* will be removed, but bacteria and viruses may flow through the filter. You might want to use filters that trap particles down to 0.0004 microns in size, which will handle viruses.

Other methods exist such as UV sterilizers that control bacteria, parasites, and viruses in shallow pools of water. These do not require chemicals and some are compact enough to carry into the woods. Other compact water filters, commonly used by campers and hikers, may require batteries.

The old-fashioned method of boiling water helps, and in many countries, people don't even bring the water to boiling point before drinking it. They use water pasteurization indicators to let them know when the water temperature reaches 149 degrees Fahrenheit (rather than boiling point, or 212 degrees), at which time, they assume all the microbes are dead.

The best bet is to heat the water above 160 degrees Fahrenheit for thirty minutes; and if the water's above 185, it will kill all pathogens after only a few minutes.

In a pinch, you can treat water with pool shock chlorination tablets or calcium hypochlorite. To do so, dissolve a tablet or a heaping teaspoon of calcium hypochlorite into several gallons of water. Make sure to use a glass or plastic container—definitely not metal, which will interact with the chemicals. Now add one part of your solution to one hundred parts natural source water.

If the water is at or below 50 degrees Fahrenheit, approximately 90 percent of *Giardia* microorganisms, which can make you very sick, will be killed after thirty minutes. If at 40 degrees, make sure to double the time you wait before using the chlorine solution.

One of the most effective methods for sterilizing water around the world is an iodine treatment, which kills more *Giardia* cysts than chlorine. For example, you can fill a bottle with source water, add iodine crystals, and then shake the bottle and let it sit for an hour. At this point, you add one capful of your iodine solution to each quart of source water.

Or you can use iodine liquid, a 2 percent tincture of iodine that requires five drops per quarter of clear water and ten drops for cloudy water.

Katniss uses iodine liquid to purify water in *The Hunger Games.* Luckily, her backpack is equipped with a bottle of iodine, as well as a half-gallon plastic bottle with a cap. (*The Hunger Games,* 154) Knowing how to survive in the wild, Katniss adds "the right number of drops of iodine" and then waits half an hour (*The Hunger Games,* 170). It's also lucky that she doesn't happen to be allergic to iodine, which isn't too common but does affect people (who are also allergic to shellfish, oddly enough).

After sterilizing water in the wild, you need some containers that you can easily carry. It obviously helps if they're leak proof and have wide lids for easier filling. At the beginning of her first Games, Katniss has the option of trying to make it to the Cornucopia and grab water containers without being killed. Wisely, she doesn't choose to do. Luckily, she does have a half-gallon plastic bottle with a cap, and Rue has a water "skin," by contrast (*The Hunger Games,* 240).

It's a while before Katniss finds a water source, and she hopes that Haymitch will send water down to her in a parachute; she hopes that a sponsor will supply a gift of water, which in the context of *The Hunger Games* is like finding a treasure in a video game and getting ten extra "lives" or a boost in health points.

In the second book, *Catching Fire,* decent drinking water is more difficult to obtain. In fact, it's a major problem. This time, the Games are held in a saltwater-centric arena, where the sun is hot and the air is moist. Not having any water makes Katniss extremely thirsty, particularly given that she must hike through a jungle in such intense humidity (*Catching Fire,* 278). Still seeking drinking water, Katniss and Peeta later try to hike left and break through the force field and far away from the Cornucopia and saltwater. Peeta thinks they might find drinking water "between the force field and the wheel" (*Catching Fire,* 287). An intelligent thought, but as with all good plans, things don't quite work out the way Katniss and Peeta hope.

When the two of them come across a large rodent with a wet muzzle, they know that water must be somewhere nearby. As in a video game, just in the nick of time, a sponsor sends a gift spile in a parachute, and again using her experience in survival techniques, Katniss remembers seeing her father insert spiles into maple trees to get sap. So this is how Katniss obtains a few drops of precious water in the second book (*Catching Fire,* 294). Had she not been incredibly skilled in wilderness survival, Katniss never would have survived the first day of *The Hunger Games,* much less the subsequent death matches in *Catching Fire* and *Mockingjay.*

As a side note, many plants other than maple trees contain water. In deserts, barrel cacti will quench your thirst, and indeed, a 3.5 foot tall cactus will supply a quart of liquid. You can also drink from the roots of plants such as the desert oak and bloodwood. In other area, you can drink water from vines, from the stalks of palms, and obviously from coconuts. In addition, all of these plants contain water that you can drink: bamboo stems, which have water in their joints; umbrella tree of tropical Africa; baobab tree of Africa and Australia; and many others.

By the time Katniss reaches *Mockingjay* and by the time she descends down the elevators into the labyrinth of living spaces, her water is purified mechanically, as is her air (*Mockingjay,* 80).

It's ironic that, when chosen for the Games, Katniss has the luxury of as much pure, clean water as she wants. Not only does the tribute train include private quarters for each child, it also provides private bathrooms with hot and cold running water. Katniss marvels at the luxury because to have any warm water at home, her family must boil it (*The Hunger Games*, 42). Later, while preparing for the Games in the Capitol, she's even more amazed by the water luxuries of her bathroom. The shower panel has "more than a hundred options you can choose regulating water temperature, pressure, soaps, shampoos, scents, oils, and massaging sponges" (*The Hunger Games*, 75). The futuristic shower reminds me of the old Hanna–Barbera *Jetsons* cartoon. If you don't know what I mean, find some old *Jetsons* clips on YouTube, and you'll see the personalized bathrooms and showers. These are so futuristic they even brush George Jetson's teeth. However, rather than using water, they're ultrasonic and don't require that people remove clothing before showering.

Water Checklist: Katniss versus Reality

Natural Sources of Water and Treatment Methods	Available to Katniss in the Games
Springwater	No, but she does find a pond in *The Hunger Games*.
Well water	No.
Rainwater	Yes, in *Catching Fire*, but the rain burns her skin.
Leak-proof wide-lid bottles	Comes in her backpack in *The Hunger Games*.
Tree sap	Yes, in *Catching Fire*.
PURIFICATION	
Particulate filtering	No.
Chlorination	No.
Fine filtering	Yes, in *Mockingjay*, the subterranean labyrinths include water and air purifiers.
Pesticide and herbicide filtering	Yes, in *Mockingjay*, the subterranean labyrinths include water and air purifiers.

UV sterilization	No.
Compact battery-powered units	No.
Boiling	At home, this is the only way Katniss's family obtains warm water. In the Games, she doesn't boil water to purify it.
Water pasteurization indicators	No.
Pool shock—calcium hypochlorite	No.
Iodine crystals or liquid	A bottle of liquid iodine comes in her backpack in *The Hunger Games*.

FOOD

Next to water, food might be the most critical aspect of surviving in the wilderness. Shelter is important, as is protection from the elements. But without food, you will definitely die.

Food, as all readers of The Hunger Games series know, is the one thing that everyone in District 12 never has enough of. Food is the key thing that Katniss has learned to cull from the woods to keep her family alive.

Not only is it important for someone who is stranded without food to find sustenance, it's also essential that he or she eat a variety of items. Katniss scrubs the forest at home for meat, grains, berries, and vegetables. There are approximately 120,000 edible plants on Earth, and Katniss can clearly identify enough of them to survive. When she's in the Games, she's still trying to hunt and gather food as she did in District 12.

In general, when without modern methods of storing, preparing, and eating food, it'll help if you have various fundamental items.

Salt is important because it preserves many foods and can often attract wild animals, which can then be hunted. Rice would be useful, as would wheat and grains. Corn, oats, powdered milk, canned fruits and vegetables, oils: these are all staples of the "we're all going to die" bunkers that we hear about from time to time. A lot of families during the Cold War kept these items stocked in their basements, which served as bomb shelters.

But for someone like Katniss (or someone who has to leave town in a hurry and hide in the woods), this type of list is impractical. Not only is she going to have a hard, albeit impossible, time trying to find powdered milk and canned fruits, she's not going to find a lot of other common bunker foods, either; foods like peanut butter, coffee, vitamin C tablets, trail mix, or energy bars.

We learn very quickly in *The Hunger Games* that Katniss's father taught her how to find food in the wilderness before he died in a mine explosion. She was only eleven when she became responsible for feeding both her sister Prim and her mother, who sank into a deep lethargic depression.

Good foods to eat from the wild include berries, nuts, freshwater fish, birds, eggs, mammal flesh, insects, crustaceans, seaweed, and soft pine needles. Katniss kills, catches, and harvests most of these foods during The Hunger Games books.

Early in the series, Katniss explains that she learned to survive by harvesting dandelions (a memory intimately connected to Peeta), pine needles, wild onions, and pokeweeds, and that she swiped eggs from birds' nests and fished using a net. Luckily, her survival skills come in handy during the first Games, which is held in a forest of pine trees. Katniss eats the soft bark that's inside the branches (*The Hunger Games*, 50–52 and 155).

During *Catching Fire,* the second book, she returns to the house in the woods where she hung out as a child, and she knows something's amiss when she smells "steaming pine needles." It's a clear indicator that she's not alone, that somebody else who knows how to survive in the woods is there with her (*Catching Fire,* 134). There are other clues, of course, but how many of us would recognize the odor of "steaming pine needles" and realize that somebody's cooking pine needle stew?

While survival skills include knowledge of foods that are *safe,* they also include knowledge about foods to *avoid.* In general, thanks to her father's forest skills and her mother's medicinal-herb skills, Katniss has learned what not to eat in the wilderness. Any survival handbook, such as the one published by the U.S. Army, spells out which foods to avoid, such as: toads, ticks, flies; insects that sting, bite, or have hairy bodies; saltwater fish with parrotlike beaks or spines; and mushrooms and other fungi that might be poisonous.

When younger, Katniss learned to creep out and slide under the fence when the electricity went down for a few hours in the evenings. She learned to keep her bows and arrows in a hollow tree, and unlike most people, she was lucky to have these weapons because her father crafted them and taught her how to use them. She and Gale learned to trade hunted meat for other foods their families needed.

In fact, securing food has always been so central to Katniss that she thinks that, without hunting, fishing, and gathering, there might be absolutely nothing left of her (*The Hunger Games,* 311).

Contrast Katniss's food-related survival skills to Peeta, who does well—don't get me wrong—but who offers her deadly nightlock berries without realizing that they're poisonous.

Providing for his family is also important to Gale Hawthorne, and in *Catching Fire,* he goes into the coal mines while Katniss hunts for his family. She does receive food from the Capitol in *Catching Fire,* but for matters of personal pride, she still hunts and gathers, and for matters of personal pride, Gale is extremely reluctant to take food from her. While it makes sense that Katniss would keep hunting, it makes little sense that Gale would not gladly receive her overabundance of Capitol-provided food to help his starving family. After all, they have been best friends for a very long time. And when your family's starving, you do what it takes.

Alas, male pride is a strange thing, so when Katniss becomes "engaged" to Peeta, Gale is furious and refuses all of her gifts, including a leather bag of food (*Catching Fire,* 93).

ENVIRONMENT AND SHELTER

The environment in which you're lost—or find yourself fighting to the death in the Games—is key to your survival. If you've grown up in a northeastern forest, will you know how to survive in the jungle, in the desert, in the ocean? Or like Katniss, will you have to figure out how to cope on the fly, using general survival skills you've acquired over the years in your home environment?

True survivors can adapt to unusual environments, immerse themselves in their surroundings. They constantly protect and analyze their resources, the hazards around them, and the patterns of their new environments. They look for clues that may help them remain alive. For example, survivors seek food, water, shelter, any way to use natural objects to their advantage. When confronted with hazards that spell certain death, or with resources that don't suffice to keep them alive, they navigate to better locations, if at all possible.

These are all techniques that Katniss uses well. She's indeed a true survivor in the classic sense.

THE THREES OF SURVIVAL

1. You must have oxygen within three minutes, or you will die. If in a poisonous gas-fog, run! Get out of there quickly!

2. You must find drinking water, or you will die within three days.

3. You must sleep, or within three days, you will be too exhausted to survive.

4. You must find protection from horrendous weather within three hours, or you will die. If in a scorching jungle with no water and food, get out. If in a blizzard with subzero weather, get out. If in a heavy wind, get out. And if like Katniss in *Catching Fire,* you ever find yourself in the path of a tidal wave, a pack of shrieking mutation monkeys, or blood rain, run as quickly as you can.

5. **Without food, you might survive for three weeks if you have enough fat in your body and if you have enough water.**

In the first Hunger Games book, Katniss must survive in an environment similar to District 12. That is, the arena resembles a pine forest with trees where she can sleep at night and hide, with foods she knows how to procure, with terrain she can manage to navigate. We're told that District 12 is located in former Appalachia, which gives us a clue about the terrain and wildlife.

The Appalachian Mountains actually range from Quebec to the southernmost Alabama and Mississippi foothills. However, the area specifically known as *Appalachia* is much smaller; though it's still a huge region, including parts of thirteen states with a total of more than four hundred counties. Appalachia encompasses portions of New York, Pennsylvania, Ohio, and Maryland, as well as portions of Mississippi, Georgia, Alabama, North Carolina, South Carolina, Kentucky, Virginia, and Tennessee, plus all of West Virginia.

Okay, so where does Katniss come from, just where *is* District 12?

At minimum, we know she hails from somewhere in the eastern part of North America.

We have a few more clues: pine trees, the types of animals and plants she eats, and possibly most important, the fact that District 12 relies on coal mining. This last tidbit narrows Katniss's region of Appalachia to either western Pennsylvania, or down south: West Virginia, eastern Kentucky, southwest Virginia, eastern Tennessee, Alabama. In Pennsylvania, the mines produce anthracite, which is hard coal containing a lot of carbon. But in the more southern areas, the mines yield bituminous coal, which is softer. Unfortunately for those of us who are trying to figure out where in Appalachia we might find District 12, our clues are dwindling: pine trees are found all over the Appalachian region, not just in one part, say, western Pennsylvania.

We have a few other clues about District 12's location. For example, District 12 has a small population of approximately 8,000 people, implying it's a tiny district. It could be geographically large, with the

8,000 people spread all over a lot of former states. A good guess is that the people are *not* spread widely, however, because the people in District 12 basically know each other, everyone can cram into the public square for the reapings, and we never hear about civilization beyond the Justice house, the public square, and the mayor's home. It's possible that everyone lives in a small area of District 12, yet the district itself encompasses a vast space—all or most of current Appalachia—which is now unoccupied due to the apocalyptic event that triggered the carving of North America in the first place. We do know that District 12 is the "end of the line," according to Katniss (*The Hunger Games,* 83).

There's been much debate among fans about the location of all the districts. But nobody knows for sure except Suzanne Collins, the author.

The most we might be able to state about District 12's pine forest is that it's a *temperate forest* much like the one in Katniss's first Hunger Games.

Temperature varies quite a bit in most temperate forests, requiring heavy clothes, layers of clothing to peel off as temperatures warm, boots for hiking. Katniss doesn't wear heavy coats, though she does wear traditional hiking clothes and boots. Her mother uses snow to heal bad wounds, so we do know that it gets cold in the District 12 mountains. In the first book, Peeta wraps his jacket around Katniss to keep her warm (*The Hunger Games,* 83). Edible plants and animals in temperate forests include birds, eggs, freshwater fish, and pine needles, from which tea can be made—remember the steam rising from the old house in the woods—as well as acorns, dandelions, maple sap, and berries. All of these items are stock fare in Katniss's world.

In the first Games, Katniss wears a jacket that has special material to reflect her body heat so she won't get cold at night (*The Hunger Games,* 145). She also wears boots with rubber soles to help her run quickly.

In *Catching Fire,* the environment of the Quarter Quell, the seventy-fifth Games, is much more difficult for Katniss. Here, her survival skills are stretched to the limit. She's in an arena concocted by Gamemakers to resemble a giant clock, with each section devoted to a different hazardous environment.

When first placed into the Quarter Quell arena, she's confronted with a circle of saltwater. Equipped with a flotation device, her belt, she must make it to a beach, and from there, to an outlying jungle.

This is a much more elaborate and difficult combat experience for Katniss. She really has to use her wits now because she's not used to the environment.

In reality, jungles vary quite a bit, with the vegetation strongly dependent on both climate and human interference. Clearly, in *Catching Fire*, human interference is anything but lacking.

Unlike the jungle in *Catching Fire*, real-world jungles can have tropical trees that mature after a hundred years. Some of these trees only attain their full height and breadth in primeval virgin forests that man has yet to destroy. The canopy of dense top growth of these old trees can be as high as a hundred feet from the jungle floor. Both light and underbrush are scarce beneath the canopy. Monkeys, birds, and bees live in the treetops.

Most jungles are similar to the one in *Catching Fire*, but there are differences. In reality, men clear the primeval jungles, cultivate the earth or use it for other reasons, and then let the land remain idle. When the underbrush creeps over the idle land, it forms thick, high mats covered in dense vines. In *Catching Fire*, Katniss is confronted with trees that have very few branches, with soil that is so rich and black that one would think centuries of vegetation has rotted here. Vines are everywhere, it's humid as hell, and the sun is "hot and bright" (*Catching Fire*, 275). Katniss's jungle merges the conditions of a primary jungle with those of a secondary jungle. She has the horrible sun of a secondary jungle that's without one-hundred-foot trees and their knitted canopies. Yet she also has the vines and underbrush of a primary jungle. The killer muttation monkeys, were they real rather than man made, might live high in the tops of primary jungle trees.

Speaking of, isn't it enough to be thrust into a jungle with no water and death at every turn without adding killer muttation monkeys to the nightmare? Thankfully—though it's not much—the tributes don't have to contend with some aspects of real jungles, such as swarms of mosquitoes and thousands of leeches.

Before traveling to jungles, people are warned to gear up to the climate and conditions. For one thing, it's wise to be fairly athletic, but experts tell us that even the most athletic people must exercise in scorching, humid climates for a minimum of four days before hiking through a jungle. And even after preparing for the trip, experts tell hikers to allow at least four to six additional days—in the actual jungle—to acclimate to the conditions. Unfortunately for Katniss and the other children in the Games, they aren't given the chance to prepare for, much less become accustomed to, the harsh environment.

In addition to the jungle, Katniss must cope with various man-made environmental hazards, including a bizarre burning gas-poison fog that causes body seizures; an enormous wave that thunders down a hill and crashes into the saltwater in the center of the arena; and even blood rain. The clock wedges contain plagues such as lightning, killer muttation monkeys, gas-poison fog, the insanely huge wave, and the blood rain. (*Catching Fire,* 326). In fact, the environment inflicts so many plagues on the tributes that it almost feels as if they're confronting something akin to the ten plagues in Exodus.

THE TEN PLAGUES: LET MY PEOPLE GO!

Do you remember the story of Exodus? The tagline might be "Enough is enough." God finally cast the ten plagues on Egypt, and Moses finally got his way after begging God to "Let my people go!"

Catching Fire has its own set of plagues, which the Capitol uses against the tributes. The districts finally revolt in *Mockingjay,* and their tagline might also be "Enough is enough." In fact, Katniss could very well be screaming, "Let my people go!" throughout *Mockingjay.*

The Ten Plagues	*Catching Fire* Plague?
Blood	Blood rain
Frogs	No, but there are tree lizards with flickering tongues.
Gnats	Not in *Catching Fire*, though *Mockingjay* includes muttation gnats.
Wild beasts	Killer muttation monkeys.
Pestilence	Weird rat-possum rodents.
Boils	Poison-gas fog burns the skin and causes seizures.
Hail	No, but there's something far icier: *President Snow*.
Locusts	All of the other "plagues" in The Hunger Games trilogy make up for the omission of locusts.
Darkness	No, but there *were* the Dark Days, which led to the nightmares of the Hunger Games.
Death of the firstborn, the most vile plague.	All the tributes who are cast into the arena to die are children. An exception is the Quarter Quell, when all winning tributes must compete again, and some of them have already become quite old.

MEDICAL SUPPLIES

Survival in the wilderness is tough without even the most rudimentary first aid kit. Most people bring items such as:

- Adhesive bandages in various sizes.
- Roll bandages for protecting larger wounds and infections, securing dressings, and wrapping broken or sprained ankles, feet, wrists, etc.
- Tape and safety pins.
- Scissors.

▓ **Antiseptics.**

▓ **Soap.**

▓ **Painkillers.**

It's hard to forget Peeta's leg infection in *The Hunger Games*—the fever, pus, swelling, and blood poisoning. Katniss hopes that a sponsor will drop a gift of anti-infection medicine before Peeta dies. She's been using chewed leaves, all that's available in the wilderness, and ineffective ointment. As for a first aid kit, forget it: The tributes are on their own. They're lucky to plunge burning flesh into cool water, and if they want bandages, they have to make them from strips of clothing. The best they can hope is that medicine and supplies drop from gift parachutes out of the sky.

This may be the one area where the tributes, including Katniss with all her wilderness skills, have no chance whatsoever. Break a bone, you're doomed. Get an infection, pray that a magical ointment falls from the sky.

TRAINING AND OVERALL KNOWLEDGE

If you're lost in the wilderness, as in the first Hunger Games, and you're with other people, it's essential to immediately identify the skills of your potential killers; or in the case of the real world, your friends. Potential killers or friends, you need to know immediately who among you possesses the following skills:

▓ **Plant identification.**

▓ **Navigation.**

▓ **Medical.**

▓ **Knowledge of local terrain.**

▓ **Knowledge of local weather.**

▓ **Builds fires, and by corollary, knowing how to extinguish them.**

- Physical strength and endurance.
- Fast runner.
- Reacts quickly and intelligently.
- Builds shelters.
- Hunts.
- Uses weapons well.
- Can make rope.

All of these topics seem like logical ones, but without training, most of us wouldn't have a clue what to do if suddenly stuck in an arena to fight for our lives. Katniss, remember, enters the arena very well trained in plant identification, navigation, weapons, and hunting. She's physically agile—imagine if Katniss was weak when sent into the arena!—and she reacts quickly and intelligently. Her mother is a healer, so Katniss knows a lot about natural medicines. As for the local terrain in the arena, if she's not in a forest similar to the one in District 12, she has to learn how to cope just like everyone else. The same is true for the local weather, which changes at whim in the arena based on what the Gamemakers want to do to the contestants. How do you train for a poisonous gas fog, for example? Or for attacks by strange muttations?

In each of her two Hunger Games, and during the revolution in *Mockingjay,* Katniss always assesses the skills of her enemies and friends. She works with friends to overcome other groups of children during the Games; for example, helping Rue as much as possible and almost dying herself when Rue is killed.

According to the Army Survival Manual, you should do the following when confronted with possible death in the wild (*The U.S. Army Survival Manual,* 3):

S—size up the situation.

U—use all your senses, exercise caution.

R—remember where you are at all times.

V—vanquish any fear and do not panic.

I—improvise by making tools, weapons, shelter, etc.

V—value living and keep fighting for your life!

A—act like the natives, note how they survive.

L—live by your wits, but make sure you have basic skills.

Of course, all tributes undergo survival training in the Capitol's Training Center. To gain sponsors and lifesaving gifts, they must impress the Gamemakers and the crowds with the skills and charisma they bring to the Games. To make up for gaps in their survival knowledge, they must practice as much as possible in areas of deficiency. They learn combat techniques, how to build fires and ropes, how to use a wide variety of basic weapons. What's missing is the element that may very well matter the most: native intelligence. And this is where Katniss excels. Sure, nobody can beat Katniss with a bow and arrow, but she's truly extraordinary when it comes to the most critical survival skills.

DOOMSDAY PREDICTIONS

AD **1910–80**

AD 1910, Halley's Comet was supposed to kill us all. People took "comet pills" to ward off the toxins that would spew from the killer comet.

AD 1914, Jehovah's Witnesses, which predicted Armageddon repeatedly, pinpointed this year as their most critical death date. You can probably guess how they arrived at 1914; yes, through math. Charles T. Russell assigned numbers to a bunch of quotes from The Book of Daniel to come up with the year of the apocalypse.

AD 1914, World War I was heralded as the end of all wars, true Armageddon.

AD 1917, along with the war came the Spanish Flu, killing many millions of people. Certainly, doomsday was upon us. Any second now . . .

AD 1919, meteorologist Albert Porta did some (care to guess?) calculations and determined that on December 17, 1919, a magnetic current would pierce the sun and cause explosions that would destroy the Earth. People were so terrified that some actually committed suicide rather than be engulfed in the sun's flames.

1940s, World War II, *enough said.*

1950s, more and more and more predictions of the apocalypse, most courtesy of aliens, UFOs, and nukes.

1960s, more of the same with the addition of new doomsday scenarios including the truly bizarre notion from Edgar Cayce that the lost continent of Atlantis would rise from the ocean, and major cities would sink while the poles shifted. Another horrific apocalypse spinoff in AD 1969 was Charles Manson and The Family, who murdered famous people to somehow gain a foothold as leaders of the post-apocalypse world resulting somehow from a race war.

1970s, more of the same with the addition of the Rev. Charles Meade's Armageddon scenario: his End Time Ministries believed the world was soon to end, so people had to prepare by not reading anything, by getting pregnant yet remaining single in their teens, by not going to doctors, and by ignoring all noncult members. Meade believed the world would end by *goo,* a sticky white semen-sounding glop that would coat and suffocate everything on the planet.

AD 1977, Salem Kirban claimed the world would end because killer bees swarming throughout the United States fulfilled the Revelation prophecy of locusts with scorpion stingers and human heads.

AD 1978, on November 18, 919 people killed themselves in Jonestown, Guyana. A doomsday cult, the followers of Jim Jones were terrified of an imminent racial holocaust and nuclear Armageddon. Obeying Jones, cult members drank poisoned Kool-Aid, then lay on the ground and died together. Any cult member trying to flee was either injected with poison or shot to death.

12

MEDICINES AND POISONS

SIMPLE AND COMPLEX

Medicinal herbs, sleeping syrups, morphling: all play key roles in the three Hunger Games books. Not only does Katniss know which plants to gather for eating and which ones to avoid, she's lucky to have a mother who is, for all practical purposes, a medicine man, or as I think of her, a *medicine mom*.

On the flip side are the poisons, most notably, the nightlock berries used by Katniss and Peeta to fake-out President Snow and his cronies. But of keenest interest are the poisons that do not involve plants, such as the tracker jacker venom that hijacks Peeta.

Katniss's mother is an expert with medicinal herbs and basically serves as District 12's healer. In *Catching Fire*, she and Prim use all sorts of herbs to cure Gale after he's whipped for possessing a turkey. As mentioned in chapter 2, "Repressive Regimes and Rebellions," real-life governments have starved millions of their own people to death, they've stolen food from citizens, and they've mercilessly beaten people for infractions as ludicrous as "thinking" the wrong ideas. So it's not a stretch that a regime as tyrannical as the Capitol would whip someone into unconsciousness over a turkey. Luckily for Gale, Katniss's mother is a healer and knows how to use salves, bandages, sleeping syrup, and herbs to reduce inflammations. She even has syringes for injecting morphling, though it's somewhat unclear how she maintains a supply of hypos and how she's able to keep them sterile. In real life, doctors use sterile hypodermic needles once and then dispose of them. On the streets, used needles are a cause of infection and spreading disease.

All that aside, it's lucky for everyone in District 12 that Katniss's mother knows what she's doing. She's a medical healer, an herbalist really, whose methods aren't connected to the idea of a God or gods or spirits of any kind.

In reality, cultures around the world have believed in faith healers and medicine men for thousands of years. The notion that one man can cure the sick and return life to the dead has been around for a very long time—since prehistoric times.

A shaman, for example, is a medicine man with magic-religious powers who cures human suffering by forming relationships with spiritual entities. The shaman goes into a trance, or spiritual state, and he asks the spirits how to heal the sick, raise the dead, and save the tribe or nation.

The word, "shamanism," comes from the Russian evolution of the Tungusic word, *saman*. We could list many examples of medicine men and shaman in all cultures. One such example might be the Tatar people, who used the shaman for most everything. For example, to cure a sick child, the shaman would hold a séance to try and bring back the soul of the child. The séance could last six hours, maybe more, during which the shaman went into a trance, traveling to the lands of the spirits. The shaman would search for the sick child's undamaged soul and ask spirits for a way to heal the child's illness.

In keeping with the universal ideas throughout history of cosmic consciousness and the interconnection of human souls, the shaman traveled from one cosmic region to another for advice and help. He was able to communicate on a cosmic plane via the cosmic consciousness.

An herbalist such as Katniss's mother doesn't travel from one cosmic region to another. She simply knows how to use plants and medicines to heal people. It's a form of folk medicine, and many modern laboratory-produced medicines are derived from natural plant sources or derivatives.

Since prehistoric times, people have used herbs to heal themselves of illnesses. The Sumerians practiced herbal medicine with thyme and laurel; the ancient Egyptians used mint, garlic, castor oil, coriander, and opium. The ancients of India used turmeric, and later more than 700 different plants for medicinal reasons. The ancient Chinese used as many as 365 medicinal plants.

The cat, Buttercup, is named after a plant; Prim is named after a plant; and even the name, Rue, refers to a plant.

While Katniss almost kills Buttercup, she ends up quite fond of the cat. When wild, Buttercup is scrappy, but when fed and cared for, she becomes almost affectionate. When raw, all buttercup plants are poisonous. When boiled or pickled—when cared for—the plants are safe for consumption.

The primrose is a delicate flower, and both the leaves and flowers are edible. Prim is cast as a delicate, innocent flower in The Hunger Games.

As for rue, it is a bitter herb that tastes horrible. The word is derived from the Greek *reuo*, to set free; historically, people used rue in an attempt to cure the plague, get rid of worms and fleas, and set the body free from other diseases. Chewing rue leaves may relieve tension headaches and anxiety.

Speaking of Rue, she chews green leaves and then applies the glop to skin in order to relieve the pain and sting from leech bites. Plantain leaves, which are common weeds, can take the sting out of bites. If you chew plantain leaves, then apply the glop to an insect bite, it'll relieve the pain, swelling, and sting. Other leaves that work well include witch hazel, oak, willow, and maple.

Katniss's first gift from a sponsor is a medicinal burn ointment (*The Hunger Games*, 188). The cooling balm instantly eradicates her pain, and she knows it's not an herbal remedy, but rather, a medicine made in the Capitol's laboratories. Apparently, the ointment heals burns. Of course, we all know that cold water helps reduce the pain of burns, as does aloe vera. Sometimes, antibiotic creams are used, as well. This is all fine if you have a first-degree burn, such as a minor sunburn; or possibly even if you have second-degree burns with blisters. But for third-degree burns, where the skin looks charred, cold water and ointments aren't going to help much: For extreme burns, you need medical assistance.

SAGITTARIA LATIFOLIA AND RELATED SPECIES

Before he died in a mining explosion, Katniss's father told her that, as long as she could find herself, she would never starve. Katniss served both as *her* name and also as the nickname given to the water plantain called *Sagittaria latifolia*. Other names for this type of plant are arrowhead, duckpotato, tulepotato, and wappato. All forms of the katniss plant produce starchy tubers, which can be consumed by humans. Roasted or boiled, they're as good as potatoes, maybe better. Katniss claims that they're "as good as any potato" (*The Hunger Games*, 52). They're found worldwide in ponds and other wet areas. For example, they are often cultivated on the edges of rice paddies.

Also of interest, the leaves of the katniss are shaped like arrowheads. Her special skill, of course, is with the bow and arrow.

In the first Hunger Games book, Katniss is hoping for a sponsor gift of medicine to save Peeta's life. Instead, she receives sleep syrup that she tells us is cheap and also common in District 12 (*The Hunger Games*, 276). We're all familiar with cough syrups that can help knock people out, but a mere cough syrup isn't going to be as addictive and potent as the sleep syrup in The Hunger Games. Of course, there are many sleeping pills prescribed by doctors, and any of these crushed into a syrup would do the trick.

Barbiturates, for example, are extremely addictive and include amobarbital sodium, phenobarbital, Numbutal Sodium, and secobarbital. Depending on the dose, they can sedate someone, make him tired and drowsy, or knock him out. Benzodiazepines such as Halcion, Librium, Valium, Xanax, and Ativan can be addictive and will sedate or put someone to sleep. Drugs such as codeine, opium, oxycodone, Percodan, Percocet, Demerol HCL, and others—typically used to relieve pain—can also become habit forming and possibly sedate users.

As for the morphling, which clearly refers to morphine, doctors prescribe this drug to people after serious surgery and it's not the sort of drug you want to take casually. It acts directly on the nervous system to reduce pain. It's no wonder that Katniss becomes a morphling addict in Mockingjay. She's in the hospital for a long time under the influence of both sleeping syrup and morphling, which makes her feel empty inside (Mockingjay, 218).

Morphine sulfate is typically a white crystalline powder, though it also comes in larger crystal form. It is soluble in water, and hence, it's possible that the sleep syrup could contain some morphling. However, given that sleep syrup is common in District 12 and morphling must be obtained from the Capitol, it's doubtful that the syrup does indeed contain morphling.

In 1804, German pharmacist Friedrich Wilhelm Adam Sertürner, isolated morphine for the first time. He named the drug after Morpheus, Greek god of dreams. In 1853, with the rise of the hypodermic needle, doctors started using morphine to relieve pain and also to attempt to cure opium addiction.

But opium-based elixirs have been around for much longer. Laudanum, an opium in an alcohol base, was cited in 1522 by Paracelsus as killing pain. In the late 1800s, it was supplied to adults and children in little kits that actually came with hypodermic needles.

As for the nightlock berries, these are probably a toxic berry named after a combination of the *night*shade and hem*lock* plants. Nightlock berries instantly kill someone, and in *Mockingjay,* Cinna makes sure that Katniss has these suicide pills in a pouch on her shoulder. As in many wars, soldiers carry suicide pills, so in case they're captured, they can die rather than undergo torture and spill secrets. Earlier, when Katniss and Peeta both threaten to commit suicide using the berries rather than sacrifice one over the other, the Capitol has no choice but to declare two winners.

Nightshades are also known as Belladonna plants and Devil's Cherries, among other names. Its flowers are purple tinged with green and have five large lobes in which the berries grow. Although the shining black berries contain sweet juice, they are deadly.

Every part of the nightshade is poisonous due to an alkaloid called atropine. Stories tell us that during the Parthian wars, nightshade was given to Marcus Antonius's troops to poison them, and Plutarch graphically recounts the effects of the deadly plants.

Poison hemlock looks like a giant parsley plant, and its seeds are light brown and shaped like barrels. All parts of the poison hemlock are deadly, especially the stems and roots. The ancient Greeks used hemlock to poison prisoners, and indeed Socrates was killed in 339 BC using hemlock. It's more likely that the nightlock berries are from a type of nightshade plant.

Another point about the nightlock berries: because Katniss and Peeta used them to circumvent the evil plans of the government during the first Games, the word, nightlock, becomes symbolic, just as the mockingjay becomes symbolic. When using the Holo, if someone in Katniss's squad says "nightlock, nightlock, nightlock," the Holo blows up everything nearby. Again, as with the nightlock berries she used with Peeta in the Games, the rebels can explode everything, including themselves, in case they are captured (*Mockingjay,* 261). Indeed, Katniss uses this technique to destroy muttation human-lizard things that kill Finnick (*Mockingjay,* 312–13).

Finally, let's talk about the venom injected by the tracker jackers. These mutated wasps were created in government laboratories (see chapter 13, "Muttations and Other Hybrids") and are huge, solid gold killers. We're told that tracker jacker venom can kill, and at minimum, they induce hallucinations and insanity (*The Hunger Games,* 185).

Of course, in the real world, we do have killer wasps, killer bees, and a large variety of venom. Real-life killer wasps don't hijack our memories, nor do they track us wherever we go.

Cicada killer wasps are huge, up to two inches long. They're black with yellow markings on their abdomens and thoraxes; and there's also a solid gold killer wasp, the great golden digger wasp, but it's not as big as the black-and-yellow version. Yellow jackets, which are sometimes called wasps, are black and yellow for the most part, and some people can die from the venom of a yellow jacket.

Asian giant hornets are the world's largest hornet, with a body length of about two inches, same as the cicada killer wasps. Their wingspans can be up to three inches wide, and the venom in the stingers is so powerful that people describe it as having hot nails thrust into them. The enzyme in the venom can dissolve human flesh.

Tracker jacker wasps probably inject venom directly into the victim's bloodstream. The venom, which contains enzymes and peptides, tears down cell membranes so the internal parts of the cells dump into the bloodstream. With neurons, the damaged cells send "pain" signals to the brain. The venom typically contains norepinephrine, which stops blood from flowing near the sting, so the damaged cells are awash in the venom and keep sending "pain" signals to the brain. Something called mast cell degranulating peptides and hyaluronidase enable the venom to melt the connective tissues between cells; and hence, the venom moves into adjacent cells, as well.

As for hijacking Peeta with fear conditioning, if the venom affects the amygdalae (see chapter 7, "The Nature of Evil"), then it has successfully hijacked his mind into being terrified about things he ordinarily wouldn't think about twice. Remember, the amygdalae is vital to our memories of emotions and also key to how we process fear; and it's part of the limbic system, which handles memories of physical sensations and makes us scared. The amygdalae transmits impulses to the hypothalamus, to the reticular nucleus, and to the nuclei of our facial nerves; and it also makes our emotions whip up and down wildly, putting us into a state of terror.

It's also quite possible that a venom can alter someone's basic attributes using genetic manipulation. Our genes determine how our bodies handle poisons, battle infections and other illnesses, digest foods, and respond to environmental conditions. Our genes determine what we look like and, in many cases, how we react to emotional stimuli and how we behave. How big a deal is it that scientists have cracked the human genome? According to Dr. Steve Kay, a geneticist at The Scripps Research Institute in La Jolla, California, "It's comparable to Darwin's theory of evolution."[1] We already know how to manipulate genes to eliminate many diseases, but think about the reverse. For example, if we know how to get rid of an illness by making sure our bodies activate particular genes, then we can just as easily manipulate genes to cause diseases, such as Peeta's delusions and extreme paranoia.

How can tracker jackers follow people around? Well, in the real world, University of Georgia researchers have already trained wasps to smell chemicals and get treats if they do the right thing. Engineer Glen Rains explains that his portable Wasp Hound, a ten-inch-long PVC pipe holding a handful of wasps, "can monitor the behavior of wasps trained to a particular scent or volatile compounds."[2]

Typically, an animal's venom is produced by one or more glands. These glands are connected to a body part that administers the venom to victims. So, for example, snakes and spiders administer venom with their fangs, bees and scorpions administer venom with stingers, fish use spikes, centipedes use pincers, millipedes use squirters, and cone shells use poisoned harpoons. The amount of venom injected into a victim varies, and most often, it is injected into the subcutaneous layers of skin; that is, the animal does not inject its venom into the victim's internal layer of skin or body organs.

DOOMSDAY PREDICTIONS

AD **1989–2000**

This era, and the two decades preceding it, saw the publication of a lot of apocalypse and post-apocalyptic books. Some were written by respectable scientists, some by nutjobs. Novels about the subject proliferated—see "Appendix B, Apocalyptic and Dystopian Post-Apocalyptic Fiction: Further Reading" for a partial reading list.

Prophecies continued, just as before. A few highlights:

AD 1992, on October 28 of this year, we were all supposed to die according to the leader, Lee Jang Rim, of the Korean Mission for the Coming Days aka the Tami Church.

AD 1993, David Koresh fixed the apocalypse for AD 1995, and wanting to get a head start, he forced his followers to resist when authorities attacked his Waco, Texas, compound. In the ensuing gun battle, four agents died along with six cult members; an additional twenty cult members were injured. After fifty-one days, Koresh was still hanging tough, and finally, tanks blasted through the compound's walls, where Koresh had conveniently placed tear gas canisters. The place went up in blazes and killed seventy-five followers, including twenty-one children.

AD 1998, thirty-one cult members of the Solar Temple group were arrested because authorities feared another mass suicide. The cult believed the world was going to end at 8 p.m. on January 8, 1998, and their dead bodies would be lifted by a spaceship.

AD 1998, this time on March 8, another cult—one in southern India—felt certain that the entire world would be destroyed by earthquakes and that India would sink beneath the seas. This is when Lord Vishnu would come, claimed the cult.

AD 1998, even stranger than the above, Hon-Ming Chen, leader of the Taiwanese God's Salvation Church, told his followers that God would arrive at 10 a.m. on March 31 in a flying saucer. Not only that, but God would look identical to Hon-Ming Chen!

AD 1998, let's face it, 1998 was another bonanza year for the doomsayers. A cult called Church of the SubGenius claimed that on July 5, 1998 Xists from Planet X would arrive in flying saucers and destroy everyone on Earth. Any ordained Church clergy paying enough money would be transported to safety.

Yes, indeed. But wait! There's more!

We can't forget AD 1999. The year to end all years, or so many people believed. Perhaps the biggest kicker was that Nostradamus in the sixteenth century claimed that July 1999 was the very month that everything would die. The year, 1999, gave us death by comets, nuclear holocaust, Nostradamus's King of Terror, Armageddon, Judgment Day, and even the destruction of modern civilization due to the infamous Y2K computer bug.

Should we all survive 1999, we had to face AD 2000, with enough doomsday predictions to rival any period in history. Perhaps we have more prophets now than before, or more likely, perhaps we just document our paranoia a lot better.

At any rate, as of January 2, 2000, the world was still here. Ditto, December 31, 2000.

13

MUTTATIONS AND OTHER HYBRIDS

BIRDS, BEASTS, AND ROSES

Really, what *are* muttations? At first, we think they're dead tributes that the Capitol has somehow engineered into hybrid killing beasts. They have the eyes of dead tributes, along with their faces and their hair. One even has a collar marked with Glimmer's district number on it. Yet I couldn't help but wonder while reading in *The Hunger Games* about the wolflike muttations *how* they could be resurrected dead tributes.

The muttations are some of the most horrifying aspects of the series, especially when we're still wondering how Rue could turn into a wolfish mutt with hatred glowing in her eyes. How can this be?

To be honest, I also wondered why Katniss had never seen these human-tribute types of muttations in the broadcasts of earlier Games.

All that aside, we eventually learn that, just like the genetically engineered mockingjays, these human-wolf muttations are made in the lab. They're not human; they're not resurrected dead people. They're artificially created animals. Just like the monkey muttations in *Catching Fire*, the human-wolf muttations are programmed to kill people.

There are the human-wolves, strange human-lizard monsters, the monkeys, the jabberjays, the mockingjays, and the tracker jackers.

The idea of artificially created animals, engineered in laboratories out of the flesh of multiple creatures, is one that's been around for over a century in science fiction literature. Way back in 1896, H. G. Wells wrote his classic novel, *The Island of Doctor Moreau,* in which upper class Edward Prendick is saved at sea by a man named Montgomery. Onboard Montgomery's ship are a wide variety of animals, including a bizarre beast-human servant named M'ling.

When the ship finally reaches its destination, a remote island, Montgomery and the crew refuses to let Prendick onto the beach. Unfortunately for Prendick, the ship sails back out to sea, and he's allowed onto the island, where he meets Doctor Moreau, who is performing mysterious scientific research involving the animals.

When Prendick hears the shrieks of pain coming from Moreau's lab, he runs into the jungle and discovers a group of beast-humans. When one of the hybrid creatures attacks him, he escapes back to Moreau's enclave, and the next morning, sneaks into Moreau's secret laboratory. There he finds a weird beast-human in bandages, and he races back into the jungle, where he comes across a colony of hybrids. The leader is known as the Sayer of the Law, and the law itself requires that the beast-humans not act like wild animals. Prendick, horrified that Moreau will carve him up and also turn him into a beast-human, tries to flee to the ocean, where there would be no escape from the island anyway. Moreau eventually explains that he's not carving humans into beasts; rather, he's turning animals, the Beast Folk as he calls them, into human form. He has been performing his experiments for eleven years, he says.

There's a lot more to the story of *The Island of Doctor Moreau,* and if for some reason, you've never read the book or seen the original film (*Island of Lost Souls* featuring Charles Laughton and Bela Lugosi), you should. There are ape-humans, leopard-humans, hyena-swine-humans, and just about every other hybrid imaginable. Eventually, after killing the pure humans on the island, the hybrids revert to completely wild form.

The beast-humans in H. G. Wells's novel (and in the film mentioned above) have human eyes that reflect intelligence and sensitivity. It's not hard to imagine, as Prendick does for so long, that Doctor Moreau has been grafting humans into animal hybrids rather than vice-versa.

In The Hunger Games series, the muttations also have human eyes and other features that make them appear to be mutated versions of the tributes that Katniss has encountered in the Games. If Doctor Moreau did it in 1896, then why can't the Capitol turn animal and human flesh into strange hybrid monsters that have human characteristics, but are wild beasts at the core?

Splicing and dicing isn't necessarily the way to make these bizarre hybrids. The term *transgenics* refers to the creation of embryos containing genes from other species. Specifically, "Not only can a foreign gene be put into the cells of an organism: the gene can actually be incorporated into the DNA derived from germ cells or embryonic cells of another organism. From this combination, an embryo can be produced that contains this gene that came originally from another species (called a transgene). Transgenic embryos can be put into an adult female . . . which will then give birth to [offspring] permanently carrying the transgene."[1]

Once you accept the concept of transgenics, you can easily imagine its applications. For example, someday we might teach toddlers about new kinds of farm animals. In addition to the traditional cows, lambs, chickens, and pigs—kept onsite for that old-time feeling— Old MacDonald's Farm will now showcase fields of docile pig-lambs, horse-chickens, petunia-cows, and lion-peacocks. It's not as silly as it sounds. Pigs will be bred to have wool coats. Sheep may have bacon-flavored meat. Chickens may shed their feathers for light horse-down, and horses may taste like Thanksgiving turkeys. Tuna-textured cows may smell like flowers rather than manure; cows may indeed serve as a source of fish, complete with all the vitamins and nutrients and none of the fat found in traditional beef. Lion manes may look like peacock sprays. And it's also conceivable that female horses may give birth to horse-chickens and petunia-lambs.[2]

The types of animals that are most easy to manipulate from a genetic standpoint will be the animals used as "genetic stock." For example, if it turns out that pigs are best suited for genetic engineering, then we'll see far more pigs than other animals in the "genetic stock" pastures or barns (or warehouses, laboratories, dungeons, prisons— wherever humans produce these poor animals; we can only pray that we'll allow animals to live in reasonably pleasant environments). On the other hand, if horses are better suited for genetic engineering, then horses will be in abundance instead of pigs.

If we genetically engineer animals to suit our purposes, then in the long run we may find that we're destroying entire species, such as the original "pure" pigs, horses, cows, and so forth. If we "manufacture" pigs that are miniature assembly plants of other animals, then the real pigs that cannot give birth to peacock-lions or tuna-cows will go the way of the dodo: extinct. It's a danger. Or will the last real pigs be in zoos? Will Old MacDonald's Farm become merely an historical exhibit of stuffed dead animals at the Smithsonian?

What I'm suggesting, and what the world of The Hunger Games portrays, isn't as farfetched as you might think. Horrifying: Yes. Realistic: Unfortunately, *yes.*

An article in *National Geographic* warned in 2005 that "Scientists have begun blurring the line between human and animal by producing chimeras—a hybrid creature that's part human, part animal."[3] The report noted that as early as 2003, Chinese scientists fused human cells and rabbit eggs; that in 2004, the Mayo Clinic created pigs that happened to have human blood instead of pig blood.

In 2010, the Arizona State Senate enacted a law that makes it illegal to create beast-human hybrids. The law relates to embryonic research, as in transferring nonhuman embryos into human wombs or "transporting or receiving for any purpose a human-animal hybrid."[4] If you want a few laughs, check out http://blogs.laweekly.com/stylecouncil/2010/06/human-animal_hybrids_top_7_now.php, which asks, "Is something weird going on in Arizona? Or are they just being preemptive? In Arizona, Dr. Moreau is not just a creepy guy, he is a class 6 felon."[5] Now-illegal hybrids cited by the *LA Weekly* blog include The Little Mermaid (fish-human), Firenze (horse-human) from Harry Potter, and the poor Wolfman.

As *National Geographic* notes:

> . . . creating human-animal chimeras—named after a monster in Greek mythology that had a lion's head, goat's body, and serpent's tail—has raised troubling questions: What new subhuman combination should be produced and for what purpose? At what point would it be considered human? And what rights, if any, should it have? There are currently no U.S. federal laws that address these issues.[6]

If we're heading toward beast-human hybrids, will we have giant red roses that smell so potent and sweet that they're nauseating? Of course. Giant roses are possible due to transgenics, and certainly, fragrance requires minimal tinkering. If President Coriolanus Snow needs hyper-sickeningly-sweet roses to cover the reek of blood from his mouth sores, genetically engineered roses would do the trick.

About the genetic engineering of roses, in particular, Michael Gross, who has a doctorate in physical biochemistry, writes:

> [Researchers] have isolated thousands of pigments from the petals of different varieties of roses, characterized them, tracked down the enzymes involved in their synthesis, and the physiological conditions required for the proper coloring.

After all of this, it dawned on them that blue roses cannot be bred as a matter of principle. All roses known lack the enzyme that would convert the common intermediate dihydrokaempferol to the blue delphinidine-3-glucoside. The only way out of this dilemma is to transfer 'blue genes' from different plant species. The DNA sequence encoding the enzyme in petunias could be identified and transferred to petunia mutants whose enzyme was deficient. In principle, it should be possible to transfer the gene into roses as well, and provide them with blue petals.[7]

KILLER ROSES

As an aside, plants—whether genetically engineered or naturally occurring—have appeared in dystopian post-apocalyptic novels as the root cause of the actual apocalypse. Forget zombies that eat human bodies. Enter John Wyndham's human-killing triffids (*The Day of the Triffids,* 1951). In Wyndham's dystopian view, humans pushed the boundaries of crop cultivation to feed an ever-growing population while satellites began circling the globe (this was written in 1951, after all). Lo and behold, with nobody really knowing where they came from, millions of triffid seeds floated down from the sky and planted themselves in soil all over the world. They were intelligent, and they ate people. Imagine for a moment: If we can make genetically engineered plants such as gigantic sickeningly sweet roses, we can also make flesh-eating plants. Such plants are known in nature, and cooked in a laboratory, we may end up with triffids some day. This isn't how Wyndham described the origin of his triffids in 1951, but in a far-future Earth, one never knows.

Finally, if we can manufacture animal hybrids and totally new types of animals in the lab, someday we might have bird muttations such as jabberjays and mockingjays. The jabberjays operate as spies, hearing and repeating conversations, used initially by the Capitol as weapons against the people. The mockingjays are the result of the mating of these jabberjays with mockingbirds. Again, this isn't as strange as it sounds. The genetic construction of the jabberjay could indeed include the possibility of mating with mockingbirds.

As for replicating sounds, birds in the wild—real birds that haven't been genetically altered in any way—are very attuned to vocal sounds and learn melodies at an extremely young age.

Some real birds, such as parrots and parakeets, can replicate human words. In fact, there's a parrot named N'Kisi that reportedly knows anywhere from 560 to 950 human words. According to *USA Today,* the parrot's abilities to communicate with humans are impressive, though along with many other sources, *USA Today* isn't quite so sure about the purported telepathic capabilities of the bird.[8] (If you had a parrot who could have conversations with humans, would you also claim a telepathy angle? Isn't it enough that the bird possesses such an amazing vocabulary?) Many researchers with impressive credentials do point out that parrots do far more than mimic sounds: They can analyze and think before they "speak."

As for replicating warbles, deep tones, and songs with multiple verses (for example, see *The Hunger Games,* 43, and *Catching Fire,* 92), real mockingbirds are known for mimicry. They imitate the songs of nuthatches, wrens, cardinals, purple martins, blue jays, kestrels, kingfishers, woodpeckers, gray catbirds, swallow-tailed kites, flickers, and other birds. A mockingbird will imitate calls from one type of bird repeatedly, then follow directly after with songs from other birds. Three phrases, four, five, six, eight: It doesn't matter to mockingbirds, for they just instinctively know how to imitate the sounds and will rapidly mix them as if they're some electronic wizard spinning sounds on mixed recordings. Within one minute, a mockingbird may produce fifteen or twenty different songs. Within ten minutes, it can produce as many as 200 songs in total. And within thirty minutes, more than 450. However, the male mockingbird does seem to make up songs as he goes along, and he also increases his repertoire and creativity when trying to attract females.

On expert, Donald Kroodsma, a Professor Emeritus of the University of Massachusetts Amherst and a Visiting Fellow at the Cornell Laboratory of Ornithology, estimates that the male mockingbird might know 100 different songs, and he points out that other expert researchers put the number at 200 different songs, at 167, and at 148. The numbers vary from bird to bird, from researcher to researcher because the "males increase their vocabulary size from one year to the next," says Kroodsma. "The mind of the mocker is dynamic, never completely settled, as he continually changes all that he can say."[9]

Among bird experts, the mockingbird is known as the ultimate learner of songs with a phenomenal ability to mimic new sounds. Any society, such as the Capitol, that can genetically create such a wide variety of animal muttations in the lab can also create a jabberjay that remembers and repeats human sounds. Assuming jabberjays mated with mockingbirds, it's not a stretch to think that the resulting mockingjays can mimic human vocal sounds and repeat songs. Just as the Capitol figures the mockingjay will never survive in the long run, they underestimate the ability of the true mockingjay—Katniss—to survive, as well.

DOOMSDAY PREDICTIONS

AD **2001**–NOW

As 2001 rolled into place and none of the apocalyptic prophecies centered on AD 1999 and 2000 came true, the predictions died down. But they didn't entirely cease, of course. That would be contrary to human nature.

Added to the doomsday mania was the terrorist attack on the World Trade Center on September 11, 2001. The horrors of this particular day somehow wasn't foreseen by any of the doomsday prophets.

And now, we're back to "same old, same old," with people predicting the coming of Armageddon, nuclear holocaust, a pole shift, aliens, UFOs, flying saucers, plagues, etc.

14

MORE WEIRD SCIENCE

A BRIEF ROUNDUP

The Hunger Games series contains quite a bit of speculative science, the stuff of traditional science fiction. Several of the most obvious are the muttations, including the mockingjays and the tracker jacker venom. But the books include other forms of science that either already exist or will exist in the very near future. Examples are the zapping force fields on the rooftops and in the arena; the night-vision glasses; the body armor; Peeta's prosthetic leg; the high-tech showers; the automatic clothing and food devices; and the Holo contraption. Because the speculative science is part of the "wow" factor of the entire Hunger Games phenomenon, we'll touch upon a few of these topics; but keep in mind that the science is really quite minor in the series compared to other subjects: hunger, survival, love, death (and its many ways of happening), evil, torture, weapons, repressive regimes, strength, honor, ethics, determination, and even compassion in the face of terrible odds.

Let's begin with the force fields, which are used several times throughout The Hunger Games series. For example, in the first book, when Peeta and Katniss are at the edge of the Training Center roof in the Capitol, Peeta tells her that he asked Cinna why the officials don't worry about tributes leaping to their deaths. The reason is that there's a force field that tosses people back on the roof if they try to jump off. In *Catching Fire,* we learn that Haymitch won his Hunger Games when the girl from District 1 threw an ax at him, he ducked, the ax flew over a ledge, and then, *bam!* the ax hit a force field and flew back up and buried itself in her (*Catching Fire,* 202). And of course, Peeta and Katniss encounter a force field, as well, during training; it protects the Gamemakers from the tributes. Finally, there's a force field in the *Catching Fire* arena.

Force fields are common gimmicks in science fiction. They seem to be in almost every episode of *Star Trek.* They're typically used like invisible walls and deflector shields. Force fields are still the stuff of science fiction more than science reality. However, some progress is being made in developing them.

In 2010, British researchers described new force-field technology that they're developing to protect military vehicles from incoming fire. As described by science correspondent Richard Gray, "When a threat from incoming fire is detected by the vehicle, the energy stored in the supercapacitor [in the armor of the vehicle] can be rapidly dumped onto the metal plating on the outside of the vehicle, producing a strong electromagnetic field."[1]

Then there's the Trophy Active Defense System (ADS) that a company called RAFAEL developed along with the Israeli Defense Research and Development Directorate. According to officials at General Dynamics, which bought the force-field technology from RAFAEL, "the system demonstrated effective neutralization of anti-tank rockets and guided missiles, high safety levels, insignificant residual penetration and minimal collateral damage."[2]

As for night-vision glasses, you can easily obtain these devices now, and they do enable you to see objects that are two hundred yards or more away—in total darkness. Rue tells Katniss that the officials supply a few kids with night-vision glasses during harvest season so the work can continue after dark.

Apparently, the Capitol has an excellent type of body armor, and when Cato's wearing it, Katniss just can't seem to kill him. But the mutts eventually chew and destroy the full-length body armor and nearly kill him (*The Hunger Games*, 335–37).

Body armor has existed since the beginning of human history. For thousands of years, every advance in weaponry brought an equal advance in personal armor, until the invention of guns and cannons in the sixteenth century changed the world. It wasn't until the mid-twentieth century that armor managed to catch up with weaponry, but just barely.

Bulletproof vests provide the user with some protection against gunfire, but all too often, not enough. A modern bulletproof vest doesn't use metal but high-tech woven fibers to protect the wearer.

This soft body armor is based on the principle of spreading the energy at the point of impact of a bullet (or other missile) over a wide area. This dispersal occurs using an interlaced net of anchored tethers that form an interlocking pattern, which absorbs the energy no matter where the projectile hits. In most bulletproof clothing, long, thin strands of Kevlar fiber make up the netting. Kevlar is a lightweight fiber made by DuPont that is five times stronger than a similar piece of steel. When thickly woven, Kevlar is extremely dense and almost impossible for a regular bullet to penetrate.

The momentum from a bullet is often powerful enough to break bones, which is why bulletproof vests are usually made from several layers of woven, twisted Kevlar netting and layers of plastic film. The plastic film helps spread the force of the impact from the bullet over a wide space, thus lessening the blunt trauma caused by the projectile. To increase the protection offered by soft body armor, ceramic and metal plates are often inserted in pockets in the front of the armor.

Even more advanced, a human exoskeleton suit consists of a robotic-type device that can be strapped on or attached directly to the human body. The device adds muscle power for heavy lifting, long-range running, and walking. It also enables the user to wear heavy armor without being affected by the weight.

It seems unlikely that the Capitol has provided tributes with exoskeletons. After all, the tributes aren't leaping extraordinary heights, running incredibly fast as if barely on the ground, or functioning as if they have artificial pneumatic muscles. Besides, if the tributes were protected by exoskeleton armor, the Games would cease to amuse the Capitol and its citizens.

As for Peeta's prosthetic metal-and-plastic leg, every reader of this book knows that these devices are available now. Prosthetic limbs are artificial replacements of flesh-and-blood limbs.

Peg legs are the simplest type of prostheses, and they have no electronic components. Another simple type of artificial appendage is an arm that ends with pincers rather than a hand with fingers; this simple limb is attached to whatever is left of the patient's real arm. It is also attached to a harness that is strapped around the patient's shoulders. When the patient moves his shoulder, the harness moves, pulling cables that open and close the hooks.

However, far more sophisticated devices do exist. Dynamic protheses contain electronic components and are based on myoelectric properties. In short, a myoelectric prosthesis contains sensors that respond to the electricity created by the movement of flesh-and-blood muscles. When a patient tenses his muscle—say, in his upper arm—the sensors in the prosthetic portion of his arm detect the myoelectric transmission and sends the corresponding signals to the artificial hand. Run by batteries, the hand opens or closes. Some prosthetic limbs even have sensors that detect temperature. These devices send hot and cold information to electrodes in the skin, enabling a patient to "feel" with his prosthetic limbs.

Today's advances include artificial feet that cushion the body on the ground as if they are real; and feet with electronic components that enable patients to balance their weight more evenly. For example, the Elation Flex-Foot contains "flex-foot technology" along with adjustable heel heights. The Elation Flex-Foot automatically adjusts its mechanical pieces—known as foot blades and rocker plates—based on the amount of weight placed upon it. If a patient is heavier than average, if he shifts his weight from one foot to the other, or if he leans heavily in one direction, the foot blade presses more strongly against the rocker plate, thus changing the cushioning or impact of the foot against the ground. According to the makers of the Elation Flex-Foot, "A narrow, anatomically correct foot cover with a sandal toe contour is bonded to the foot, making it suitable for dress shoes, sandals, cowboy boots and other types of footwear."[3]

For amputees who have lost limbs at the hip level, modern medicine provides artificial hip joints made of laminated plastic or a thermoplastic.

Prosthetic devices are commonly made from carbon fibers, titanium, and polypropylenes, which are flexible plastics. Prostheses can be constructed of a bulletproof material called Kevlar. To make limbs really strong, a prosthetic can be devised of a layer of carbon, a layer of Kevlar, and another layer of carbon.

According to *Medical Device & Diagnostic Industry Magazine*,[4] much research is being done to create materials that emulate human muscles. For example, a full-size plastic skeleton named Mr. Boney roams around the University of New Mexico Artificial Muscle Research Institute. Mr. Boney's microprocessor-controlled heart pumps a chemical fluid through his body, and this fluid is what actuates his artificial muscles.

One major "wow" feature of The Hunger Games series are the high-tech shower, closet, and food dispenser that Katniss uses in the Training Center. She can choose more than a hundred options for her water, shampoo, oils, and sponges; and she can also instruct her closet to create clothing for her. Right out of the old Jetsons cartoon, she can mention the name of a tasty food, and within a minute, get a plate of it (*The Hunger Games,* 75).

So how is all of this done?

I wrote a novel called *TechnoLife 2020* (ECW Press, 2001), in which Joe Leinster, my main character, uses a lot of smart devices: doors that recognize him and open; home butler systems that prepare foods and clothing; showers that adjust to his needs; surfaces that require no dusting.

By combining artificial intelligence, robotics, sensors, micro-machinery, distributed processing, and other technologies, scientists will create a wide variety of smart materials and devices over the next couple of decades. According to a company that specializes in creating them, smart materials are "any material that shows some form of response (often physical) such as mechanical deformation, movement, optical illumination, heat generation, contraction, and expansion in presence of a given stimuli, such as electricity, heat, light, chemicals, pressure, mechanical deformation, exposure to other chemicals or elements. The response may be useful in converting the applied energy into a desired motion or action."[5]

Smart devices are those that are created using smart materials and computer systems. For example, in *TechnoLife 2020*, Joe's condo cabin comes equipped with an array of very sophisticated smart devices. Here's one description of the wall in his living room:

> There were ten depressions in the wall that perfectly fit his fingertips. Depending on the combinations he pressed, Joe could choose his clothing, his facial mask; his eye color, hair color, mindset; his food.
>
> The walls were electronic membranes, reinforced by genetically engineered impenetrable rock. The place was wired with embedded circuitry and microprocessors, everything tuned to enhance his moods, relax him, stimulate him, feed him, nourish him in all ways. What he needed, and when he needed it. At all times.

And a few minutes later, when Joe steps into the shower, more smart devices shift into action:

Each stream of water hit him in a preset location: scalp and face; back and chest; rearend and lower torso; and finally, his lower legs and feet. There was no need to adjust the temperature: it was perfect. The first water streams that hit him included body-cleansing droplets, and the water pulsed in such a way as to lather him thoroughly. Then the water streams stopped the pulsing massage and released a spring rain: all water, no bacteria, no soap, no dust, just spring water in a fine tingling spray. The stream shifted briefly, massaging his body again, this time with a small amount of skin-darkening tint, meant to last 24 hours then fade back to normal skin color. His body was flush, glowing, clean.

Five minutes into the shower, the water turned to mist, spraying everywhere but his head. He pressed his face gently against the face groove to his right. The groove fit the contours of his face. A waft of Ancient Spice: the cream was released from micropores in the face groove, rubbed onto his whiskers, lifting all hair from his face. He turned, letting the cream penetrate and remove all stubble from his scalp.

Before long, our clothes will eat their own stains and odors, our houses will maintain perfect temperature and air flow, our paint won't peel, and our metal tables, bikes, and cars won't rust. We'll have sensor systems that monitor environmental conditions—temperature, humidity, toxins, pollen, pollution, and so forth, and these systems will trigger the use of ventilators, air filters, water purifiers, and other mechanisms. Smart device systems in our walls, keyboards, and clothes will emit chemicals and medications that help us sleep, that stimulate or arouse us, that boost our creativity. These systems, worn perhaps on a belt or embedded in our skin, will monitor our health twenty-four hours a day. Indeed, smart implants may target and release medications, and may help control body functions and synthetic organs using biomembranes. Smart implants may produce hormones and aid in the repair of tissues.

If you've watched enough *Star Trek,* then you know all about holographic devices and holodecks. If you've visited a major museum, you've probably seen holographs.

In *Mockingjay,* the hand-held Holo is like a holographic GPS device that zooms in and out of a map, showing whatever is in specific locations. If you go to Google Earth, you can see 3D views of pretty much anything you want: oceans, surfing and diving locations, and even 3D-historical imagery that you can zoom and pan. You can go all over the world, street by street, and see whatever you want. Sure, we're not looking at holographic images of Bombay, Hawaii, London, or wherever, but we can see if someone has a certain type of car parked in front of his house, whether he's built a shack, and if a delivery van is down the street. The views set up all over the world via satellite are not real time, of course, as in *Mockingjay*'s Holo system. It seems that the Holo must use constantly current data to supply information about weapons/pods and people that are possibly hidden from view. (Why the holographic images are necessary is something I don't quite understand, though I admit it's cool.)

In short, holography records light emitted from objects, then reassembles the light later to display the objects in realistic simulations; as if interacting with a virtual reality system or playing a first-shooter 3D video game, the recorded holograph appears fully 3D to the viewer. Holography is an optical mechanism that's been used since the 1960s.

In 2011, MIT created a streaming holographic television video made out of a Microsoft Xbox gaming Kinect camera. The results are rudimentary, but still, the effect is that of a real-time holograph.[6]

If we set aside the mysterious reason for using *Star Wars*-like Holo imagery, we can easily see how 3D real-time images might be collected and displayed. Distributed micro-sensors could pick up images and transmit them to some central node, where they would then be collated and massaged by algorithms to display 3D realtime images.

DOOMSDAY PREDICTIONS

The future of an old prophetic legacy

By the time this book is printed and in your hands (or on your screen, as the case might be), AD 2012 may have already passed. The forces of nature are supposed to gang up on us in December 2012. Armageddon will come, with the ancient Mayan calendar being the culprit. I'm not the betting type, but even I would bet that we'll all still be here in January 2013. Mayan tradition actually doesn't place the end of the world in 2012; so hopefully, 2012 will be a period of enlightenment.

AD 2033, this may be the 2,000th anniversary of the crucifixion, so watch out!

Approximately AD 5 billion, the sun will grow old and lash out at us. The sun's hydrogen will fuse into helium, its core will collapse, and the whole sun will blow. We'll all be fried.

APPENDIX A

END·OF·THE·WORLD
SCENARIOS

A s readers, we never learn much about why Katniss Everdeen lives in a post-apocalyptic world. We know that environmental problems caused some type of apocalypse, that a major rebellion took place seventy-five years ago, that the Capitol basically destroyed the population of Panem, and as punishment, divided them into thirteen districts and subjected their children to the Hunger Games to teach them all a lesson in obedience. As for the reasons behind the apocalypse, I give you my best guess in chapter 1.

As I write this companion guide, people are rebelling in half a dozen nations against repressive governments. The world is receiving daily news about these events, and other countries are expressing diplomatic concerns and otherwise trying to ease tensions and help the citizens cope. As I write this chapter, Japan has just experienced an estimated 8.9-magnitude earthquake and tsunami with nuclear reactor repercussions, and current news reports fear that 10,000 people have already died. The world is reaching out to help the Japanese people.

It's true that governments do not always lend sufficient support when major catastrophes occur (Stalin and other dictators slaughtering their own people, hurricanes such as Katrina, and so forth). But the world knows about such suffering, and support is *usually* available at least to *some* extent.

So where is everybody and everything? I give you my best guess about this issue in chapter 1, as well: that maybe the survivors in other parts of the world are too busy coping with their own issues, that maybe communications systems have been mangled.

Only Suzanne Collins—and possibly her editor and agent—knows the background of the Hunger Games apocalypse.

Post-apocalyptic fiction has been around for a long time (see Appendix B for examples). So has apocalyptic fiction, which takes the reader *through* the end-of-the-world scenarios. A typical example of apocalyptic fiction is Stephen King's 1978 novel, *The Stand,* in which a worldwide plague wipes out most of the human race. But King's novel is also a post-apocalyptic work because it traces not only the plague, but what happens after the plague kills everyone.

This is a common technique used by writers: show us the apocalyptic event as well as the post-apocalypse aftermath. Richard Matheson, who served as one of King's strongest literary influences, composed a frightening novel of biological warfare in the near future in 1954's *I Am Legend.* In the story, a deadly artificial plague infects mankind and there is no cure. Only a few humans are immune to the disease that turns the rest of the population into vampires who feed on blood. Matheson's description of the breakdown of civilization was amplified by King to great effect in *The Stand* a quarter of a century later.

The atomic bomb was the weapon of choice in novels of humanity's destruction in the 1960s and 1970s. Biological weapons seemed very hit or miss when compared with the total devastation brought about by an atomic bomb. Plus, zombies created by atomic radiation were all the rage. As I write this book, zombie fiction has been making a huge comeback.

But clearly, the depressing future portrayed in The Hunger Games series does not involve zombies. Nor has a killer comet struck Panem, as far as we know. The Capitol didn't beat down the masses because an asteroid smashed into North America, as far as we know. There were no supermassive black holes or volcanic eruptions that we know of. District 12 wasn't hit by bizarre gamma rays from outer space. Vampires don't roam the earth.

It is not within the scope of this book to describe all of these apocalyptic scenarios in great detail:

- Plagues and biological warfare.
- Chemical warfare.
- Nuclear armageddon.
- Artificial intelligence, nanobots, and cybernetic revolts.

- Genetic warfare.
- Killer comets and asteroids.
- Supermassive black holes.
- Earthquakes.
- Volcanoes.
- Global warming.
- Gamma rays.
- And that all-time favorite, alien invasion.

But it is worth looking at some of the more common scenarios, particularly those that might fit slightly into the framework of the world of The Hunger Games.

PLAGUES AND BIOLOGICAL WARFARE

If a natural-born plague gripped the Earth, it's possible that all the major nations and cities would be wiped out, leaving only pockets of people here and there. An evil government could condemn these remnants of a former country to poverty, misery, slavery, and gladiatorial games by use of traditional force. Similarly, if major nations subjected each other to man-imposed biological warfare—that is, a plague purposely set loose upon humanity—the effects could be the same. In the case of the manmade biological warfare, we might assume any evil government and leader that survives has an antidote. The natural-born plague is trickier because it seems less logical that a specific government and its evil authorities would know *beforehand* that a natural plague would break out, and hence, happen to have a supply of antidotes to save their own lives and their loved ones.

Most diseases don't remain lethal after being transmitted three or four times. Their effects diminish with the age of the virus. However, if a disease constantly mutates from one flu strain to another, it remains deadly long after most other plague germs have lost their potency.

How quickly would the Earth's population be decimated? For the sake of simplicity, let's assume that each infected person has contact with five other people each day. And, after that, these newly infected five people only meet five people each day. The geometric progression of the infection is therefore:

- On the first day, 1 person infected.
- Second day, 5 people infected.
- Third day, 25.
- Fourth day, 125.

- Fifth day, 625.
- Sixth day, 3,125.
- Seventh day, 15,625.
- Eighth day, 78,125.
- Ninth day, 390,625.
- Tenth day, 1,953,125.

So in this very simplistic view, in which a person only has contact with five people in a day, by the tenth day, close to 2 million people would die from a plague disease, whether naturally made or created by man. Most likely, the disease would spread even more rapidly.

And by, say, nineteen days into the plague, how many would be dead? 19,073,486,328,125 or in approximate numbers, in nineteen days the plague would have been spread to 19 trillion people, more than enough exposures so that everyone on Earth would have been infected a thousand times over by the plague.

Once a geometric progression starts in earnest, there's nothing in the world that can stop it, other than nipping the sequence off at one of the early stages. In other words, the plague has to be contained immediately, or it cannot be stopped.

If there's a secret laboratory somewhere in the Rocky Mountains, and government scientists are working on a deadly strain of flu virus for which no antidote exists, and someone infected with the disease goes home that night, then the world is doomed. Unbelievable as it sounds, it could happen. On a somewhat smaller scale, with a slightly less virulent virus, it already has. More than once.

THE BLACK DEATH

The greatest disaster in *recorded* history took place during the years 1347 through 1350. It was a disease outbreak that became known as the Black Death, and it killed an estimated 34 million people, approximately one-third of Europe's population. Records from the Far East and the Middle East show that the Black Death was part of an even larger bubonic plague pandemic (a pandemic is defined as an epidemic over a wide geographic area and affecting a large percentage of the population) that struck much of Europe, Asia, and Africa. The total number of people killed by this pandemic will never be known, but some historians estimate that, in total, over 60 million people died due to the plague.

Bubonic plague, the main cause of the Black Death, returned to haunt Europe again and again until the beginning of the eighteenth century. Recurrent episodes of the Black Death included the Italian Plague of 1629–31, the Great Plague of London (1665–66), and the Great Plague of Vienna (1679).

According to modern researchers, the Black Death most likely began in the steppes of central Asia, though some historians believe it might have originated in northern India. The cause of the disease was a bacteria named *Yersinia pestis,* which was carried and spread by fleas. Plague fleas were transported by rats across half the world. It was the unchecked spread of rats through Asia, Europe, and the Middle East that brought the Black Death. No other bacteria had so much of an effect on human history.

There were three types of plague. Bubonic plague was the most common. A flea bite deposited the bacteria into the victim's lymphatic system. The disease was characterized by *buboes,* large, inflamed, and painful swellings in the lymph glands of the groin, armpits, or neck, depending where the flea bite occurred.

In *septicaemic* plague, which was almost always fatal, the bacteria entered the bloodstream directly, rather than through the lymphatic system where they might be contained. Like bubonic plague, the *septicaemic* variety of plague was caused directly by flea bites. Death usually took place within twenty-four hours of catching the disease.

Pneumonic plague was the most deadly form of plague. It was usually fatal and wasn't caused by a flea bite. When the plague bacteria reached the lungs of a victim, it caused severe pneumonia. The bacteria were present in water drops spread by coughs and choking. This third variation of the plague was highly contagious. Death from the *pneumonic* plague occurred within three or four days.

In all three versions of the plague, internal bleeding caused large bruises to appear on the skin. This bruising resulted in the plague being called the Black Death.

Biological warfare, also known as germ warfare, is the use of any organism, including bacteria, virus, or some other disease-causing organism or poison found in nature to wage war. Biological warfare is designed to kill enemy soldiers, and in some cases, enemy civilians. Biological warfare also means attacking nature in the area where the enemy is located—destroying his food supplies, destroying his environment, destroying his habitat.

The creation and stockpiling of biological weapons was outlawed by the Biological Weapons Convention of 1972, which was signed by over one hundred countries. Biological weapons were deemed too extreme for warfare as they could cause deaths in the millions and major economic disasters in countries throughout the world. In a strange bit of wording, the treaty prohibited the creation and storage of the weapons, but did not outlaw the use of these weapons.

Biological warfare was used as far back as the sixth century BC, when the Assyrian armies poisoned enemy wells with a mind-altering fungus that would drive their enemies mad. In 184 BC, Hannibal of Carthage had his army fill clay pots with poisonous snakes and instructed his soldiers to throw the pots onto the decks of Pergamene ships.

During the Middle Ages, the Mongols threw diseased animal bodies into the wells and drivers used by their European enemies for drinking water. Before the Black Death hit all of Europe, Mongols were notorious for catapulting diseased corpses into cities they were besieging, hoping to infect the population with the plague.

The practice of throwing the corpses over city walls only grew worse after the plague enveloped Europe. The last time infected corpses were used as weapons of terror was at the beginning of the eighteenth century.

During the Sino-Japanese War of 1937–45 and World War II, Unit 731 of the Imperial Japanese Army conducted experiments on thousands of prisoners, mostly Chinese. In certain military campaigns, the Japanese used biological weapons on soldiers and civilians. The Japanese secretly fed their Chinese prisoners poisoned food. They also contaminated the water. Estimates suggest that over 500,000 people died, due to the bad food and also plague and cholera outbreaks.

Suspicious of reported biological weapons development in Germany and Japan, the United States, United Kingdom, and Canada initiated a Biological Weapons development program in 1941 that resulted in the weaponization of anthrax, brucellosis, and botulinum toxin. The center for U.S. military Biological Weapon research was Fort Detrick, Maryland. Biological weapons research was also conducted at "Dugway Proving Grounds" in Utah. Research carried out in the United Kingdom during World War II left Gruinard Island in Scotland contaminated with anthrax for the next forty-eight years.

Despite having signed the 1972 treaty, the Soviet Union continued research and production of offensive biological weapons in a program called Biopreparat. The United States was unaware of this program until Dr. Kanatjan Alibekov, the deputy director of biopreparat defected in 1992.

During the Cold War era, considerable research was performed by the United States, the Soviet Union, and other major countries on biological warfare.

In 1986, the U.S. government spent $42 million on developing defenses against infectious diseases and toxins, ten times more money than was spent in 1981. The money went to twenty-four U.S. universities in hopes of developing strains on anthrax, Rift Valley fever, Japanese encephalitis, tularemia, shigella, botulin, and Q fever.

At present, several countries are developing biological warfare programs.

According to the defense department; these countries include Russia, Israel, China, Iran, Libya, Syria, and North Korea. The characteristics of effective biological weapons are that they are highly infective, have a high potency, can be delivered as an aerosol, and vaccines are unavailable for the victims.

Diseases considered for use as weapons or known to have been used already as weapons include anthrax, Ebola, bubonic plague, cholera, tularemia, brucellosis, Q fever, Machupo, Coccidioides mycosis, glanders, melioidosis, shigella, Rocky Mountain Spotted Fever, typhus, psisticosis, yellow fever, Japanese B encephalitis, Rift Valley Fever, and smallpox. Naturally occurring poisons that can be used as weapons include Ricin, SEB, botulism toxin, saxitoxin, and many mycotoxins.

While it's quite possible that plague and biological warfare could wipe out the world's populations, it's unlikely they could destroy skyscrapers, suburbia, infrastructures, and entire cities across the globe. All of these manmade items would eventually weaken and collapse. So while an evil government could conceivably employ biological agents against its own people and somehow protect government leaders, such an empire would also have to use other means to destroy the actual cities and infrastructures.

CHEMICAL WARFARE

Unlike bombs, which of course explode, this form of warfare uses nonexploding chemicals. Like biological warfare, stockpiling of chemical weapons is forbidden, in this case by the Chemical Weapons Convention of 1993.

As with biological warfare, it's conceivable that an evil empire might use chemical warfare on its citizens; however, the use would have to be limited unless everyone in the Capitol, for example, wore gas masks during the Dark Days of the war in Panem. Unlikely scenario; biological agents would make more sense because government researchers could also create the antidotes for the leaders' use.

In more general terms, a worldwide apocalypse based on chemical agents is less likely than one caused by a plague, for example, which spreads rapidly from victim to victim.

Chemical warfare comes in various forms:

- Pulmonary agents that attack the lungs and suffocate victims. Examples are chlorine and phosgene.
- Blood agents that attack how the body uses oxygen. An example is cyanide.
- Blister agents attack the skin, making flesh break out in massive bloody blisters. An example is mustard gas.

- Nerve agents, which are far more lethal than pulmonary, blood, and blister agents, attack and destroy acetylcholine neurotransmitters in the victim. An example is sarin.
- Hallucinatory agents, which may not kill victims but would certainly incapacitate their abilities to function normally. Probably not the weapon of choice for an apocalyptic scenario unless used in conjunction with something lethal.
- Tear gas, which may not kill victims, but again, incapacitates them. Again, probably not the weapon of choice for an apocalyptic scenario unless used in conjunction with something lethal.

NUCLEAR ARMAGEDDON

Because the government and District 13 both possess nuclear weapons, there's a truce of sorts between the two. The Capitol allows District 13 latitude but keeps its existence secret from the other twelve districts. The government fears nuclear missiles and radiation should officials attempt to nuke District 13 (*Mockingjay*, 138). Twill tips us off that there was indeed an apocalypse of *some* kind in District 13: "We think the people moved underground when everything on the surface was destroyed" (*Catching Fire*, 147). This may explain the devastation of District 13, but it doesn't explain what happened to the rest of the world during the period of war.

In terms of the possible destruction of the entire world by nuclear weapons, this horrific scenario has been feared since World War II. As with plagues and biological warfare, a nuclear holocaust could wipe out the world's populations and in this case also destroy the cities and infrastructures. Possibly, as with plagues and biological agents, pockets of humanity somehow survive the apocalypse, such as the districts of Panem. And then, as mentioned earlier, an evil Capitol could step in and subdue the survivors using military force, starvation, and other measures.

In general terms, a nuclear bomb uses the forces that hold the nucleus of an atom together. In particular, nuclear bombs deal with atoms that possess unstable nuclei.

Atoms release nuclear energy in two ways. With nuclear fission, the nucleus is split into two fragments; isotopes of uranium or plutonium are typically used. With nuclear fusion, two atoms are brought together; hydrogen or hydrogen isotopes are typically used.

There are many ways of devising and detonating bombs. Some of the most common nuclear bomb designs are:

- Fission bombs (the earliest type of bomb).
- Gun-triggered fission bombs.

■ Implosion-triggered fission bombs.

■ Fusion bombs.

To understand how a fission bomb works, you need some basic knowledge about nuclear radiation. We're sure you remember from chemistry class that everything consists of atoms and that groups of atoms form molecules. For example, two hydrogen atoms plus one oxygen atom equal one water molecule. The Periodic Table lists all the types of atoms, which are also called elements.

Each atom consists of subatomic particles: protons and neutrons form the atom's nucleus; electrons orbit the nucleus. Protons have positive charges, while electrons have negative charges. Usually, the number of protons and electrons in an atom are the same. The role of the neutrons is basically to keep the protons together in the nucleus. Because the protons all have the same charge, positive, they would repel one another. You might recall that opposites attract. The neutrons do not have a specific charge, such as positive or negative.

Some elements have more than one stable form. By stable, we mean that you could leave the element alone for five hundred years, then return to find that it hasn't changed at all. If you accidentally leave a chunk of stable copper in a garbage bin, then return in five hundred years to find your chunk of copper still sitting in the garbage, then this means two things: first, that the trash collectors have been on strike for five hundred years; and second, that the copper is in a stable form.

In fact, speaking of copper, 70 percent of all natural copper is called copper-63, and the other 30 percent is called copper-65. Each type of copper has twenty-nine protons, but a copper-63 atom has thirty-four neutrons and a copper-65 has thirty-six neutrons: similar, but slightly different. Both copper-63 and copper-65 are stable forms of the element.

Both are called *isotopes* of copper.

Now some isotopes happen to be *radioactive*. In the most simple terms, radioactivity means that an isotope is unstable. For example, one of the hydrogen isotopes, which is called tritium, is radioactive. It has one proton and two neutrons. Over time, it transforms—by means of *radioactive decay*—into the more stable isotope called helium-3, which has two protons and one neutron.

There are three ways that a radioactive isotope will decay: alpha decay, beta decay, and what we're interested in talking about here, spontaneous *fission*. This is, by the way, how alpha, beta, gamma, and neutron rays are formed.

The actual word, *fission*, means "splitting." So if an atom undergoes spontaneous fission, the atom splits. For example, a fermium-256 atom, which is really heavy, may split and turn into one xenon-140 atom and one palladium-112 atom, and in the process, shed four neutrons. These four neutrons may crash into other atoms and cause various nuclear reactions.

Induced fission means that an element can be forced to split. Uranium-235 is a good example of such an element. It is often used in *fission bombs*. If a Uranium-235 nucleus is hit by a free-floating neutron, then the nucleus instantly becomes unstable and splits. This kind of thing happens to cause a nuclear explosion.

In a *gun-triggered fission bomb*, explosives ignite, thus propelling a bullet down a barrel. The bullet hits a generator, which launches the fission reaction. Detonated over Hiroshima, Japan, during World War II, Little Boy was a gun-triggered fission bomb. It had a yield equal to 14,500 tons of TNT. If Lex Luthor dropped a Little Boy a mile outside of Smallville, Clark Kent's hometown would not fare any better than Hiroshima.

In an *implosion-triggered fission bomb*, explosives ignite and create a shock wave, which then compresses the core of the bomb. The fission reaction occurs, and the bomb explodes. In World War II, Fat Man was an implosion-triggered fission bomb. It wiped out Nagasaki, Japan. It would wipe out Smallville within seconds.

Which brings us to *fusion bombs*, also known as thermonuclear bombs. Before we describe this type of device, it's well worth noting that a fusion bomb is far more powerful than either Little Boy or Fat Boy. In fact, estimates place the deadly power of a fusion bomb at seven hundred times more than the deadly power of Little Boy.

Basically, the fission part of the bomb implodes, and resulting X-rays heat the inside of the bomb. Pressure causes shock waves that initiate the fission in a plutonium rod, which in turn gives off radiation, heat, and neutrons. Combined with high pressure and temperature, these neutrons are used to create fusion reactions. The fusion reactions create yet more radiation, heat, and neutrons. In a horrific cycle, the neutrons from the fusion create yet more fission, and round and round we go until the bomb detonates.

Irreversible damage is in the form of: (a) intense heat and fire, (b) intense pressure, (c) radiation, and (d) radioactive fallout. The fallout alone would enter the water, cling to the air, be carried to far distances by winds.

Big Boy's explosion was that of 12,500 tons of TNT. A 1-megaton hydrogen bomb possesses eighty times the deadly power of 1945's Big Boy. Within a 1.7-mile radius of a hydrogen bomb, everything would be destroyed, including 98 percent of the people.[1] Within a 2.7-mile radius, everything would be destroyed, including 50 percent of the people, with 40 percent of the remaining population seriously injured. Moving to a 4.7-mile radius, most buildings would be destroyed, with 5 percent of the people dead and an additional 45 percent of the population seriously injured.

OTHER APOCALYPTIC SCENARIOS

At the beginning of this appendix was a list of other possibilities:

- Artificial intelligence, nanobots, and cybernetic revolts.
- Genetic warfare.
- Killer comets and asteroids.
- Supermassive black holes.
- Earthquakes.
- Volcanoes.
- Global warming.
- Gamma rays.
- And that all-time favorite, alien invasion.

Most are too farfetched in terms of The Hunger Games to explore here. For example, we have absolutely no reason to believe on any level that aliens invaded the Earth and killed everyone except the people of Panem. That's just absurd.

Similarly, we have no evidence of genetic warfare on Earth in The Hunger Games series. It's true that scientists have already devised complex forms of genetically mutated creatures. However, it's a big stretch to leap from the mutations to a worldwide apocalypse caused by mutated genetic lifeforms. Surely, in this case, we'd see *some* evidence of these killer lifeforms within the district's human populations. But there are no human mutations in the districts, and nobody ever talks about how "Aunt Jane gave birth to a wolf-human that devoured the whole family." Again, this scenario of apocalypse seems absurd in The Hunger Games context.

When I considered all the possibilities, I determined that The Hunger Games apocalypse had to be caused be global warming, melting of the ice caps, and then war. But as pointed out in chapter 1, only Suzanne Collins knows for sure.

APOCALYPTIC AND DYSTOPIAN POST-APOCALYPTIC FICTION: FURTHER READING

The popularity of apocalyptic fiction, which concerns end-of-the-world scenarios and their aftermaths, and post-apocalyptic fiction—only the aftermaths of the collapse—have become extremely popular during the past few years. The post-apocalyptic form may feature a world in which former technology and science has been destroyed. It may feature a world in which most of the survivors live in hunter-gathering sorts of communities, yet futuristic technology is oddly juxtaposed among an elite subset of the survivors; The Hunger Games series is an example of this form of post-apocalyptic fiction.

As explored fully in this book, The Hunger Games series is clearly dystopian in nature. The books contain classic dystopian features, such as: (1) warning us that we're heading toward repression and suffering if we don't change the way we function now, (2) putting a totalitarian and highly repressive government in charge of the surviving population, and (3) making it clear that the vast majority of people have no freedom, live in poverty, and are subjected to military brutalities.

The popularity of this form of fiction rises and falls depending on what's happening in the real world. As discussed earlier, the genre surged after World War II with images of nuclear annihilation, as well as plagues and alien invasions; plus a host of other doomsday scenarios.

It's possible that the current hopelessness that many readers feel about the world in which we live is now driving the current surge in sales of these types of novels; perhaps it helps people realize that "It could always be worse." If people are mistreated now in their own lives, or if they perceive even falsely that they're undervalued, misunderstood, manipulated by their governments, or outrightly abused, they may find solace in reading extreme forms of post-apocalyptic fiction. It underscores their feelings that "If we keep heading down this path, this is how bad it could get, so you'd better listen to me and my friends and stop this [war, government abuse, economic destruction, elimination of freedom and civil liberties, etc.]"

Not a cheerful subject, but it's been around for a long time. If you're interested in reading more fiction about the world going to hell, this Appendix offers some suggestions organized by publication date.

This list is by no means comprehensive. If you really want to find extensive booklists, I suggest you scour the Internet for resources. I'm listing only books that I've personally read and enjoyed; and in some cases, I'm including books that may not top my favorites list, but may be enjoyable to other Hunger Games fans. You'll notice that half the books I suggest are classics in the genre, and the other half are recently published. If you read the classics, you'll probably find the newer books far more interesting.

For example, having read science fiction novels since I was a child, when I first read The Hunger Games, I was struck by: (1) how well written it is—the voice and style are superb, (2) the post-apocalyptic and general science fiction ideas it uses from the classics, and (3) the freshness it offers by twisting together reality television, the ancient Roman gladiatorial games, plastic surgery and fashion obsessions, hype over substance, etc.

Anyway, without further ado, here's a partial reading list to get you started:

1898	H. G. Wells, *The War of the Worlds*
1943	Fritz Leiber, *Gather Darkness*
1949	George R. Stewart, *Earth Abides*
1949	George Orwell, *1984*
1951	John Wyndham, *The Day of the Triffids*
1953	Ray Bradbury, *Fahrenheit 451*
1952	Andre Norton, *Daybreak—2250 A.D. (Star Man's Son)*
1954	Richard Matheson, *I Am Legend*
1955	John Wyndham, *The Chrysalids*

1957	Nevil Shute, *On the Beach*
1959	Pat Frank, *Alas, Babylon*
1961	Walter M. Miller, Jr., *A Canticle for Leibowitz*
1968	Philip K. Dick, *Do Androids Dream of Electric Sheep?*
1977	Jerry Pournelle and Larry Niven, *Lucifer's Hammer*
1978	Stephen King, *The Stand*
1979	David Graham, *Down to a Sunless Sea*
1982	Frank Herbert, *The White Plague*
1985	David Brin, *The Postman*
1993	Octavia E. Butler, *Parable of the Sower*
1993	Lois Lowry, *The Giver*
1997	Jack McDevitt, *Eternity Road*
1997	Jean Hegland, *Into the Forest*
1997	Garth Nix, *Shade's Children*
2003	Jeanne DuPrau, *The City of Ember*
2003	Margaret Atwood, *Oryx and Crake*
2004	S. M. Stirling, *Dies the Fire*
2004	M. T. Anderson, *Feed*
2004	Meg Rosoff, *How I Live Now*
2005	Scott Westerfeld, *Uglies*
2006	Susan Beth Pfeffer, *Life As We Knew It*
2006	Cormac McCarthy, *The Road*
2007	Neal Shusterman, *Unwind*
2007	Peadar Ó Guilín, *The Inferior*
2007	Peter Hautman, *Rash*
2008	Susan Beth Pfeffer, *The Dead and Gone*
2008	Suzanne Collins, *The Hunger Games*
2008	James Kunstler, *World Made by Hand*
2008	Clare B. Dunkle, *The Sky Inside*
2009	Suzanne Collins, *Catching Fire*
2009	Carrie Ryan, *The Forest of Hands and Teeth*
2009	William R. Forstchen, *One Second After*
2010	Suzanne Collins, *Mockingjay*
2010	David Macinnis Gill, *Black Hole Sun*
2011	Ann Aguirre, *Enclave*

NOTES

1. The Hunger Games Trilogy

1. Jeffrey Kluger, "Earth at the Tipping Point: Global Warming Heats Up," *Time*/CNN, March 26, 2006, www.time.com/time/magazine/article/0,9171,1176980-3,00.html#ixzz1HckqZwJl.
2. Spencer Weart, American Institute of Physics, "The Discovery of Global Warming," http://www.aip.org/history/climate/floods.htm, citing: Oppenheimer, Michael, "Global Warming and the Stability of the West Antarctic Ice Sheet," *Nature* 1998, 393: 325–32; IPCC (Intergovernmental Panel on Climate Change), *Climate Change 2001: The Scientific Basis. Contribution of Working Group I to the Third Assessment Report of the IPCC,* edited by J. T. Houghton, et al. Cambridge: Cambridge University Press, 2001, online at http://www.ipcc.ch/; Weertman, Johannes, "Glaciology's Grand Unsolved Problem," *Nature* 1976, 260: 284–86; and Van der Veen, C. J., and J. Oerlemans, eds., *Dynamics of the West Antarctic Ice Sheet. Proceedings of a Workshop Held in Utrecht,* May 6–8, 1985.

2. Repressive Regimes and Rebellions

1. G. William Domhoff, "Wealth, Income, and Power," University of California at Santa Cruz, January 2011, http://sociology.ucsc.edu/whorulesamerica/power/wealth.html.

2. Gus Lubin, "15 Mind-Blowing Facts About Wealth and Equality in America," *Business Insider,* April 9, 2010, www.businessinsider.com/15-charts-about-wealth-and-inequality-in-america-2010-4.

3. Ibid.

4. Don Miller, "Housing Crisis Could Peak in 2011 as Foreclosures Rise to Record," Money Morning, January 13, 2011, http://moneymorning.com/2011/01/13/housing-crisis-could-peak-2011-foreclosures-rise-to-record/.

5. Les Christie, "Foreclosures make up 26% of home sales," CNN, February 24, 2011, http://money.cnn.com/2011/02/24/real_estate/foreclosure_sales/.

6. Jonathan R. Laing, "Banks Face Another Mortgage Crisis," *Barron's,* November 20, 2010, http://online.barrons.com/article/SB50001424052970203676504575618621671054514.html#articleTabs_panel_article%3D1.

7. Harvey Katz, "The Real Unemployment Rate—January 13, 2011," Value Line, January 13, 2011, www.valueline.com/Markets/Commentary.aspx?id=10133.

8. Mallie Jane Kim, "The Wealth Gap Around the World," *U.S. News & World Report,* February 3, 2011, www.usnews.com/opinion/articles/2011/02/03/the-wealth-gap-around-the-world.

9. Domhoff, op. cit.

10. "Presidential hopefuls report their wealth," CNN, May 17, 2007, http://articles.cnn.com/2007-05-17/politics/candidates.wealth_1_financial-disclosure-candidates-edwards?_s=PM:POLITICS.

11. Marlys Harris, "Millionaires-in-chief," *Money,* December 10, 2007, http://money.cnn.com/2007/12/10/magazines/moneymag/millionaires_in_chief.moneymag/index.htm.

12. David Dukcevich, "America's Richest Politicions," *Forbes,* October 29, 2002. www.forbes.com/2002/10/29/cx_dd_richpols.html.

13. Kim, op. cit.

14. Walter C. Langer, The United States Office of Strategic Services, *Hitler As His Associates Know Him,* 51, www.nizkor.org/hweb/people/h/hitler-adolf/oss-papers/text/oss-profile-03-02.html.

15. David Biello, "A Deep Thaw: How Much Will Vanishing Glaciers Raise Sea Levels," *Scientific American*, 090508, www.scientificamerican.com/article.cfm?id=how-much-will-global-warming-raise-sea-levels.

16. James DeFronzo, *Revolutions and Revolutionary Movements* (Boulder, CO: Westview Press, 2007), 19.

17. Jay Stanley and Barry Steinhardt, "Bigger Monster, Weaker Chains, the Growth of an American Surveillance Society," reprinted in *Civil Liberties vs. National Security in a Post-9/11 World* (Amherst, NY: Prometheus Books, 2004), 54.
18. http://epic.org/privacy/choicepoint/

3. Hunger

1. World Hunger Education Service, "2011 World Hunger and Poverty Facts and Statistics," www.worldhunger.org/articles/Learn/world%20hunger%20facts%202002.htm.
2. World Food Programme, "Hunger Stats," www.wfp.org/hunger/stats.
3. Medicine for Africa, "Kwashiorkor," www.medicinemd.com/Med_articles/Kwashiorkor_en.html
4. Ibid.
5. For details about the 1960s study, see L. H. Lumey, Aryeh D. Stein, Henry S. Kahn, Karin M. van der Pal-de Bruin, G. J. Blauw, Patricia A. Zybert, and Ezra S. Susser, "Cohort Profile: The Dutch Hunger Winter Families Study," *International Journal of Epidemiology*, 36, no. 6 (December 2007): 1196–1204, http://ije.oxfordjournals.org/content/36/6/1196.full.
6. Susan Jeffrey, "Victims of War Famine Provide Prenatal Clues to Schizophrenia," *The Medical Post*, November 7, 1995, www.mentalhealth.com/mag1/p5m-sc01.html.
7. See www.news.leiden.edu/news/dutch-hunger-winter.html and Mark Henderson, "Imprint of famine seen in genes of Second World War babies 60 years on," *The Times*, October 28, 2008, www.timesonline.co.uk/tol/news/uk/health/article5029679.ece.
8. Jacqueline Hansen, "The Truth About Teaching and Touching," *Childhood Education*, Spring 2007, http://findarticles.com/p/articles/mi_qa3614/is_200704/ai_n19431206/pg_4/.
9. Gavin Hewitt, "Ethiopian Children Face Starvation," *BBC News*, June 11, 2008, http://news.bbc.co.uk/2/hi/africa/7449523.stm.
10. Damien Cave, "Fighting Starvation, Haitains Share Portions," *New York Times*, January 25, 2010, www.nytimes.com/2010/01/26/world/americas/26hunger.html?_r=1.
11. "Blaine Begins Starvation Stunt," *BBC News*, 090503, http://news.bbc.co.uk/2/hi/entertainment/3083066.stm.
12. "Doctors Feed Blaine After Stunt," *CNN World*, 102003, http://articles.cnn.com/2003-10-20/world/britain.blaine_1_stunt-box-water-supply?_s=PM:WORLD.

13. Molly G. Morrison, "Connecting with the God-Man: Angela of Foligno's Sensual Communion and Priestly Identity." http://tell.fll.purdue.edu/RLA -Archive/1998/italian-html/Morrison,%20Molly.htm.

14. Office for the Liturgical Celebrations of the Supreme Pontiff, "Alexandrina Maria da Costa (1904–1955)," vatican.va/news_services/liturgy/saints/ ns_lit_doc_20040425_da-costa_it.html.

4. Tributes

1. "A Conversation with Suzanne Collins, Author of The Hunger Games Trilogy," Scholastic, Inc., www.scholastic.com/thehungergames/media/qanda .pdf.

2. Bob Minzesheimer, "Collins leaves young love unresolved in 'Catching Fire,'" *USA Today*, August 8, 2009.

3. George Rolfe Humphries, *The Art of Love* (Bloomington: Indiana University Press, 1957).

4. Matt Cartmill, *A View to a Kill in the Morning: Hunting and Nature through History* (Cambridge, MA: Harvard University Press, 1993), 40–41.

5. J. P. V. D. Balsdon, *Life and Leisure in Ancient Rome* (London: Bodley Head, 1969), 308.

6. "New Interview with Author Suzanne Collins Talks 'Mockingjay,'" August 1, 2010. Full interview at: Rich Margolis "The Last Battle: With 'Mockingjay' on its way, Suzanne Collins weighs in on Katniss and the Capitol," *School Library Journal*, August 1, 2010, www.schoollibraryjournal.com/slj/ printissue/currentissue/885800-427/the_last_battle_with_mockingjay .html.csp. http://mockingjay.net/category/suzanne-collins/page/2/.

7. Pat H. Broeske, "The Glory That Was Hollywood," *Los Angeles Times,* April 21, 1991, http://articles.latimes.com/1991-04-21/entertainment/ca-559_1 _hollywood-movie.

8. Jon Solomon, *The Ancient World in the Cinema* (New Haven, CT: Yale University Press, 2001), 55.

9. Examples are in interviews of Suzanne Collins by the Library of Congress in 2010. See www.loc.gov/bookfest/kids-teachers/authors/suzanne_collins .html, www.usatoday.com/life/books/news/2009-08-31-suzanne-collins -catching-fire_N.htm, www.scholastic.com/thehungergames/media/qanda .pdf, along with many others.

10. Susan Dominus, "Suzanne Collins's War Stories for Kids," *New York Times*, April 8, 2011. www.nytimes.com/2011/04/10/magazine/mag-10collins-t .html.

11. See www.slate.com/id/46344/, www.phoenixnewtimes.com/1998-02-12/ news/john-mccain-breaks-up-a-fight/3/, www.usatoday.com/life/people/ 2006-12-04-ultimate-fighting_x.htm.
12. www.fila-official.com/index.php?lang=en.

5. Weapons

1. To learn about KA-BAR knives, see www.kabar.com/index.jsp.
2. International Knife Throwers Hall of Fame, www.IKTHOF.com/Ranking _Tests.html.
3. W. Dale Nelson and David Eisenhower, *The President is at Camp David* (Syracuse: Syracuse University Press, 2000), 40.
4. Ed Garsten, "Congressional Bomb Shelter Outlives Usefulness," CNN, November 7, 1995, www.cnn.com/US/9511/gimme_shelter/index.html.
5. Volta Torrey, "How We Fight Japan with New Incendiary Bombs Packed with Gel-Gas and Pyrogel Raze the Enemy's Factories and Shipyards," *Popular Science* 146, no. 5, (May 1945), 100.

6. Torture and Execution

1. www.nytimes.com/2011/04/10/magazine/mag-10collins-t.html.
2. Culled from the more extensive information at Tony R. Kuphaldt, "Ohm's Law (again!)," *All About Circuits*, www.allaboutcircuits.com/vol_1/chpt_3/ 4.html
3. Kerry Ressler, MD, PhD, and Michael Davis, PhD, "The amgydala is the primary brain region involved in fear-conditioned learning," *Journal of the American Academy of Child and Adolescent Psychiatry* 42, no. 5 (May 2003), 612–15.
4. Eric Kandel "Cell and Molecular Biological Studies of Memory Storage," Howard Hughes Medical Institute, www.hhmi.org/research/investigators/ kandel.html.
5. Richard Gray, "Scientists find drug to banish bad memories," *The Telegraph,* July 1, 2007.
6. Quoting Nader, ibid.
7. Interview transcript, "Joseph LeDoux on Replacing Fear Memories," National Institute of Mental Health, January 4, 2010, www.nimh.nih.gov/ media/video/ledoux.shtml.

7. The Nature of Evil

1. http://biblescripture.net/Galatians.html.
2. Susan Neiman, *Evil in Modern Thought* (Princeton, NJ: Princeton University Press, 2004), 9.
3. "Moyers in Conversation," PBS, 091201. www.pbs.org/americaresponds/moyers912.html.
4. "British Scientists discover criminal gene," ABC Science Tech, May 8, 2002, http://abc.net.au/news/scitech/2002/08/item20020802225123_1.htm.
5. Anjana Ahula, "The Get out of Jail Free Gene," *The Times*, 11709, www.timesonline.co.uk/tol/news/science/genetics/article6919130.ece.
6. Michael Shermer, "Demon-Haunted Brain," *Scientific American*, (March 2003), 32.
7. Olaf S. Blanke, T. Ortigue, T. Landis, and M. Seeck, "Neuropsychology: Stimulating Illusory Own-Body Perceptions," *Nature* 419 (September 19, 2002), 269–70.
8. Michael A. Persinger, *Neuropsychological Bases of God Beliefs* (New York: Praeger, 1987), and Persinger, "Paranormal and Religious Beliefs May Be Mediated Differently by Subcortical and Cortical Phenomenological Processes of the Temporal (Limbic) Lobes," *Perceptual and Motor Skills* 76 (1993), 247–51.

8. Killer Kids

1. Francis Mading Deng, *The Dinka of the Sudan* (Prospect Heights, IL: Waveland Press, 1972), 68–73.
2. Stephen Buckley, "Loss of Culturally Vital Cattle Leaves Dinka Tribe Adrift in Refugee Camps," *Washington Post,* August 24, 1997, www.washingtonpost.com/wp-srv/inatl/longterm/africanlives/sudan/sudan.htm.
3. Emmy E. Werner, *Reluctant Witnesses: Children's Voices from the Civil War* (Boulder, CO: Westview Press, 1998), 2.
4. Ibid., 9.
5. Graça Machel, *Impact of Armed Conflict on Children* (New York: United Nations Publications, 1996).
6. http://www.amnesty.org/en/children.
7. Peter W. Singer, "Books: Children at War," *The Washington Post,* June 12, 2006. www.washingtonpost.com/wp-dyn/content/discussion/2006/05/22/DI2006052200785.html.
8. "Child Soldiers," United Nations Cyberschoolbus, www.un.org/cyberschoolbus/briefing/soldiers/soldiers.pdf.

9. Singer, op. cit.
10. Julian Borger, "Darfur's Child Refugees Being Sold to Militias," *The Guardian,* June 6, 2008, www.guardian.co.uk/world/2008/jun/06/sudan .humanrights.
11. Ibid.
12. BBC News, February 23, 2010, http://news.bbc.co.uk/2/hi/africa/3496731 .stm.
13. Mike Pflanz, "Rwanda 'recruited child soldiers for Congo rebels,'" *The Telegraph,* December 11, 2008, www.telegraph.co.uk/news/worldnews/ africaandindianocean/rwanda/3708901/Rwanda-recruited-child-sol diers-for-Congo-rebels.html.
14. GlobalSecurity.org, "Niruyeh Moghavemat Basij Mobilisation Resistance Force," www.globalsecurity.org/intell/world/iran/basij.htm.
15. Ali Alfoneh, *Iran Primer: The Basij Resistance Force,* October 21, 2010, www .pbs.org/wgbh/pages/frontline/tehranbureau/2010/10/iran-primer-the -basij-resistance-force.html.
16. www.un.org/cyberschoolbus/briefing/soldiers/soldiers.pdf.

9. Hype Over Substance

1. Maria Gonzalez, "'Keeping Up with the Kardashians' Breaks Rating Records," Buddy TV, December 20, 2009, www.buddytv.com/articles/ keeping-up-with-the-kardashians/keeping-up-with-the-kardashian-33413 .aspx.
2. Perez Hilton, January 25, 2011, http://perezhilton.com/2011-01-25-kourt ney-kim-take-new-york-premieres-with-3-million-viewers-most-watch-of -series.
3. James Hibberd, "'Jersey Shore' ratings go nuclear: most-watched MTV series telecast ever!," *Entertainment Weekly,* January 7, 2011, http://insidetv .ew.com/2011/01/07/jersey-shore-ratings-record/.
4. James Hibberd, "'Jersey Shore' ratings: Yup, they did it again," *Entertainment Weekly,* January 14, 2011, http://insidetv.ew.com/2011/01/14/jersey -shore-ratings-new-record/.
5. Robert Seidman, "Bravo's 'The Real Housewives of Beverly Hills' Sets Records with Total Viewers," January 14, 2011, http://tvbythenumbers .zap2it.com/2011/01/14/bravos-the-real-housewives-of-beverly-hills-sets -records-with-total-viewers/78756?utm_source=feedburner&utm_medium =feed&utm_campaign=Feed%3A+Tvbythenumbers+%28TVbytheNum bers%29.

6. Lynette Rice, "'Real Housewives of New York City' finale draws record ratings," June 5, 2010, http://insidetv.ew.com/2010/06/05/real-housewives-of-new-york-city-finale-draws-record-ratings/.

7. "'Real Housewives of New Jersey' episode earns record ratings," CNN Entertainment, 071510, http://marquee.blogs.cnn.com/2010/07/15/<#212>real-housewives-of-new-jersey<#213>-episode-earns-record-ratings/.

8. "'Real Housewives of Atlanta' Finale Breaks Ratings Record," VIBE.com, 020211, www.vibe.com/posts/real-housewives-atlanta-finale-breaks-ratings-record.

9. "Bravo's 'The Real Housewives of Orange County' Returns on March 6 at 10pmET/PT," J!-ENT Entertainment Worldwide, 012711, www.nt2099.com/J-ENT/news/american-entertainment/bravos-the-real-housewives-of-orange-county-returns-on-march-6-at-10pm-etpt/.

10. James Poniewozik, *Time*/CNN, August 9, 2010, http://tunedin.blogs.time.com/2010/08/09/some-hope-for-america-real-housewives-of-d-c-ratings-only-ok/.

11. According to a Bravo TV press release, as reported on The Futon Critic, October 20, 2010, www.thefutoncritic.com/ratings/2010/10/20/bravos-the-millionaire-matchmaker-earns-highest-rated-season-premiere-among-all-key-demos-665112/20101020bravo01/.

12. www.eonline.com/on/shows/kardashians/index.html, accessed in February 2011; also see http://tv.ign.com/dor/objects/14218278/keeping-up-with-the-kardashians/images/keeping-up-with-the-kardashians-20090304101417582.html.

13. Jocelyn Venna, "'The Hills' Cast Addresses Mysterious Finale Scene," MTV News, July 14, 2010.

14. David Hinckley, "The Real Housewives of New Jersey are fake but impressive," *Newsday,* May 10, 2009, www.nydailynews.com/entertainment/tv/2009/05/11/2009-05-11_the_real_housewives_of_new_jersey_are_fake_but_impressive.html.

15. "Kardashian Reality Show Completely Fake So Says Khloe's Ex," *Anything Hollywood*, 110509, http://anythinghollywood.com/2009/11/kardashian-reality-show-completely-fake/.

16. Piers Morgan, "The Kardashians get real—about what's real and fake," CNN, January 27, 2011, http://piersmorgan.blogs.cnn.com/2011/01/27/piers-preview-the-kardashians-get-real-about-whats-real-and-fake/.

17. "VH1 'Love Shows' Pronounced Fake," *Reality Rehash*, 050808, http://realityrehash.com/index2.php/rant/vh1-love-shows-pronounced-fake.

18. "The Real World: Fake Storaayyy," January 6, 2009, http://videogum.com/43951/the_real_world_fake_storaayyy/tv/reality-tv/.

19. "Sarah Palin Lays into Obama, Uses Crib Notes, Says Nothing of Substance," *The Hollywood Gossip*, 020710www.thehollywoodgossip.com/2010/02/sarah-palin-lays-into-obama-uses-crib-notes-says-nothing-of-subs/.

20. "Biden on Palin's Speech: Style but No Substance," CNN, September 4, 2008, http://articles.cnn.com/2008-09-04/politics/Biden.Palin_1_joe-biden-sarah-palin-debate?_s=PM:POLITICS.

21. Tracey Lomrantz, "Hillary Clinton Pulls a Pantsuit Out for the DNC: The Woman Knows What Works," *Glamour*, August 27, 2008, www.glamour.com/fashion/blogs/slaves-to-fashion/2008/08/hillary-clinton-pulls-a-pantsu.html.

22. "Power Dressing," *The Guardian*, March 17, 2008, www.guardian.co.uk/lifeandhealth/gallery/2008/mar/17/fashion.photography.

23. www.huffingtonpost.com/news/michelle-obama-style.

24. Daniel Mendelsohn, "The Mad Men Account," *The New York Review of Books*, February 24, 2011, www.nybooks.com/articles/archives/2011/feb/24/mad-men-account/.

25. Mimi Hall, "Jackie Kennedy Onassis: America's quintessential icon of style and grace," *USA Today*, September 26, 2010, www.usatoday.com/news/washington/2010-09-26-jfk-jackie-kennedy-onassis_N.htm.

26. Press Release, "Plastic Surgery Rebounds Along with Recovering Economy; 13.1 Million Cosmetic Procedures Performed in 2010, up 5%," American Society of Plastic Surgeons, February 7, 2011, www.plasticsurgery.org/Media/Press_Releases/Plastic_Surgery_Rebounds_Along_with_Recovering_Economy.html.

27. Henry I. Miller, "Better Genes for Better Living," *Wall Street Journal*, August 21, 1999, B1.

28. Andy Dehnart, "At last! The secrets of 'Survivor' revealed," MSNBC, October 7, 2008, http://today.msnbc.msn.com/id/26726792/ns/today-entertainment/.

10. Theseus and the Minotaur

1. "A Conversation: Suzanne Collins, Author of the Hunger Games Trilogy," Scholastic, Inc., www.scholastic.com/thehungergames/media/qanda.pdf.

2. Ibid.

12. Medicines and Poisons

1. Carol Clark, *On the Threshold of a Brave New Work,* as reproduced by CNN at www.cnn.com/specials/2000/genome.
2. Glen Rains, www.uga.edu/aboutUGA/research-wasphounds.html.

13. Muttations and Other Hybrids

1. Frederick B. Rudolph and Larry V. McIntire, ed., *Biotechnology: Science, Engineering, and Ethical Challenges for the 21st Century* (Washington D.C.: Joseph Henry Press, 1996), 12.
2. Lois H. Gresh, *TechnoLife 2020* (ECW Press, 2002).
3. Maryann Mott, "Animal-Human Hybrids Spark Controversy," *National Geographic,* January 25, 2005, http://news.nationalgeographic.com/news/2005/01/0125_050125_chimeras.html.
4. Andy Barr, "Arizona legislature targets 'human-animal' hybrids," April 30, 2010, www.politico.com/news/stories/0410/36594.html.
5. Gendy Alimurung, "Top 7 Human-Animal Hybrids Now Illegal Under Arizona Law," *LA Weekly,* June 1, 2010, tp://blogs.laweekly.com/stylecouncil/2010/06/human-animal_hybrids_top_7_now.php.
6. Mott, op. cit.
7. Michael Gross, *Travels to the Nanoworld: Miniature Machinery in Nature and Technology* (Cambridge, MA: Perseus Publishing, 1999), 177.
8. Tara McKelvey, "'Psychic' parrots expected to ruffle scientific feathers," *USA Today,* February 12, 2001, www.usatoday.com/life/2001-02-12-parrot.htm.
9. Donald Kroodsma, *The Singing Life of Birds* (Houghton Mifflin Company, 2007), 73.

14. More Weird Science

1. Richard Gray, "Star Trek-style force field armour being developed by military scientists," *The Telegraph,* March 20, 2010, www.telegraph.co.uk/technology/news/7487740/Star-Trek-style-force-field-armour-being-developed-by-military-scientists.html.
2. www.defense-update.com/products/t/trophy.htm.

3. Roger Wolfson & Associates, Medical Orthotists Prosthetists, www.reger wolfsonandassociates.co.za/w-prosthetic-components-display.php.

4. Gregg Nighswonger, "New Polymers and Nanotubes Add Muscle to Prosthetic Limbs," *Medical Device & Diagnostic Industry Magazine,* August 1999, www.devicelink.com/mddi/archive/99/08/004.html.

5. See the Biomimetic Products Inc. Web site at www.biomimetic.com/faq .html.

6. Kate Taylor, "MIT unveils holographic TV system," January 24, 2011, www .tgdaily.com/hardware-features/53703-mit-unveils-holographic-tv-system? utm_source=feedburner&utm_medium=feed&utm_campaign=Feed %3A+tgdaily_all_sections+%28TG+Daily+-+All+News%29

Appendix A: End-of-the-Word Scenarios

1. "Megaton Surface Blast: Pressure Damage," *American Experience PBS,* www .pbs.org/wgbh/amex/bomb/sfeature/1mtblast.html.

The twilight Companion

The unofficial guide to the bestselling twilight series

Lois H. Gresh

The Twilight series by Stephenie Meyer follows an unlikely couple: Bella, a gawky teenage girl stuck in a new town, and Edward, a gorgeous vampire who has sworn off human blood. Added to the mix is Jacob Black, a werewolf who also loves Bella. Seductive and compelling, the four-book series has become a worldwide phenomenon.

With legends and lore about vampires and werewolves, insight into the lives and loves of the characters, and loads of exclusive facts and quizzes, this guide is a must-have for fans of the Twilight series.

D4RK

INSIDE

JEYN ROBERTS

'SOMETHING BAD IS ABOUT TO HAPPEN. A LOT OF PEOPLE ARE GOING TO DIE AND IT'S ONLY THE BEGINNING.'

A murderous rage has been unleashed. Moments after earthquakes rock the world, people start to change in the most terrifying of ways. Friends turn on friends, girlfriends on boyfriends, brothers on sisters. Nobody can be trusted.

For those who survive the first wave of killing, the world is a different, deadlier place. Michael, Aries, Mason and Clementine must battle to stay alive in a world determined to kill them. All they have is one another . . . but can they even be sure of that?

AN APOCALYPTIC, HEART-STOPPING SAGA OF RAGE, HOPE AND SURVIVAL

GL◯W

SKY CHASERS

AMY KATHLEEN RYAN

HER HEART WILL DETERMINE THE FUTURE . . .

Teenagers Waverly and Kieran believe their future is written in the stars.

They are part of the first generation born in space.

They are in love.

They have never seen a stranger before . . . until the day they are wrenched apart and suddenly find themselves fighting for their lives.